VOICES FROM THE HILLS

VOICES FROM THE HILLS

Pioneering women fell and mountain runners

Steve Chilton

Foreword by
Jasmin Paris

SANDSTONE PRESS

First published in Great Britain in 2023 by
Sandstone Press Ltd
PO Box 41
Muir of Ord
IV6 7YX
Scotland

www.sandstonepress.com

Editor: Robert Davidson

ISBN: 978-1-914518-19-5
ISBNe: 978-1-914518-20-1

Sandstone Press is committed to a sustainable future.
This book is made from Forest Stewardship Council ® certified paper.

Printed an … 4YY

To every female athlete I have
coached who has enriched my life

People who end up as 'first' don't actually set out to be first. They set out to do something they love.

CONDOLEEZA RICE
former USA Secretary of State,
on changing acceptance of women in sport

We should always remember the ones who went before, as they made a path for us.

SARINA WIEGMAN
manager of the England Women's football team
on winning the Women's EURO Championship 2022

Contents

List of photographic plates

Photo credits

Plate 1 – Duncan McPherson
Plate 2 – Boston Herald
Plates 3, 4, 6, 8, 10, 11, 17 – Tommy Orr
Plate 5 – Joan Glass
Plate 7 – Jean Dawes
Plate 9 – Jean Lochhead
Plates 12, 15, 19, 21, 23, 24, 26, 27, 28, 35 – Dave Woodhead
Plate 13 – Brenda Robinson
Plate 14 – Carol McNeill
Plate 16 – Anne-Marie Grindley
Plate 18 – Fiona Wild
Plate 20 – Angela Brand-Barker
Plate 22 – Véronique Marot
Plate 25 – Helene Diamantides
Plate 29 – Kirstin Bailey
Plate 30 – Anne Stentiford
Plate 31 – Elaine Wright
Plate 32 – Dave Hughes
Plate 33 – Sarah Rowell
Plate 34 – copyright not known
Plate 36 – Angela Brand-Barker
Plate 37 – Christine Menhennet
Plate 38 – Wendy Dodds

Foreword

I started fell running as an adult in 2008 and was struck immediately by the warmth and inclusivity of the fell running community. In a midsummer evening race close to home in the Peak District, I experienced for the first time the camaraderie of that shared effort as I followed the line of runners to the summit trig point, and then the adrenaline rush of the fast, scarcely controlled descent across heather and mud to cake and tea at the finish.

That day was the start of a new passion, which has brought me intense joy, great satisfaction and, I believe, a better understanding of who I am and what I'm capable of. I love the humbleness and lack of elitism that fell running entails, and the way in which enjoyment of the hills brings people together, regardless of their differences. When I won the Montane Spine race outright in 2019, setting a course record in the process, the running community was overwhelming in its support. Given the history of female endurance hill runners like Helene Diamantides, they were also probably not as surprised as the media seemed to be.

It seems scarcely believable therefore that, less than fifty years ago, women were not allowed to compete in fell races at all. Facing longstanding tradition and gender expectations, it took a string of passionate and committed women, pursuing the pleasure of running in the mountains, to change the pervading attitude amongst the running community and the public in general.

In this book, Steve Chilton has turned his attention to exploring the stories of those female pioneers, their motivations, experiences, and challenges. Building on his previous books about the history of fell running, Steve combines meticulous research with personal interviews to shine a light on those that paved the way for the gender equality we enjoy today, from the record breaking champions to those who played a quieter but equally important role behind the scenes.

On a personal level I've often referred to my own fell running female heroes, including Angela Mudge, Helene Diamantides and Wendy Dodds, all of whom are covered here. Yet I realise how little I knew about so many others; those who raced before they were allowed to, sending in entries with first name initials only and registering with coat hoods pulled up to disguise their female identity; and those who took part in the face of blatant criticism, such as Véronique Marot when she raced around Ennerdale for the first time, resplendent in long sleeved gloves.

My own experiences of gender discrimination in running have been negligible, typically relating to prize giving rather than the sport itself. In 2014, when I finished third overall and first lady in the Wasdale Fell race, narrowly beaten to second place in a sprint finish off Lingmell, I was surprised at the prize giving when the first two men both received a trophy (one being for a veteran over 40), but one didn't exist at all for the ladies. I joked about needing to run faster next year to finish in the top two, nevertheless I was pleased to see a female trophy appear for the next edition of the race.

I'm immensely grateful to the women who paved the way for my generation to compete in fell races as equals with our male counterparts, free to run the same courses neck and neck, sharing the highs and lows, and ultimately the joy that time spent in the mountains brings. Throughout this book, many of those ladies point out that at the time they were simply enjoying running in the hills and didn't consider themselves to be pioneers. Yet it needed that group of fearless women, ready to pursue what they loved to do, and to defy expectations and constraints of society, to open the floodgates for the involvement of women in fell racing, to normalise their presence and to push increasingly for equality in terms of opportunity as well as achievement on the hills. Thanks to this book those trailblazing women will be recognised for the contribution they made, and continue to make, for the fell running dreams of women today and in the future.

I believe that the progressive participation of women in fell running shows what can be achieved when passion and self-belief work as a force for good, and I hope the same can now be achieved in terms of ethnic diversity in our sport for the future. I believe wider enjoyment of the hills and mountains will foster further understanding and desire to protect them, essential for not only our generation but for those to come.

JASMIN PARIS
Edinburgh
Scotland, 2022

Prologue

In researching this book, I spoke to many people involved in the early days portrayed within. I have tried to reconstruct the story of this era (the second half of the twentieth century), and the issues and actions involved, with a fairly arbitrary cut-off of the turn of the millennium. The basis of the story is the barriers and struggles encountered and the personal courage and self-confidence shown by athletes doing things because they wanted to. What I hope makes for interesting reading is that it is predominantly told through the words of those early pioneer women, many of whom have said how much they enjoyed looking back over their running careers, some of which are still ongoing.

The many interviews with athletes that provided the basis for the book took place throughout 2021, mostly when we were in various stages of lockdown due to the Covid-19 pandemic. This meant that in-person interviewing was out of the question. When offered a choice between telephone or email conversations approximately half chose each option. Both options allowed me to explore each athlete's background and their place in the evolving story.

In one conversation Ruth Pickvance said, 'I think it's so great that you're doing this [book].' She then dropped a bomb by saying, 'A few years ago I said to Helene Diamantides/Whitaker, "Shall we write a book about women's fell running?" We both thought it was a good idea, but life's pressures took us in other directions!' Ruth later added an unprompted remark that could have been a precis of the subject. 'It is not just about women going running. It is about, why was it like that at the time, and what else was going on? How did the people involved feel about it? I feel very differently now looking back at it than I probably did at the time.' I had exactly that in mind when I started researching the manuscript, and hope that by speaking to a good number of the pioneers I have managed to give a real feel for what it WAS like through the eyes, and memories, of some of the participants. Ruth, and Helene, may of course have written a very different book, but for now this is *a history* of early female fell runners.

[Note: in most cases I have used athlete's surnames as they were at the time of competition (i.e. how it would have appeared in results), with a note of name changes where relevant.]

Introduction

Dawn. A bitter, damp Welsh mountain morning. The special train lay hissing and clanking, awaiting its one lady passenger. Reaching the end of the line by 8am, Esme Kirby could finally set off on her epic challenge to climb fourteen mountain summits faster than any woman had done before, and achieve lasting fame. Having caught the specially arranged train up to the summit of the first mountain, she had a quick drink of coffee and set off at a trot just before eight o'clock in the morning. It was damp and mightily cold. Esme had trained hard for this, but nagging away at the back of her mind was the slightly strained ligament she had experienced a few days ago. She and her pacer, her friend Thomas, set off into the mist.

The clag had set in for the day, meaning that finding the fourteen summits was often difficult. Esme eventually limped up to the shelter on the last summit. She had taken nine hours and twenty-nine minutes. It was exactly one hour faster than the previous record, which had been set by a man. Having finished the challenge, there was still five miles to go to get back to their car.

This was back in 1938, and Esme had just traversed the Welsh Three Thousands in a new record time (although her husband and two friends had only taken 8 hours 25 minutes, having set off an hour after her). Esme's name is not one that comes to mind readily when recalling pioneer female runners, but she was certainly ahead of her time. Her husband at the time was

Thomas Firbank, author of the best-selling book *'I Bought a Mountain'*. Both of their exploits garnered huge publicity and certainly raised a few eyebrows in the mountaineering establishment, such that Firbank's two companions felt it necessary to write an apology letter in the Climber's Club Journal – about turning the mountains into a competitive arena. Thomas Firbank did not like the fuss that was being made, but Esme seemed to enjoy it immensely, particularly being invited to London by the BBC and being featured in several of the national newspapers.

Esme Kirby's single-minded approach certainly showed the way for later females to challenge themselves in similar ways. She went on to become a leading conservationist and founded, with her second husband Peter Kirby, the Snowdonia [National Park] Society in 1958, to try to ensure the mountains were protected from inappropriate development.

CHAPTER 1

You can't do that

Female Frailty: Fiction or Fact?
Pedestrianism, The Olympics and Marathons.

'Allowing women in sports would harm their feminine charm and degrade the sport in which they participated.'

This attitude, as espoused by Baron de Coubertin (founder of the International Olympic Committee) solidified one of the greatest barriers to women's participation in sport.

When writing a history of any topic it is often not easy to know where to start (or indeed stop). Are the instances of pioneering women in other branches of the sport of running directly relevant to a history of women in fell and mountain running? What they DO show is that women have faced incredible obstacles to their participation in endurance sports, both on grounds of their (perceived) frailty as a gender, and of the perception of their role within society.

The myth of female frailty was an unproven medical belief that strenuous sport would damage a woman's body and make her infertile. Girls were told that they would become masculine and sterile if they took part in vigorous sporting activity. It was suggested that their uteruses might fall out, and it was even seriously considered, by some with extreme views, that women were born with a finite amount of energy and if they used it up on active sports, they would not have energy to give birth. Furthermore, Patricia Vertinsky noted[1] that the thinking in the

1. *The Eternally Wounded Woman: Women, Exercise and Doctors in the Late Nineteenth Century*, Manchester University Press, 1990.

medical profession in Victorian times was that 'in addition to the monthly menstrual drain of energy, at each birth a portion of a woman's vital energy was transformed and imparted to the new-born child. As each child was born, the mother experienced a physical loss to her over-drained body'.

Women had been forbidden from participating in the Ancient Olympics, way back before the Modern Olympics. A woman who was caught even as a spectator at those Games could face execution. Women in ancient Greece held their own festival to honour the goddess Hera every four or five years – the Heraean Games. There is hardly any historical record of these games, which probably started around 776 BC. About the only source of information is a set of writings from the Greek geographer Pausanias. Only women could compete in the Heraean Games, and Pausanias suggests they had to be virgins. As opposed to competing in the nude, like competitors in the male-only Panhellenic Games, the women wore knee-length tunics that left the right shoulder and breast exposed. The event took place in a stadium, with several running events, possibly ranging from 177 metres to about 3 miles.

It is worth looking at several instances in later times, where pioneering women went against the grain, and the expectations of them, in the era before it was normal for them to be involved in endurance events alongside men. In all cases the participants showed great strength of character.

Pedestrianism was a nineteenth-century form of competitive walking, often professional and funded by betting, from which the modern sport of racewalking developed. It also produced some of the earliest formal endurance records. The exploits of nineteenth-century (male) 'pedestrians' such as Robert Barclay Allardice, and the gloriously named duo of Corky Gentleman and the Flying Pieman, provide some of the highlights of this stage of the development of men's endurance sport.

Pedestrianism was not the exclusive domain of men, though. Emma Sharp (1832 to 1920) was an athlete famous at the time for her feat of pedestrianism. She completed a 1,000-mile walk in 1,000 hours, the event first completed by Allardice in 1809. She is thought to be the first woman to complete the challenge, finishing on 29 October 1864, having started on 17 September. She is reported to have dressed like a man for the event, and to have used the proceeds of the walk, which exceeded £500, to set up a rug making business.

A report of the event is available on the web,[2] which includes the following detail:

> She took the same approach as Captain Barclay [Allardice] by walking a roped off course of 120 yards for 30 minutes at a time, which was equivalent to about two miles, before taking a 90-minute break. She would continue this routine for six weeks straight, walking day and night, until she completed her last mile.
>
> Others threw burning embers in her path, some tried to drug her food, and still others simply resorted to trying to trip her at random times. As things escalated, for her protection, eighteen police officers disguised as working citizens were assigned to her on the final days of the race. In addition to that, during the night, a helpful citizen walked in front of her with a loaded rifle. Emma also walked the final two days with a pistol, which she had to fire in warning a reported 27 times in total to ward off unruly spectators.

She was not universally welcomed, then. She was an early example of someone pushing herself to overcome what was put before her. Despite doing virtually no training for the event, the only major physical issue Sharp experienced during the walk was painfully swollen ankles early on, but that soon went away as the days went on. Initially the female pedestrians astutely exploited the advantage of novelty, and Emma Sharp was not the only female pedestrian of note.

When the Olympics were revived in 1896, women were

2. http://www.todayifoundout.com/index.php/2016/05/time-emma-sharp-walked-1000-miles-1864-just-prove-woman/

again excluded. Despite this, Stamata Revithi became the first woman to run a marathon when she covered the Olympic course from Marathon to Athens. Revithi ran one day after the men had completed the official race, and although she finished the marathon in approximately 5 hours and 30 minutes and found witnesses to sign their names and verify the running time, she was not allowed to enter the Panathinaiko Stadium at the end of the run. She intended to present her documentation to the Hellenic Olympic Committee in the hope that they would recognise her achievement, but it is not known whether she did so. No known record survives of Revithi's life after her run. According to contemporary sources, a second woman, Melpomene, also ran the 1896 marathon course. There is debate among Olympic historians as to whether or not Revithi and Melpomene are the same person.

Societal disapproval of female runners was not universal though. Women among the Tarahumara in Mexico ran for hours without coming to any harm, as did many Native Americans, it being part of their chosen lifestyle.

In 1919 Alice Milliat started discussions with the International Olympic Committee (IOC) and the International Amateur Athletic Federation (IAAF) to also include women's track and field athletics events in the 1924 Olympic Games. The suggestion was turned down. On 31 October 1921, Milliat formed La Fédération Sportive Féminine Internationale (FSFI) with a plan to oversee international women's sporting events. Milliat organised a competition in 1921 called the Women's Olympiad in Monte Carlo; further editions were held in 1922 and 1923, and then in 1924 the Women's Olympiad was held at Stamford Bridge in London. The IOC objected to the FSFI using the word *Olympiad* in the title of its events. After further negotiations the IOC and the IAAF agreed to include five women's athletic events in the 1928 Olympic Games, and in exchange Milliat altered the title of the FSFI event to Women's World Games. They didn't include any endurance events.

Thirty years after Revithi's run in Athens, Violet Piercy of

Great Britain was the first woman to be credited with a world best time for the marathon, when she clocked 3-40-22, in what appears to have been a solo effort on 3 October 1926, although historians have questioned its veracity. On 16 December 1963, American Merry Lepper ran a time of 3-37-07 to improve slightly on Piercy's record, having gatecrashed a marathon race. To add further confusion to the matter, sources such as the IAAF and ARRS (Association of Road Racing Statisticians) do not agree on details of some of these early marathons, or indeed recognise their existence in some cases.

Things did not move on smoothly for women in the Olympic movement. In 1928 women were allowed to compete at the Olympics at just five events: the 100m, 4 x 100m relay, high jump, discus and the 800m. One of the women's races at that Olympiad, held in Amsterdam, set things back dramatically.

There was controversy surrounding the 800m race, stemming from the perception that nearly all the women collapsed upon finishing the race, which took place on 2 August 1928, with nine women starting and finishing the race, with six runners breaking the previous world record. Lina Radke of Germany won the gold medal, finishing in 2 minutes, 16 and 4/5 seconds, a full seven seconds faster than the previous world record, which Radke also held.

The media, at least in part, were responsible for stirring up the controversy and many newspapers reported the event as a disaster. Sportswriter William Shirer reported in the *Chicago Tribune* that, 'five women collapsed after the race and that Bostonian and fifth-place-finisher Florence MacDonald needed to be "worked over" after "falling onto the grass unconscious" at the end of the race'. In the eyes of the male-dominated media, these competitors had shown that they were too weak to complete two laps round the track.

The background of the inclusion of women's track and field events in the Amsterdam Games also provides some insight into the controversy surrounding the 800m race. The traditional views of the IOC, championed by the founder of the modern

Olympic movement, Baron Pierre de Coubertin, excluded women from competition and made the addition of events for women extremely difficult. Baron de Coubertin believed that 'allowing women in sports would harm their feminine charm and degrade the sport in which they participated'. The 800m was not re-introduced to the women's programme until the Rome Olympics in 1960.

In Great Britain, there had been a race up and down Ben Nevis, the highest mountain in Britain, nearly every year since 1895. Kathleen Connochie was the first woman to run the race, in 1955. Kathleen was no stranger to the race as her father was the medical adviser, and the acting vice-chairman of the organising committee (Duncan MacIntyre) was a family friend.

Her family were all sitting at home one evening about three weeks before the race talking about the arrangements. Out of the blue, Duncan MacIntyre said to her: 'Do you think you could run the Ben race yourself?' She replied: 'I don't see why not!' Immediately, Duncan offered to train her.

Her son, Duncan Macpherson, recently re-told the story to me. 'The following morning at 8am Duncan MacIntyre was there to take her out running. They ran in out of the way places so as not to be seen. Then went onto the hills and on to the Ben two weeks before the race.' For the next three weeks, Kathleen and Duncan trained in secret on the peat track at the back of Fort William, and in the forests between Torlundy and Leanachan. Although she didn't want people to know that she was running, Fort William was a small place, and eventually people began to find out, and Kathleen Connochie soon became the focus of attention in the build-up to the race.

Duncan Macpherson added that, 'she was entered as a woman, and was accepted', but the plan was nearly scuppered by the Scottish Amateur Athletic Association (SAAA) bureaucracy. A message had arrived before lunchtime on race day to say that Kathleen was being forbidden to run. Duncan MacIntyre was furious and withdrew from the race, with others supporting his stance. An approach was made to the race committee, and they agreed to make the race facilities available to Kathleen, who was set off two minutes after the main body of runners.

Hugh Dan MacLennan's Ben Nevis race history[3] reported the race:

> The day itself was dry with a light wind. There was mist, but no snow on the summit. Eddie Campbell won the race in one hour fifty minutes, and Kathleen came home in three hours and two minutes. Kathleen said at the time she would never forget the surge of adrenalin as she approached the finish field. 'I felt really fresh, and we had a great time coming down the hill. At one stage Duncan disappeared to go and wash himself having fallen in a bog and I know there was consternation at the finish when it was announced that we had been separated. Then I passed the SAAA official on the way down and that gave me a lot of pleasure. I still have the ladies' washbag I was given as a prize. It is a treasured possession.'

Happy with the outcome, Kathleen Connochie never ran the race again, although she and her family continued to support it. She said: 'I had done what I set out to do, and I didn't really see any point in doing it again. It was for other people to pick up the challenge and we got a lot out of it as a family over the years. I suppose in many ways I did it for Duncan. It was fun and we have all enjoyed every minute of it.'

Having Kathleen Connochie running in the 1955 Ben race was quite probably of huge benefit to the race itself. The media exposure it attracted may well have been responsible for the fact that double the number of runners completed the course the next year. However, women weren't officially invited to run the race until 1980.

Moving on to the challenge of the marathon: Dale Greig became the first woman to break 3 hours 30 minutes for the marathon distance. Her record, of 3-27-25, was set on 23 May

3. *The Ben Race: The supreme test of athletic fitness*, Ben Nevis Race Association, 1994.

1964 at the Isle of Wight Marathon, where she was followed around the course by an ambulance. Greig was made to start four minutes ahead of the men. This meant that her run could be called a time trial, rather than a race against the men. It was her first attempt at the distance. She was also the first woman to run two ultramarathons: the Isle of Man 40 in 1971 and the 55-mile London-to-Brighton race in 1972 – seven years before female competitors were officially allowed.

The Secretary of the sport's governing body, the Women's Amateur Athletic Association (WAAA), Marea Hartman, was concerned to protect the 'rules' that were in place at the time, and certainly saw no need to encompass change in women's sport. She was quoted in the Daily Express,[4] two days after the event (i.e. in 1964), with this position statement. 'We have no races over [*more than*] 4.5 miles. It's felt these distances are too much for women. As for women running against men – No. The discrepancy is too great.' The Isle of Wight Marathon race organisers, Ryde Harriers, were reprimanded by the area athletics authority for allowing a woman to run in their marathon.

Before 1972, women had been barred from the most famous marathon outside the Olympics – the Boston marathon – although that rule did not keep women from running it. In 1966, Roberta Gibb hid behind a bush at the start, sneaking into the field and finishing the race in an unofficial time of 3-21-25, to become the first woman known to complete the arduous Boston course. Gibb had been inspired to run by the return of her race entry with a note saying that women were not physically capable of running a marathon. 'I hadn't intended to make a feminist statement,' said Gibb. 'I was running against the distance [not the men] and I was measuring myself with my own potential.' Roberta Gibb's run has largely been forgotten because of the fuss made over the next woman who ran the Boston Marathon.

The following year, number 261 in the Boston Marathon was assigned to entrant K. V. Switzer. In lieu of the pre-race medical

4. See: *There'll be no prizes for women*, Katie Holmes, Like the Wind magazine #25, 2020

examination, Switzer's coach took a health certificate to race officials and picked up the number. Not until two miles into the race did officials realise that Switzer was a woman, twenty-year-old Kathrine Switzer of Syracuse University. Race director Will Cloney and race official Jock Semple tried to grab Switzer and remove her from the race, or remove her number, but her teammates from Syracuse fended them off with body blocks. Switzer eventually finished the race after the race timers had stopped recording, in 4-20. Although Switzer knew that they were not expecting women to enter, she has claimed that she had not used her initials on the entry form to deceive the race officials, but was merely a fan of J. D. Salinger and liked the sound of her initials. While Switzer was creating a stir with her unauthorised entry, Roberta Gibb again ran the race, this time being forced off the course just steps from the finish line, where her time would have been 3-27-17.

Photos of the race officials chasing after Switzer appeared in the national papers the next day and brought the issue of women's long-distance running into the public consciousness. The officials defended their actions, saying they were only enforcing the rules – that forbade men and women from competing in the same race and barred women from races of more than one and a half miles.

'I think it's time to change the rules,' said Switzer. 'They are archaic.' Switzer's story and the surrounding publicity had made the quest for equality in road racing for women a political issue. Coming as it did in the midst of the women's liberation movement, it galvanised women in the belief that it was time for change. Soon race directors wanted her (unofficially) in their races, and she was given unofficial trophies at several events. In May 1967, in Toronto, thirteen-year-old Maureen 'Moe' Wilton was paced to a 3-15 marathon, then the world best for women, in a race Switzer also took part in.

In the late 1970s, Kathrine Switzer, retired from competitive running, and was one of the people who led the way toward the inclusion of a women's marathon in the Olympics. In 1977, Switzer, then director of the Women's Sports Foundation, met an executive for the Avon cosmetics company who told her the company was interested in sponsoring a running event for women. Switzer wrote a seventy-five-page proposal describing how Avon might sponsor a series of events, and the company liked her idea so much they hired her to plan the races. The first Avon International Marathon was held in Atlanta, Georgia, in March of 1978, drawing women from nine countries. On 3 August 1980, 200 women from twenty-seven countries ran in the third of the Avon sponsored marathons. It was held in London, starting in Battersea Park, and was won by New Zealander Lorraine Moller in 2-32-44. This was one year before the London Marathon was launched, which really opened up the event to mass participation by women.

In 1979 the International Runners Committee had been set up to campaign for the inclusion of the marathon, 3000m, 5000m and 10,000m in the IAAF World Championships and the Olympics, and in 1980 the American College of Sports Medicine had released a statement in support of the creation of the women's Olympic Marathon. It stated:

> There exists no conclusive scientific or medical evidence that long-distance running is contraindicated for the healthy, trained female athlete.

After years of hard work and lobbying by passionate female and male athletes alike, the women's Olympic Marathon was finally included in the Los Angeles Olympics, in 1984. Joan Benoit became the first female gold medallist in the event. This was eighty-eight years after the first men's Olympic marathon had taken place.

Joan Benoit later said of running into the Olympic stadium: 'Once I passed through that tunnel, I knew things would never be the same.' The women that followed on from Kathleen Connochie also ensured that fell and mountain running would never be the same again.

CHAPTER 2

Beginnings

Opportunites and Competition Open Up:
The 1950s and After.
Profiles: Carol McNeill, Joan Glass

'The fields had some very narrow stiles, and some very odd things happened at these stiles.'

Such was the scene at an early running competition on the fells, which can be traced back to the 1860s. The first 'fell race' was the Hallam Chase, which has been hailed as the sport's oldest amateur race, being first run in 1863. The Hallam Chase is best described as a cross-country race, which was originally held over a 10-mile course on the edge of Sheffield. The Grasmere Guides Race was first held in 1868, going to the top of Silver Howe and back initially. It was a professional race, with three pounds being the first prize.[5] The full history of these and other early fell races, and the amateur/professional divide, is documented elsewhere by this author,[6] and is not directly relevant to the theme of this book, as women were not allowed to compete in those early amateur or professional races.

Towards the middle of the twentieth century, we see women beginning to assert themselves by competing in off-road endurance events. Even before the exploits of Kathleen Connochie on Ben Nevis (in 1955), there had been a couple of cases of women

5. Roughly equivalent to £145 today.
6. *It's a Hill, Get Over it: Fell Running's History and Characters*, Sandstone Press, 2013.

being accepted into, rather than being turned away from, UK fell and mountain races.

The Lake District Mountain Trial was the first event in England to promote a women's fell race. The event had been inaugurated (with a men-only race) in 1952. It was organised by the Lakeland Region Group of the Youth Hostels' Association, to celebrate the group's twenty-first anniversary. They had originally planned on holding it on just that one occasion. The event was a mountain challenge, starting at the Old Dungeon Ghyll and covering about sixteen miles, for YHA members – with the stipulation that they wore boots or stout shoes. It used one-minute interval starts, in the same way that cycle time trials have usually done, probably because it was suggested by Harry Chapman, who was a former racing cyclist.

It was such a success that it was repeated in 1953, to celebrate the coronation of Queen Elizabeth II. This time there was also a women's race, going up Rossett Gill, across to Esk Pike and Bowfell, then back down the Band. It is worth noting that there were just fifteen starters in the men's race. Bill Smith reported on the women's event in his history of the sport:[7]

> There were 4 competitors, of whom Jane Allesbrook of Cark-in-Cartmel was easily the fastest in 2-14-39, being accompanied by her two dogs; and she was followed by 17-year-old C. H. Mawson of Windermere in 2-46-12; Hazel Myers, assistant warden at Coniston Youth Hostel, in 2-48-30; and 41-year-old Mrs M. O'Hara, wife of the Coniston YH warden.

There was a women's race again in 1954, over the same course. There were three entrants, Hazel Myers again, together with C. M. Bleasdale and M. Metcalfe (from Preston Harriers), with only Myers finishing, in 2-46-10. After that, Mrs Jane Buckley (of Kentmere) finished twenty-seventh out of a total of thirty-one competitors in 1956; and then there were three

7. *Stud Marks on the Summits: a History of Amateur Fell Racing* 1861–1983, SKG Publications, 1985.

female entrants in 1968. The Lake District Mountain Trial Association booklet[8] records that last event:

> Three women were given special guest entries as another precursor to the Women's Trial, but the course proved to be too demanding. LDMTA Records indicate all ran within sight of each other and that Carol McNeill of the Devizers, who was to win the Women's Trial in 1991, retired at Slight Side while Sophie Rex and Hazel Hill, both of Southern Navigators, were timed out at Great Knott.

A patchy start to women's competition, then, and still not really being welcomed by the organisers. Despite the 'precursor to the Women's Trial' quote above, it was another decade before the women's trial was run again. This was in 1978, by which time Sue Courchee was Organiser, a post she held for seven years.

Orienteering was ahead of fell running in its attitude to females. Southern Navigators, to which two of the competitors above belonged, was founded in 1965 by Chris Brasher and John Disley. The British Orienteering Federation (BOF) was established in 1967 and held the first British Championships that year. There was equality of competition right from the start, with both a men's and women's competition, won by Gordon Pirie and Carol McNeill respectively.

Carol McNeill was a competitor who went on to make a significant mark as a fell runner, and in orienteering (as she won the BOF Championships six times). She recalls that Lake District Mountain Trial in 1968. 'We had been putting pressure on organisers to allow us to run. Sadly, none of us finished – it was from the Old Dungeon Ghyll, and I had to retire because of feeling ill. This was a real shame because I thought it would have fuelled the argument against women competing. It was a few years later when women were allowed in again.'

---

8. *Fifty Years Running: a History of the Mountain Trial*, LDMTA, 2002.

Carol McNeill

When I first contacted Carol she agreed to get out all of her fell running maps to help her to remember the past years, times and positions in events. She also dug out her training diaries as a further guide. Straight off she confirmed that she is still running competitively, and proudly noted that she had competed in twenty-six Mountain Marathons and many fell races. Although claiming not to have been a pioneer she was certainly challenging the status quo by pressuring the Lake District Mountain Trial organisers to be allowed to compete.

Carol was born in 1944 in Crosby, Liverpool. She trained as a PE teacher, taught in Wiltshire (where she started orienteering and running), then moved to Scotland to work in Outdoor Activities at the Benmore Outdoor Centre near Dunoon. She then moved to the Edinburgh University PE department; to the Dunfermline PE College Outdoor department; and then ran an outdoor centre for Dumfries and Galloway at Castle Douglas. She moved to the Lakes in 1983, eventually teaching at John Ruskin School, Coniston.

She was not a runner at school, mainly playing hockey and tennis. As an adult she carried on the hockey and tennis, and added orienteering, cross-country skiing and mountaineering. She didn't start running until she was twenty-two years old.

She says now that she ran some cross-country and a half-marathon – all as part of her training and fitness for orienteering. 'I was never at the front, I wasn't a natural athlete, better at running over rough terrain than on roads. But I trained really hard from 1978 to 1993, averaging 50 miles a week with a peak of 80 miles per week in 1979.'

According to Carol's records she next raced in a fell race at the Moffat Chase in 1978, aged thirty-four. 'I think I must have done the Carnethy 5 when I lived in Edinburgh, which would have been sometime between 1969 and 1981, and also the Ben Nevis race. I do remember when they changed the Carnethy course. They started on the other side of the A702 instead of the school in Penicuik. When it was really foggy there was concern that the runners wouldn't see the cars coming and vice versa.'

With her love of the hills, it was natural for Carol to run on them. Initially she trained with several other runners, some of whom ran on the fells, and she recalls there was general banter and encouragement to do some fell races. Despite the Scottish connection she only ran the Ben Nevis race once, in 1982, finishing out of the medals in 2 hours 1 minute. She was, however, there as well when the Ben race was cancelled due to thick mist in 1980. She came second (to Anne Bland) in the two-lap cross-country race the organisers put on instead.

Carol certainly hadn't been training specifically for the fells by the time of her first race on the hills. 'I was doing a lot of hill intervals as part of my training and running in the hills for fun. I started doing Mountain Marathons in 1976.' She was a member of three orienteering clubs (Interlopers Orienteering Club of Edinburgh, then Solway OC, and then Lakeland OC) before she joined Ambleside AC around 1983. She has notes in her training log which show that she joined the midweek training runs there in the late 1980s.

Looking back on those early days, Carol didn't have any specific problems with race organisers and their attitude to female competitors. 'I can't think of any in particular. There certainly weren't any negative vibes coming through. There weren't that many women at races in the beginning, but I never thought of myself as a pioneer.'

Whilst not being particularly active in trying to make changes happen, Carol was very aware of inequalities, particularly with regard to prizes. 'I remember commenting at a Borrowdale race that winning a pair of socks didn't compare well with the men's rucksack or similar prize. Also, at a KIMM our winning socks (again!) undervalued our result – we got them changed for a fleece, which I still have.'

Carol emphasises that she took up running to train for

orienteering, which she started doing in 1965. 'Whilst in Scotland I ran in some fell races for fun and in 1983 I moved to the Lakes and increased the number of races considerably. I really enjoyed the contrast of trying to keep up with a pack compared to navigating on my own in O-races. All my training was aimed at and motivated by succeeding in O-races – right up until the 1990s when I was aiming to win the veteran category at fell races, and I did.'

Carol feels that her Joss Naylor Challenge was one of her most satisfying achievements. 'I had a go at this when I was fifty-ish – soon after it was established. I was confident I could do it in the 14 hours allowance we had at that age but was sick going up Gable on a really hot day. I did finish but out of time (in 15 hours). I told myself I would wait until I had 24 hours to do it again. One does slow down with age. It wasn't as easy as I had anticipated, although I trained with a small group doing sections. I had a couple of bad patches which I got through thanks to my support team.'

She also did the Bob Graham Round, in 1993, getting home just inside the 24 hours. 'I was the oldest woman to do it at the time. I was forty-nine. I am not sure if that has been superseded – maybe Wendy Dodds has done it again?' Wendy Dodds did a Bob Graham Round (a 53 Peaks at fifty actually), and Julie Carter a 55 at fifty-five in 2019, so Carol is no longer the oldest female Bob Graham Round completer.

Although she hasn't done any other big rounds, she did do the Three Peaks Yacht Race a few times – Barmouth to Fort William – as a runner. Once with women runners (three women, three men), with Jean Dawes and Anne-Marie Grindley; then she raced with all women's teams two or three times. She also did the KIMM every year from 1996 to 1998 and has been controller a couple of times.

Carol did the Lowe Alpine Mountain Marathon (LAMM) a few times, including Harris in 2019. She also did one mountain marathon in Norway with Ros Coats and tells a story from that event. 'At one point we swam across a lake. The advantage was that we beat the Bloor brothers into the finish; the downside was that we had chosen a bad place where it was quite wide, and Ros declared she wasn't a strong swimmer!'

When asked about her finest race or achievement in the sport, Carol McNeill says it was the Dunnerdale in 1991. 'I was training for the Vets World Cup (Orienteering) in Australia, so I was training hard while the others were cruising through the winter. I was just enjoying the run when I caught up with Helene Diamantides and wondered if she was maybe ill. I asked her if she was OK and she said, "of course I am, keep going Carol you are having a blinder" (or something similar). Then some of the men started running with me to keep me going to the end. I was second behind Yvette Hague, in 48 minutes, which would be a good time even now.' Not a win then but pushing herself to a great second place.

Carol adds that, although she set no race records, she did win the Lake District Mountain Trial once, in 1991, which she was really chuffed with. Having been second a few times she was pleased to win once. Of her twenty-six Mountain Trials – seventeen were Medium and nine were Short, which she started doing soon after that option was added and open to everyone. 'On the web page they only count Classic and Medium. I was disappointed that they haven't acknowledged the older people. Joss Naylor has done a few Shorts too.'

Talking through those that had the most impact on the sport in the 1970s and 1980s (male or female), she said: 'Interesting – I can't really remember. Joss of course, and Billy Bland. Selwyn Wright, Ros Coats, and Ruth Pickvance.' But she had no doubt about whose overall record on the fells most impressed her, looking back. 'Joss's multiple achievements, which went on and on. Amazing.'

Still with unfulfilled ambitions, Carol McNeill concluded by saying she hoped to carry on doing the Lake District Mountain Trial (the short version). She had done the 2021 Short course and beaten Joss Naylor, although admitting that 'he is a bit older than I am'. Carol McNeill was the first of the female athletes who pushed for their inclusion in events, and then went on to have a long and varied career as an orienteer and fell runner.

While there were scarce opportunities for fell race action for women in the 1950s and 1960s, several of the more walker-focused events did give openings for women to do endurance events. In a less competitive sense women had been leaving their mark much earlier. For instance, Louise Dutton was an exceptionally strong walker and was the first woman to walk the Pennine Way, soon after it was designated.

The Chevy Chase started as an organised walk in 1955 and had a formal runner's class added in 1967. However, some male athletes had run it prior to that, and in 1962 sixteen-year-old Eleanor Puckrin won a women's race over a much shorter course, with Eileen Dobson winning it in 1963. Reports of this event from later in the decade don't mention female finishers.

Other events in which women were allowed to participate include the Fellsman Hike and the Lake District Four 3,000 Foot Peaks Marathon. The Fellsman started in 1962, and accepted women from 1968. It is a high-level traverse covering more than sixty miles over very hard rugged moorland. The event climbs over 11,000 feet, going from Ingleton to Threshfield in the Yorkshire Dales. The Fellsman list of winners, starting with Hazel Costello in 1968, became a veritable who's who of female endurance athletes over the years.

The Lakes 4 x 3,000s[9] (which is no longer held) started in 1965, and also accepted women from 1968. The route covers

9. The Lakes 4 x 3,000s was a race over the four highest mountains in England – Scafell Pike 3,029ft, Scafell 3,162ft, Helvellyn 3,117ft and Skiddaw 3,054ft.

about forty-six miles with 11,000 feet of ascent but did include a good deal of road running. Pat Kenley (of Ulverston) won the first women's edition in 1968, and then two more times in 1970 and 1973. The participation by a good number of women in these very long endurance events certainly shows there was an appetite for events for females to be added to the calendar. It is a sign of the times though that both Fellsman and Lakes 3,000s have the women's information relegated to the very last paragraph in their respective chapters in Bill Smith's *Stud Marks on the Summits*. Recent Fellsman organiser, Phil Carroll, confirms that at least seven female competitors completed the 1971 event, which is a good number for the time. Janet Sutcliffe was an early pioneer and was often competing at the Fellsman in the 1970s.

Even England's national game was not immune to prejudice. There was massive excitement in England after the football World Cup win in 1966, with high hopes of a repeat in Mexico in 1970. However, the sport had not been welcoming of women's involvement. In 1921 the sport's governing body, The Football Association, had declared the game to be 'quite unsuitable for females', before barring women from playing on grounds belonging to affiliated men's clubs. That ban was lifted in 1970 to allow a slow revolution in women's involvement in the national game. There was soon to be a parallel change for women in fell and mountain running, which was more of an evolution than a revolution, as the sport became more formalised.

Two years after the Fellsman and Lakes 4 x 3,000s had accepted women into their events an organisation to manage fell running was set up in 1970. The Fell Runners Association (FRA) was initially run by men for men. It was reported that Brenda Robinson, the wife of one of the committee members elected at the first meeting, had to 'wait outside in the car' during that first meeting. However, it turns out that wasn't quite the full story. It was actually worse, and Brenda wrote in *The Fellrunner* (the FRA magazine) that she was, 'locked out of the car in the freezing car park playing with my seventeen-month-old son in the snow as dusk approached'.

The first FRA newsletter was published in September 1971, and on page three listed the first 117 members who had paid their 25p annual subscription. At the foot of that page was a footnote:

> At least one enquiry has been received from a lady re membership! – How about lady members? – our constitution doesn't specify sex!

Not exactly a welcoming message from the editor. For the record, Item 3 of the Constitution of the FRA, adopted at its opening meeting, states: 'The Membership of the Association is open to *all persons* who support the Association's objectives [*my italics*].' These objectives were: 'to encourage and foster better standards of Fell Running and allied mountain races in the United Kingdom and to provide service to competitors and race organisers.' The Long Distance Walkers Association (LDWA) was founded in 1972 and offered long walking events for all, up to their annual 100 mile event.

The Autumn 1972 issue of *The Fellrunner* carried a two and a half page 'recent history' of the Ben Nevis Race by Jim Smith, and quietly mentions right at the end that the 'women's record stands at 3 hours 2 minutes, set by Kathleen Connochie of Fort William in 1955.' Earlier the *Press and Journal* reported, in Sept 1971 in an article entitled '*174 men – and 1 girl – in gruelling battle of the Ben*', on another female athlete running in the Ben Nevis race:

> Fifteen minutes before the start, Miss Dale Greig, Tannahill Harriers, Paisley, already making a name for herself in marathon running circles, set out to try and beat the 1955 record of 3hrs 2 mins set up by a Fort William girl, when she limped in in 3hrs 3min 2sec with her shoes soaked in blood from blisters. First to greet her was that girl runner of 16 years ago, Kathleen Connochie, now Mrs George McPherson, wife of the Ben Nevis Race Association's president.

The Welsh 1,000m Peaks race had first been held in 1971, with the full race going from Aber, taking in the four highest peaks in Wales and finishing on the summit of Snowdon. The first (shorter) women's Welsh 1,000m Peaks Race, from Ogwen to the summit of Snowdon, took place the next year (1972), but was called 'Class D for Women Mountaineers', with Joan Glass entering in 1973. Carol Walkington and Joan Glass entered as mountaineers in 1974 and Joan won in 3-02-33. They returned the next year, finishing in the same positions, Joan winning with 2-28-50 to Carol's 2-34-35. The women continued to run a shorter course for several years.

That Welsh 1,000 metres race, in 1973, was the first mountain event that Joan Glass had ever entered – as she had noticed that there was a class for 'lady mountaineers', over a shorter route than the men. She adds, 'to my surprise and delight I won, and also the following year, but I didn't train as such – just good days walking in the mountains.'

Joan Glass

The first thing that Joan Glass did when I contacted her was to offer the contact details for one of her long-time race rivals whom I had been trying to reach. She then proceeded to diligently respond to my multiple emails requesting details of her career and then asking supplementary questions as I sought clarification of the fine detail, particularly of challenging the Ben Nevis race organisers.

Joan Glass, whose maiden name was Gallagher, was born in Liverpool on 11 September 1939. As a youngster Joan didn't really do athletics in school but was selected to run in the 400 yards and 200 yards hurdles for an inter-school meeting just before Easter 1953. She was selected on the Friday evening but on the Tuesday when she should have been competing, she was on her way to hospital, having been taken very ill, as she explains. 'I didn't return to school until the new school year in

September. I had contracted osteomyelitis in my pelvis. It was originally thought to be polio.'

On returning to school, she was told she wouldn't be able to do any sports. 'Aghast, I did proceed to play hockey and netball, and had always loved swimming, which was a family favourite. I didn't do any running before fell running. In fact, I came to running on the fells by default.'

Dennis, her husband, was the catalyst. He was organiser for an event for a YHA club (Liverpool Area Club) that they belonged to, that had first taken place in the 1950s. It was from Llangollen Youth Hostel to Maeshafn Youth Hostel. Joan says it was, 'approximately twenty-six miles, consisting of some road sections and a super route over the Clwydian hills.'

The first event Joan competed in was this club 'marathon' in 1961 (but unofficially). 'It was a mixture of walking and a bit of running downhill, and I ended up first female. Initially the route for the women was shorter, but after some persuasion we were able to do the longer route. My strength is stamina, not speed, so it suited me fine.'

Joan and Dennis Glass moved to Llanberis in 1964 to take up a position of managing Llanberis Youth Hostel and had three children, in 1965, 1969 and 1972. Joan comments that, 'some good walking on the mountains was how I kept fit, with a baby in a papoose on my back.'

There wasn't a running club in the area. The nearest was Wrexham Athletic Club, which they joined in order to enter some Lakeland races. 'There were no fell races in North Wales. Dennis had joined the FRA in 1972. His number is 224. I joined later but was not a member for long, as hip problems interfered greatly with my running.' Eventually, in September 1977, Dennis and Joan were among the founder members of Eryri Harriers.

Joan Glass had protracted issues when trying to run in the Ben Nevis race in the early days, as she explained. 'Dennis and a friend were entering in 1975 and suggested I entered too. My entry was refused because it was a men's race, and they returned my entry fee. However, we persisted because there was a ladies' record and we pointed this out. We asked if I could have a go at beating that time.'

The next letter, in July 1975, from race secretary Derek Button to Dennis Glass, (quoting Connochie and Greig's previous efforts) said that 'subject to confirmation by the Committee we shall endeavour to arrange a similar event for your wife.' Button confirmed in yet another patronising letter that, 'your time will be recorded by the official Timekeepers, and we shall do our best to ensure that you do not get lost on the Ben.'

They permitted Joan to run, but she had to start one minute after the men. 'I ran that year in 1975, and I broke the women's record, and won again in 1977 when other women entered. But we still had to start separately from the men until 1980, when the first official women's race was included.'

A new race secretary, Krys Chmielewski, wrote to invite Joan personally to that first official women's race, saying:

> You will want to know that the Association has taken the necessary steps to organise an official Ladies Ben Nevis Race. The Committee is confident that this development will be welcomed by the running fraternity.

With deep irony Joan points out, 'alas the weather was so atrocious it had to be cancelled!' According to the Ben Nevis race book: 'For the first time ever, "Britain's toughest Race" had to be cancelled because of weather conditions. The dramatic moment came when the 400 runners, including fourteen women taking part in the first official women's race, were led to the starting line by the Lochaber Junior Pipe Band.' But there was a silver lining for Joan. 'I went for a run with the other girls up Glen Nevis. It was super running with just ladies, a novelty for me!'

Despite her success in getting to run the Ben Nevis race before it was officially allowed, Joan says she never considered herself a pioneer. 'I just happened to discover running when there weren't many women running on the hills, but I was quite determined that we should be able to compete the routes the same as the men when I realised that we were quite restricted in some events.'

She also entered the Avon Ladies' Marathon in London in August 1980. 'Imagine being able to run along the streets of London, just women only, it appealed tremendously. This race was organised to prove that women were capable of running the marathon distance. It was brilliant! Two hundred women from twenty-seven countries ran the streets of London. This was the year before the first London Marathon and John Disley was the only familiar face I saw when I attended the pasta party the evening before. He was there checking out the logistics for organising a city marathon before he and Chris Brasher started the London Marathon the next year. Dennis and I also ran in that first London Marathon in 1981. My time for the Avon was 3 hours 20 minutes and my London I think was 3 hours 15 minutes. I thought I could go under three hours if I trained properly (there was a lot more information available by then) and I attempted to train seriously, but unfortunately my childhood hip problem was becoming more troublesome. I'd been trying to ignore it because some days I could run without any problems but the next day I was in agony.'

In February 1981 Joan saw her consultant in Liverpool. He had warned her when she was aged fourteen that she would have problems as she got older. 'I had check-ups every two years, and he told me that I was going to need a replacement hip, and then that after twenty-eight years looking after me, he was retiring! He had been brilliant.'

She carried on running and competing when she could. 'I'd take Solpadeine tablets before I set off and if I got through the first twenty minutes, I was then OK until I stopped. It was SO frustrating. I needed to find an understanding orthopaedic surgeon, and fortunately, I did.'

Joan had her first hip replacement in November 1984. It went well and she had no pain and managed movement she hadn't had for years. 'I was told I wouldn't be able to run again, but I couldn't accept that and told the surgeon, who was amazing, that I couldn't promise. I competed the following July in the Snowdon Race. For the next seventeen years I continued running, representing Wales in cross-country, and doing my first triathlon in 1985 at Plas y Brenin (which included canoeing, cycling and running up Moel Siabod), and many other events – occasionally winning my age group.'

Unfortunately for her, the Bangor surgeon was headhunted by Great Ormond Street, so when she needed a revision, she went to Gobowen Orthopaedic Hospital. Sadly, that surgeon was not at all understanding about anyone wishing to run. 'I couldn't really run again after that operation. I had needed a lot of bone grafting, and although the pain had gone it just didn't feel it was aligned correctly. The surgeon wasn't someone I could ask for guidance, and it only lasted two years. I had my second revision in 2007 and thankfully had another brilliant surgeon who keeps an eye on it. I see him every two years.'

Now she still walks on the mountains and does quite a bit of cycling, which was her initial love after her mother bought her a 'sit up and beg' bike when she came out of hospital all those years ago. 'I did an 80-mile bike ride for my eightieth birthday. I haven't gone electric yet, but living where we do – in the mountains – it's very tempting!'

In conclusion Joan modestly doesn't really consider any of her races as great achievements. 'I'm just really pleased I enjoyed running and was rewarded with a few record runs. I particularly enjoyed being part of a ladies-only race.' She also mentions the Avon Marathon and managing to get into the Ben Nevis Race, despite their initial opposition because she was a woman. 'I guess also winning the Snowdon Race, three times on the run, was great because it is such a local event and helped to get fell running established here in North Wales.'

Joan didn't wish to single out any particular female whose record on the fells most impressed her. 'There have been so many brilliant runs by ladies it is difficult to select just one. What I do miss, is the fun and camaraderie of the very early days. Organisers considered it was not possible for ladies to run as hard and as long as the men, and it's very satisfying to belong to the group of early lady fell runners who proved that we can!' Joan Glass determinedly chased the Ben Nevis organisers to let her run and from then onwards showed what women are capable of.

The Autumn 1972 issue of *The Fellrunner* has an extensive report and results for the 1972 Fellsman Hike – but it fails to mention that Susan Hargreaves was the fifth winner of the women's category for the event. Similarly, a report on that year's Lake District Four 3,000-foot Peaks Marathon Walk has no mention of women competitors.

It is important to remember that it is not just about competition. Although there is much detail in this book of races, records and achievements, there are those who are happy just being out in the fells. Several of the pioneers interviewed for this book mentioned that the competitive aspect wasn't as important to them as the freedom to just be out running and exploring in the mountains.

An interesting view on the competitive urge is expressed by Nan Shepherd in her excellent treatise on a life lived in the Cairngorms.[10] She writes:

> To pit oneself against the mountain is necessary for every climber: to pit oneself merely against other players, and make a race of it, is to reduce to the level of a game what is essentiallly an experience. Yet what a race-course for these boys to choose! To know the hills, and their own bodies, well enough to dare the exploit is their real achievement.

10. *The Living Mountain*, Aberdeen University Press, 1977.

She does admit on the very next page that it is 'merely stupid to suppose that the record-breakers do not love the hills'.

In 1953 Gwen Moffat had become the first British female to be certificated as a mountain guide. Before this, females had been denied this possibility, either formally or informally, and so there were no females in the professional Guides races, such as Grasmere or Ambleside, until the sport became 'open'. Let us not forget that women had been ascending mountains, including those in the Alps, from the end of the eighteenth century, although admittedly usually with male guides.

Writing about the Cuillin Ridge (on Skye),[11] Moffat gives her thoughts on the competitive urge:

> The main ridge is seven or eight miles long with about sixteen peaks of over three thousand feet. The average time taken for the traverse was ten to thirteen hours, some parties took twenty-four, others were bringing the record down to fantastic times, as on the fourteen-peak walk in Snowdonia. We hated records: we decided to be different. We would take our time, sunbathe, enjoy the views, carry food for two days, sleep out on top of the ridge; we would set up the record for the longest time spent on the Cuillin traverse. [*They took thirty-nine hours*]

Notwithstanding that, Shepherd and Moffat set fabulous examples to other females to get out and explore the mountains, and can be said to have broken through some barriers for females in the same way as the runners highlighted in the introductory chapter did.

11. *Space Below My Feet*, Penguin, 1976.

CHAPTER 3

Competing unofficially

Governing Bodies Rule.
FRA and Race Organisers Awaken.
The Sex Discrimination Act.
Profiles: Carol Walkington, Bridget Hogge,
Anne-Marie Grindley

'I couldn't get enough of the mountains', commented one runner, taking to the hills in the 1970s.

Women were beginning to compete more, and over longer distances, consequently showing others the way. Bill Smith reported (in *Stud Marks*) on an anomalous occasion. 'The first fell race to be run (nominally) under AAA Laws with female competitors (unofficially, it would seem) was the inaugural Edale Skyline in 1974. The programme included three women, each of whom started. Lesley Evans (Castle Climbing Club) retired, but Lynne Mitchell (Manchester Rambling Club) and Katherine Peek (Castle Climbing Club) both completed the full 22-mile course, finishing 55th and 71st respectively out of 100 starters, of whom twenty-nine retired.' Three women competing on the fells, who from their club affiliations were from climbing and walking backgrounds. There was no mention of the women in *The Fellrunner* race report, as though it never happened. Note that 22-mile distance though, and the fact that the furthest that female athletes could run at the Olympic Games at this time was 1500m (just under 1 mile). Outstanding pioneers right there then, who paved the way for others to have the freedom to do their own endurance running and racing. Lynne Mitchell was also the fastest lady in that year's Lakes 3,000 Marathon, an achievement she repeated in 1975.

The problem for women, or more particularly for race organisers, was that the rules of athletics' governing body did not permit women and men to race together at that time. All the events mentioned up to now, (the Lake District Mountain Trial, the Chevy Chase, Fellsman Hike, Lakes 3,000, Welsh 1,000m, Ben Nevis and Edale Skyline races), were technically guilty of breaking the rules by accepting female entries. As can be seen, the acknowledgement of this, and adjustment of the arrangements to allow it, varied from event to event.

Later in 1974 Carol Walker came sixth overall with Jim Smith in the 'B' Class of the Karrimor International Mountain Marathon, winning the mixed team prize. *The Fellrunner* did slip in a mention of the leading woman at the Fellsman in 1974, the aforementioned Miss L. Mitchell.

Carol Walker/Walkington/Campbell

I contacted Carol at a bad time as she had just had an accident with her bike on black ice and had badly fractured her femur. After rehabbing for a while she was then able to concentrate on the questions I had sent her, including ones on her running unofficially in races before being allowed in by race organisers.

Carol Walker was born in July 1952, in Bolton. She married Pete Walkington in 1977 and became Carol Campbell in 1991. From her early school years Carol loved all things sporty, as she explains. 'In junior school we had great teachers that offered netball and athletics for ages nine to eleven, and I was in the teams. I joined Lichfield Athletic Club in 1963, and then in 1966 we moved back to Bolton.'

During the 1966 to 1970 school years she was involved in many team sports, and was introduced to badminton, where she represented Bolton schools and played inter-league matches for her club. 'In athletics I ran 880 yards (the furthest distance girls could run), threw the javelin (and was Bolton schools champion three years running), but would try any athletic events. Jim Smith (at Bury AC) was a history teacher who started a cross-country club and I found I really loved running the longer distances. Over the four years I represented Bolton schools on a number of occasions.'

Carol's love of the Lakeland fells started with trips organised by the art teacher, on day and youth hostel trips. 'Sergeant Man was my first summit. That was me, hook line and sinker.'

For three years, from 1970 to 1973, Carol was doing her teacher training, with PE her subject, in Matlock in Derbyshire. 'This involved loads of outdoor education. In my free time I continued with the badminton and cross-country, and was introduced to climbing on Stanage. I also did orienteering and joined the fell walking club.'

In 1973 Carol returned to Bolton for a teaching post and met Peter Walkington, a colleague in the PE department, and by November 1973 they were a couple. 'I was soon helping with Youth Hostel trips in the Lakes, and completed my Mountain Leader training in 1975. Pete was already an established and successful fell runner and cyclist, and he was keen for us to be in the mountains. We cycled a lot. Weekends were spent in the Lakes, holidays in Scotland and the Alps. In the Alps we did a variety of walking, mountaineering, climbing, snow and ice climbing on 4,000m peaks, and running.'

At Easter in 1974 they had traversed the Aonach Eagach and Pete thought they would get back quicker if they ran down. 'It was very exhilarating and the start of fell running for me. I started to run to work, continued our various activities at weekends and looked for a race. I've always loved to compete at whatever I did, and still do! The only 'race' available in 1974 for women was the Welsh 1,000m from Lake Ogwen to the top of Snowdon, but it had to be done dressed as a mountaineer, carrying a 10lb sack. I finished second to Joan Glass, a local, and I was hooked. I returned over the years for the race, Joan and I became friends and completed the KIMM in 1975 together, finishing first women's team in the B Class.' Prior to that Carol teamed up with Jim Smith, who was a friend of Pete and in 1974 Jim and Carol competed in the A Class Cheviot KIMM, finishing as first mixed couple.

Carol joined Kendal AC in 1974 and ran in the Mid Lancs cross-country league races and on the fells with Anne Bland. Carol claims she never really had a training plan in the 1970s, but just tried to do something active every day. Carol ran the Fairfield Horseshoe race unofficially for two years in 1975 and 1976. She adds ruefully, 'I did run in the first official race in 1977 but with a very disappointing time and recall having run faster unofficially!'

In those early days Carol looked up to Grete Waitz and also Ingrid Kristiansen, as they were putting women's marathon running on the map. Grete was the first female in history to run under 2.5 hours. Turning back to the fells, Carol mentions that in fell running, 'there was Joss Naylor. We travelled together with him and Mary for the first Sierre-Zinal race, and they borrowed a tent from us. It was probably the first and last time they ever camped! I didn't race that year, as I hadn't been running very long.'

West Cumbria offered several races for women in the mid-1970s, separate to the men, which Carol says were, 'such good, low key fun. A must to do if you were free, but generally only five or six competing on average, not always the same ones, but generally from different backgrounds like myself, that is fell walking, mountaineering, orienteering, climbing and cross-country running. The Copeland Chase, an orienteering-style event, and the Kinniside race were popular. The most welcoming as I remember was definitely CFRA [*Cumberland Fell Runners Association*]. At the time they had individual race organisers. Joe Long (RIP) was always happy to use Ennerdale Scout camp as a venue for low key events in which women were welcome, including orienteering-style events like the Copeland Chase.'

Carol relates a telling story about those days and the attitude some of the athletes had. 'I remember the first women's Kinniside race, five women, excited at the start, our own race. I know Joan Lancaster and Janet Sutcliffe were there. Chatting and jogging along, not overly fast, staying together and still together as we came up to the summit and checkpoint. All together five abreast, I think we had to be reminded it was a race. Unfortunately, there were a number of people watching us from the sports field through binoculars who were greatly amused!'

Carol explains her frustration at the attitude of some men at the time. 'I think, for me in the early days I loved to run, but it was all about equal opportunities. What gives men (the race organisers) the right to say women are not able to participate in these events? We were more than capable. It was the same in teaching PE. If girls could run 1.5 miles cross-country in the winter, why were they only allowed to run 800m and not 1500m on the track? I made sure I was on the appropriate committee to initiate change.' This committee work included the Bolton Schools Athletics Association and being Bolton rep at the Lancashire Schools (later Greater Manchester after reorganisation).

By 1977 there were more race organisers offering women's races. 'The Ben Nevis race was probably the last prestigious race to offer women entry and that was thanks to Ros Coats,' says Carol. At the Spring 1978 FRA AGM Carol Walkington was the first female to be voted on to the committee. [In 1976 Ann Joynson had been FRA Secretary for a while but was a temporary stand-in for someone so not an elected member.]

The 1979 season saw the first Women's Championship races, pushed forward by Carol. On further reflection she describes the thought process that went on in setting up the Championships. 'I remember the CFRA (via Tommy Orr) was only thinking of getting us ladies involved, it wasn't a takeover. I liked Tommy very much. After hearing his suggestions, I personally thought, why adapt the men's to "suit" (or what many male organisers thought) the ladies. Could it be different, easier, even? I don't recall ever being asked what we would like to see put in place, and there always had been a reluctance to put on the same race as the men for the ladies. We had to "prove ourselves". Why? Again, you can see my equal opportunities thinking coming to the fore again.'

All that reminds me of a great quote that I recently saw (but couldn't ascertain who to attribute it to), which was: 'we don't want to take over, we just want to take part.'

As it happened, it was really bad planning, because Carol and Pete's first daughter was born in May 1979, followed by two more daughters in 1981 and 1984. 'Inevitably, I ran very little (I was still competing in badminton and netball, as always) but didn't race between 1979 and 1982. Anne Bland was running on the road by now and encouraged me to get fit for the Derwentwater 10 in November 1982. This gave me the impetus to get back on the fells in 1983.'

Carol ran in one of the races famously affected by atrocious weather on the day. It was the Kentmere Horseshoe, in 1983, a Championship race. 'It was freezing, misty, snowy conditions. I was very pleased to finish in one piece, Nan Bield pass was treacherous.' Carol finished seventh, in what was a strong women's field for the time. Twelve of the fifteen female competitors finished.

Pete and Carol Walkington trained, raced, and looked after the girls between them, often with an early start. 'Pete would often do a morning time trial and me an afternoon fell race. I trained in the evenings when Pete was home from work. I always kept up the cross-country races for speed!'

Carol did her first Sierre-Zinal race in 1978, which felt good as there were plenty of women running, a distinctly more enlightened European scene. 'It was such a huge climb up into the woods from the busy Rhône Valley below, beautiful running after the climb and a short steep 1.5-mile descent where I could pass so many less able descenders. I've done this race a number of times with my best time being just under 4 hours.' The Walkington's interest in the race came about in 1974, when they were planning to be in the region doing some mountaineering. Joss Naylor, Harry Walker, Mike Short and Jeff Norman all had invites and so Pete Walkington entered. 'I felt I wasn't experienced enough to race but I probably would have been fine,' Carol recalls. 'Harry Walker was second that day, I remember the excitement like it was yesterday. I raced the following years until 1979 when our daughter was born, and again once or twice in the eighties and nineties. In 1983 I competed in the Crete Vosges race, a great runnable race and finished third.'

The year 1983 was a good one for Carol. Her expectations were to compete and get back on the fells. She was surprised to find herself as a contender for the British Championships and finished runner-up to Angela Carson/Brand-Barker. *The Fellrunner* report noted: 'It wasn't until Burnsall that she [*Angela Carson*] overtook Carol Walkington, who had led for most of the season. Carol did well, finishing second after four years off to raise a family'. Carol hadn't run at Burnsall, as she was away on holiday. 'Instead, I travelled up to Fort William to race in the Melantee, where I finished second. Short races were never my forte. This was a long return day trip with some of the Horwich men.'

Although over the years Carol won a number of races all over the Lakes, most of her wins would be more local in north-west Cumbria. She also supported and paced many Bob Graham Round attempts in the 1970s and 1980s, and she also recced and planned her own attempt. But the time was never right, which she is very sad about, looking back now.

One particularly strong memory for her is when she set the record for the Lakes 4 x 3,000 foot Peaks, at 10 hours 53 minutes. This was in 1986, when she knocked over three hours off her previous best. She also won the Three Peaks race in 1983 and 1986, albeit in 1983 with an agreed tie with Wendy Dodds. 'It was Wendy's suggestion to run in together, after we had run down from the summit of Ingleborough more or less together.'

Carol made very occasional ventures off the fells, including competing at the tough (six events in a week) Tour of Tameside twice. She came second in 1985, and third in 1986.

She also did a marathon, in Barnsley in 1987, winning in 2-58-52, on what was not an easy course. 'I only entered because I was feeling fit and had had a good fell season. I had entries in the London Marathon for the next two years, but unfortunately I was injured. I always felt I had a faster race in me. I was extremely pleased with my time, I had wanted to get under three hours and ran even splits, the weather was horrendous, wet, windy and cold. I remember my legs seizing up afterwards. The presentation was on the top of the Town Hall steps (lots of them). I struggled to get up and down them.'

In July 2000 Carol suffered a double fracture of her ankle and for the next few years she had big problems with her feet, making running difficult. She is still active in many ways, including cycling, Nordic walking, cross-country skiing/guiding, golf and walking. She is also a 'guided walks' leader for HF Holidays in Europe and the UK.

Carol Walkington/Campbell finished by mentioning not being in the 'Ladies' chapter in Bill Smith's *Stud Marks on the Summits*, as she explains. 'Bill sent out individual questionnaires, but I didn't receive mine. I remember being disappointed with my lack of inclusion at the time of buying the book, but it seems our questionnaire had gone astray.' Carol very much deserves to be included in this book though, as she has championed women's equality in many ways over the years.

A year after the Edale race noted above, the Autumn 1975 *The Fellrunner* carried a piece, entitled 'Growing demand for women's races' that said, 'mention should be made of Miss L Mitchell's excellent time of 13 hours 45 minutes (position 24th out of 183) in the Lakeland 4 x 3,000 ft Peaks event', and also noted several other individual women's performances in 1975, including 'Carol Walker's 5th position in the Standard B Class of the Two Day Mountain Marathon, and Anne Bland's 15th position in the same event.'

Bill Smith notes in *Stud Marks on the Summits* that, 'at least two race organisers were approached around this time with a view to inaugurating a ladies' race with their event, but both replied to the effect that "a woman's place is in the home – not running up and down fells".' On this occasion it was not that women were not considered capable, but more that it was socially inappropriate. Some work to do on changing some race organisers' attitudes, then.

This attitude produced an unattributed rant, which Eileen Woodhead reported in an article in *Up and Down* magazine reflecting on these times (in the Jan/Feb 1992 issue).

> Sooner or later someone is going to take certain organisers to the sex discrimination board! I suppose it is a bit like the fight to allow women to run marathons, yet look at the number of men Grete Waitz can beat. I don't see any reason why women can't run any fell race, and start in the same race as the men. I really think women should be judged on merit and not on sex. The number of absurd reasons put forward is ridiculous – it's not safe; not lady like; not meant for women. As far as safety goes, if it is not safe for us, then it is not safe for a lot of men either, because a weak, feeble, pathetic female like me can beat them!'

All this was so unnecessary. The Sex Discrimination Act of 1975 should have helped women get equality of opportunity. It stipulated 'that employers could not discriminate against people on the grounds of their gender.' It may have helped in the workplace, but the spirit of the law really needed to be embraced by race organisers.

The Fellrunner had a report on the Welsh 1,000m Race in which it was noted that 'in Class D, for lady mountaineers, Joan Glass, the wife of Llanberis YH warden Dennis Glass, reduced her own record of 3 hrs 2 mins by more than half-an-hour. In second place was Pete Walkington's girlfriend, Carol Walker, who also broke the old record by 27-25.' The wife/girlfriend tag is a form of downplaying or trivialising female performances, which sadly can still be seen in some media reporting even now.

The Ben Nevis race book says of the 1975 race:

> 175 completed the race with a solo woman runner, Mrs Joan Glass from Wales, completing the run in 2-17-50. She was not allowed to take part in the official race and set off some minutes after the men. The mother of three received a special prize from Mrs Nan MacFarlane.

In her profile in the *The Fellrunner* (in February 2004) Joan Glass says of the occasion, 'I was the only woman (embarrassing, a solitary figure in the middle of the field, waiting for a minute to pass) but I set off and achieved the objective, which because it was a 'walking' record wasn't difficult.'

The Spring 1976 *The Fellrunner* notes on page two that the new Secretary of the FRA is Miss Ann Joynson, thus being the first female to do FRA Committee work. She gets due recognition on page three of the Spring 1977 issue, where it says Ann was thanked for her 'secretarial work for the association ... paid tribute to Ann's effort in compiling the most comprehensive calendar yet'. *The Fellrunner*, in Autumn 1976, noted that the Welsh 1,000m race secretary was Mrs Jones (wife of race organiser Dr Ieuan Jones). At that Welsh 1,000m race, on the first weekend of June 1976, the record was broken for the race (in the 'D Class for lady mountaineers'), with Bridget Hogge beating Joan Glass by around five minutes.

Bridget Hogge

When I spoke to Bridget, she wanted to explain why she was on the fells and how she felt when she was on them. Although she was extremely successful in races she seemed to want to play down the competitive element. 'I really don't know about records. I can't remember any of that because it wasn't really important to me.' Later in our conversations she had a slight change of emphasis, saying: 'I'm not sure those that I ran with would agree that I was not competitive – not sure I do now!' She added: 'I still maintain that I was a fortunate to be running when I was and I hold dear the spirit engendered by the people involved.'

That Welsh 1,000m race was Bridget Hogge's first ever, and she says she had no idea that people 'ran' on the hills, as she reflects now. 'I don't think women were allowed to compete in the long race which was fortunate for me. Had I been allowed I would not have contemplated the longer race. Even the shorter event seemed an impossible distance; however, it finished uphill and I like uphill. There were specific rules on what we had to carry with us, and my footwear might well have been light boots on the Welsh 1,000m progressing to something like Dunlop Green Flash – leather not canvas! – for the Snowdon Race. Shoes that I used then could be described as an improved plimsoll.'

The first Snowdon Race followed that Welsh 1,000m and in the weeks between the two events Bridget recalls training by going up and down Snowdon a few times. 'I didn't have a car, so I cycled to and from work and waited for lifts to places. Training was thus varied. I don't remember how many women there were in the Welsh 1,000m, but there were only three in the Snowdon Race. Joan Glass was unable to run that year. My friend John Evans who was an all-round mountaineer with a thorough knowledge of the locale was instrumental in showing me running routes over the Welsh hills and later on he introduced me to running in the Lakes and Scotland. From the start I have had generous and supportive running companions.'

In 1976 Bridget's friends were climbers and walkers, not runners. 'My background was as an instructor in the outdoors – walking, climbing, kayaking, etc. I don't recall any kind of prejudice in these sports and nor did I meet any when I joined the fell racing community.'

Running became Bridget's sport, on fells, road, or cross-country. 'I was more comfortable in longer races in whatever category, but remember some vicious short fell runs – Meall an t-Suidhe for example, maybe on an 'unofficial' Ben Nevis weekend – details forgotten, but not the doing of it! When I was in Wales I could train from work and Padarn Country Park, Moel Eilio, Elidir and the Snowdon Horseshoe were all accessible. Joan Glass became a running and training partner and we had fun as I remember it. Enjoyment was not just in training. Joan and I were Mountain Marathon partners, and a lot of laughing and chatting took place on those events. As I started to take part in events in the Lakes, Anne and Pete Bland and family were kind and generous to me, and I can still 'picture' training runs in Kentmere. Later, when I was living in Manchester and Lancaster, I could train in the Peak District and the Lakes, and with friends in support.'

Bridget took part in many races from 1976 to 1981, and again after 1982. In mid-1981 she was diagnosed with a stress fracture of the pelvis. 'It was first treated as a hamstring injury. When I was helping to load the kit for the Welsh 1,000m competitors Chris Brasher remarked that a hamstring shouldn't be taking that long to heal. He suggested somewhere to go and get it looked at properly. X-rays showed up the stress fracture and the only treatment was an instruction 'not to put on any weight'. In *Stud Marks on the Summits* Bill Smith remarked about me that I 'just disappeared'. Indeed, I did. I couldn't go on the hill, let alone race and later that year I went abroad. I started running again in early 1982, and I competed again for two or three years or so, stopping again in early 1985. After a run at the Edale Skyline race I woke up to find I couldn't walk without limping. It got worse. I didn't get a definitive diagnosis, and I did have to stop running. When after about two years I was once again mobile I was so thankful to be able to at least be on the hill that I stayed satisfied with that. I ran again but not at any particular standard, but with great relish.'

Despite Bridget saying she can't pick out any one particular race as being the best, she reels off a fascinating list of memories. 'I recall enjoying the Three Peaks – not much chance to slow down; the Wasdale, Langdale and Borrowdale events – having to slow down; the Snowdon Race – no comfy running; the Vaux Mountain Trials – mistakes in navigating at speed; the Bob Graham Round made possible by a Dark Peak Team [thank you all so much]; that fiendish KIMM in the Rhinogydd which Paddy Buckley devised [I couldn't manage that route inside five days now!]; Ben Nevis in horrid conditions; Kentmere in a white-out; the Eryri marathon – a wonderfully varied course with a testing finish, and in the shorter races the pain of not being able to take in sufficient oxygen! Lying in streams fully clothed to cool down in the summer; getting in the lake before a 'hot day' Snowdon Race; eating squashed sandwiches on the start line of some of the classics in the Lakes. All these and so much more live somewhere in the memory.'

Bridget says she has a poor recall of the politics of the fell racing world or of the efforts of the women, and men, who campaigned to allow the women to compete alongside the men. 'Some of the women's race alternatives when the men's events were closed to women meant a long journey for a short race. Things changed. I was fortunate to be in the group of women who benefitted at that time. Not being aware of the early years of fell running, I did not appreciate the work that had gone on – and continued to go on – to open up events equally to men and women. I thank them heartily. My recall is of people pushing for equality: Carol McNeill and Sue Harvey from orienteering, Anne Bland and Joan Glass from fell racing. It wasn't only women pushing for equality in fell racing. Doors were opening.'

Her overriding memory of being part of fell racing is of 'a community of people – organisers, supporters and competitors – whose love of the hills was a common thread. An egalitarian mix where the wind, rain, sun and mud soon got rid of any pretensions, where taking part was as laudable as winning and where what I considered to be superhuman skills were in evidence.'

'The number of people out on the hills now running and walking is remarkable. I see Eryri club runners out and these include lots of women and youngsters. This is so different from in 1976, when there were a small number of women racing in Wales, and many more in the Lakes. I have friends and neighbours who run and compete, and although I don't follow current stars or their times, I do know that the times achieved these days are striking. Any records that I held anywhere have been broken long ago, except for the slowest winning time for the Snowdon Race! Those who race now haven't had the joy of upgrading from boots to plimsolls to fell shoes and then to improved fell shoes. The problem now seems to be one of deciding which fell shoes to use for which event!'

Bridget Hogge loved being part of this community and says it is great to see it so popular. 'I am glad that I was there at the time that I was and that I maintain my love of being out in the hills. The distances that I used to cover with relative ease I now struggle to complete, but I do shorter distances frequently. Pioneering is not a term I would use for myself. I was there at a particular stage in the development of the sport, and I took part enthusiastically. There were competitors to strive to match and I had very generous and kind companionship and support.' A true lover of the sport at its most basic level.

The Spring 1976 *The Fellrunner* issue had a report, from Alan Barber, on the first Snowdon race. It was held in conjunction with Llanberis Carnival, and on the same day as the Olympics opened. In all probability, being such a small event the organisers didn't even consider what the governing body might have thought. 'The ladies event was won by B Hogge 65-20 summit and 100-15 at the finish. Perhaps some of the ladies who have been showing an interest lately will enter next time, I hope so.' *Stud Marks* reported that 'she gave nothing away on the descent, winning by the wide margin of 16-15 from runner-up Anne-Marie Grindley with a time of 1-40-15.' Barber also reported that at the summit 'we were all given a can of lemonade, perhaps the only mistake that the organisers made.'

There was also an interview with John North, the FRA chairman at the time, in which he is quoted as saying he was greatly in favour of women's fell running. 'There are quite a few women keen to take part and why not. If they want to take part in the same races as the men I've no objections. If they beat us fair enough – it is up to us to train harder and prevent it.' At last, some positive encouragement, with a slight macho tinge.

Finally, the magazine lists new FRA members, including 'number 649 Mrs A-M Grindley'. She is the fourth female member (although others might be hidden behind the use of initials rather than full names). The first was number 295 Miss H. Hamer (as noted in the Autumn 1972 issue of *The Fellrunner*). There had also been number 520 Edith Henry, and 525 J. Dawes. That year Anne-Marie Grindley joined Clayton-le-Moors Harriers, who had no female members up till then, and the club soon had one of the strongest female teams in the sport.

Anne-Marie Grindley

Anne-Marie admitted on our first email thread that Linda Lord had just rung her and they had a bit of a reminiscence session. 'We used to train together and also ran together on Clayton training nights. Unlike Linda, I haven't kept all my old results but with a bit of thought can dredge up the info from the depths of my recollections.' She also said that many of the comments were from memory which she hoped was accurate. 'It has given me great entertainment looking back over results and talking to my husband, Will, about what we can remember.'

Anne-Marie Grindley had entered a fell race before the Snowdon race noted above. In early 1976, her husband Will was recovering from an injury, and he agreed to run with Anne-Marie as she entered her first race, the Edale Skyline. At 21 miles and 4,500 feet of ascent, she was certainly jumping in with both feet. 'With my background of hiking, this suited me better than entering a short, fast race. We came last, but I was the only lady in the race, and I figured I had beaten the sixteen or so drop-outs. It was the third time that race had been run, and from the start, ladies could enter. Lynne Mitchell, daughter of Eric Mitchell, won the first two events.'

Anne-Marie Grindley's maiden name was Osborn. She was born in Colne, Lancashire, on 28 September 1947. At school she says she did athletics just before, and on, the annual sports day, running the 100 yards and 440 yards. She played netball and, if forced, tennis and hockey (badly, as she puts it). Later she played netball for the firm where she worked.

She explains how she got her love of the countryside early in life. 'My main interest from being really young, was hiking. My parents took my two brothers and I walking from an extremely young age. Our first Lake District holiday was when I was about thirteen years old, at a CHA centre in Grasmere.'

Anne-Marie did no other running before she started fell running, but had walked the Pennine Way. 'This was with Will and my father. It took us twelve and a half days in 1968, averaging almost twenty miles a day, carrying our camping equipment. Will and I walked all the Cairngorm 4,000 foot peaks in one day in 1967, after spending 6 weeks in the Swiss Alps. There we had climbed about a dozen peaks, which were not too demanding in terms of rock climbing, as I was not much above a *v diff* grade climber.'

She is the middle one of three children. Both her brothers, Michael and John Osborn, started running in their teens and joined Clayton-le-Moors Harriers. John subsequently moved to Blackburn Harriers with John Calvert, Harry Walker and Ken Smith. Michael was a member of Clayton when the club ran the Pennine Way Relay in 1970. 'Will and I provided the telephone headquarters for runners to check into. We then reported on to other runners about when they could expect to start their leg. Of course, that meant that we came to know a lot of the runners.'

The following year, Will Grindley, a strong walker, entered the Karrimor International Mountain Marathon, held that year (1971) in North Wales, with Anne-Marie's elder brother, Michael (who was already a good fell runner). 'They didn't even complete the first day (of the two-day event), but Will was most impressed with the super fit runners and started training himself. His fitness rapidly increased, but by then I had two young children and had lost my hiking fitness.'

Anne-Marie had something of an epiphany during a walk in the Lake District, when she was struggling to keep up with Will. She decided to take up jogging to get fit for walking. 'I started by running from our house down to the local canal and then walking back until I could run the whole distance. I slowly increased my mileage. My parents lived close by and were happy to look after our children on a Sunday morning while we jogged together. Walking and running, we would cover about a dozen miles. At some point, Will deemed me fit enough to join the Clayton Tuesday night training sessions with the slowest group. I used to carry a map and ten pence for the phone in case I got dropped and got lost!' She says she enjoyed the Sunday morning runs with Will and they gradually extended the distance.

Anne-Marie readily admits that she had no great interest in road running, except as a way to get training miles in. So, as much as possible, she ran in the countryside and on the local moors. 'I lived about six miles from Pendle Hill and a similar distance from the Forest of Trawden moors. I progressed to running long distances on my own and then, when Linda Lord and other local ladies started fell running, we would sometimes go out as a group.'

She says that, without a doubt, Wendy Dodds was the person in the sport she looked up to in those early days. 'Already, before I started running, she had completed the Karrimor, an event I aspired to enter. Will and my brothers described Wendy in the Karrimor, busying herself pitching the tent single-handedly, while her male partner lay flat out after the day's efforts!' Wendy remains someone Anne-Marie admires immensely. 'Wendy continues to be an inspiration for ladies in the sport. Other ladies I wanted to emulate included Jean Dawes and Joan Glass. They were both entering long events and obviously enjoyed the fells for their own sake.' Other names that Anne-Marie mentioned include Bridget Hogge and Jean Lochhead, and finally someone else who received very high praise from her. 'When Ros Coats started fell running, she was much better (in my estimation) than the rest of us, competing with a lot of the men at their level.'

The men Anne-Marie admired were mostly in Clayton-le-Moors Harriers – Stan Bradshaw, who gave her loads of encouragement, Alan Heaton, Alistair Patten, John Haworth, all people who had completed the Bob Graham Round. 'Help also came from various slower members of Clayton who put up with me tagging along, Roy Phillips, Harry Hartley and others. As for the very top, the men outside my immediate sphere, there were people like Joss Naylor, Billy Bland, Harry Walker – just so many great runners.'

Will and Anne-Marie's two sons were born in 1970 and 1971, a few years before she started running, and she explains how things were at the time. 'As was often the case in those days (when there was no maternity leave or right to keep your job), I did not work outside the home for about eight or nine years. As I have already said, I had a lot of encouragement from Will and my parents. After a few years when I had more fitness, my elder brother, Michael, and I would go for a 20-mile plus run around our local area on a Saturday morning.'

Anne-Marie adds another reflection of the lack of maternity leave. 'That worked very much to my advantage once I started serious running. I'd walk John and Jamie to school, then had two and a quarter hours to run to Pendle and back. Home in time for the boys' lunch time at twelve o'clock. I wasn't brave enough to turn up at school in running gear though. It was covered up, and I called home to remove my trousers, then went off to Pendle. We camped many times in the Lake District with

John and Jamie, in the early days, with Will running longer races. Often other spectators would look after the boys while I ran a short race.'

Anne-Marie recalls joining Clayton late in 1976, after entering a few races. 'My younger brother suggested I join Blackburn, as Hilary Matthews was already running with them, but I was already running on Tuesday with Clayton and receiving a lot of encouragement from them. I think there were a few of the men in Clayton who were not too happy about me muscling in on their Club. However, they were much fitter than I ever got so I was not a threat to their egos. Later female fell runners, such as Ros Coats and Vanessa Peacock, would have ruffled more feathers if they had been members around that time.'

A lot of long races, for example Borrowdale, Ennerdale, and Wasdale, were in those days restricted to male entries, and there were short races, up and down the nearest hill, which Anne-Marie says were, 'organised to pacify the women. I entered these but was hopeless at fast descending. I was first at the top of Dale Head once, but was third or fourth at the finish, because of my poor descending skills.'

Anne-Marie notes that some race organisers took the view that if you just put your initials on the entry form, they didn't know if you were male or female, so let you in. But she was conscious of some discrimination. 'The worst example I can remember was one year at the Ben Nevis Race. Lord somebody or other had come to set the men's race off. The ladies were set off ten minutes later by a race official. Good female runners, such as Ros Coats, then had to fight their way through all the slow men to get up near the front where they should have been from the start. I was never going to do well in that race, not being good at rough descents, so it didn't bother me too much, but I felt for the fast women.'

Playing down her own abilities somewhat, Anne-Marie says that at first she felt she was just tagging along behind the pioneers (here citing Jean Dawes, Joan Glass and Bridget Hogge). 'But then, as our numbers grew, I did feel to be part of a pioneering movement, particularly when I completed the Bob Graham Round.'

Not just content with having an opinion, she also took positive action for change, as she explains. 'With the help of Stan Bradshaw, Jean Lochhead and I got ourselves on to the Three Peaks Committee to convince them that ladies were quite capable of navigating the course and completing the event in a reasonable time. I am proud of that contribution to ladies' fell running.'

Anne-Marie Grindley's first races were in 1976. The first, as already mentioned, was the Edale Skyline, which she says, 'was definitely my sort of race, a long one over moors with plenty of ascent.' The same year she did the races at Pendleton, Thieveley Pike, Stoodley Pike and Snowdon. 'I don't remember much about any of them, except a feeling of nervousness at the start and hoping I wouldn't be last. I do remember the crag part way up the hill on Thieveley Pike and the energy it took for the leap across the stream near the end when I was trying to put on a burst of speed for the line.' Snowdon came about because a friend, Harry Manning, wanted to run the inaugural Snowdon race. Their families were friends, so they went to camp in Snowdonia so that Harry and Anne-Marie could enter the race.

Will and Anne-Marie Grindley put in a lot of training and recces for their Bob Graham Round. 'We invented a local Three Peaks of Boulsworth, Great Hameldon and Pendle Hill, a distance of over 30 miles. I ran that twice on my own as part of my training. Will and I went to the Lake District on several occasions to train and familiarise ourselves with the ground.' They did sections like Swinside to Wasdale, anticlockwise on the Bob Graham Round route, and back by a shorter route; Dunmail Raise to Threlkeld at night to see how they coped in the darkness. By the time they set off on the Round, the only short stretch Anne-Marie hadn't done was over Broad Stand.

Anne-Marie sums it up. 'The main feeling on the Bob Graham was the enjoyment of being on the fells with wonderful friends.

We were extremely lucky with the weather, not too hot or cold, good going underfoot, excellent navigators, attentive roadside support. During the day that included my parents with our children. My younger brother had completed his BGR a few weeks earlier in extreme heat, which caused him some difficulty.'

The following year, her elder brother Michael completed the round in quite a fast time. 'We all did it the Clayton Way, anticlockwise. I don't suppose there are a lot of siblings all to have done the Round.'

Jean Dawes was the only woman to have completed the Bob Graham Round by the time Anne-Marie tried. Some of the male runners were sceptical of Anne-Marie's prospects of success. 'I had been given various yardsticks with which to measure my chances – running the Three Peaks in a certain time, completing a marathon in under three hours. Neither of those was I ever going to come near to achieving. However, I worked on the principle that I was confident and that I could keep up an average of roughly 3.5 miles an hour with an ascent of about 1,200 feet an hour for twenty-four hours.' Anne-Marie rightly credits the community aspect of big rounds. 'It is very humbling that so many people turn out to help others on challenges such as the BGR, willing to pitch in, sort out problems as they arise, run with you or climb up to mountain passes even in the middle of the night, cosseting you as you rest, delighting in your achievement.'

The next year, 1979, Anne-Marie had a crack at the extended Bob Graham Round, which at the time was at the standard 42 peaks, but it had an element of controversy as to how she added the peaks. Anne-Marie confirms that she and Will checked all their plans with Fred Rogerson, who was the BGR guru and record keeper. 'He had supplied us with an information sheet entitled *In quest of the ultimate in mountain endeavour.* It lists all the summits on various attempts. Will settled on a definition for my extra peaks, which Fred sanctioned (bear in mind, we are numbers ninety-eight and ninety-nine in the Club, so quite a small band and we knew a lot of the other members). Will proposed, and Fred agreed, that we could include any summit already part of a successful attempt or ones that fitted our definition of a new summit as being over two thousand feet with two fifty-foot contours around the summit, as shown on the one-inch Lake District map in use at that time. This gave us the two (controversial in a few runners' eyes) summits, an extra peak on Kirk Fell and Stirrup Crag on the way to Yewbarrow.'

She did have to have a break in the mid-1980s, when she suffered a prolonged debilitating episode of glandular fever. She was ill, on and off, for about a year, with the after-effects lasting about another year. 'After that, every time I tried to get back to what I considered race fitness, I would have a minor illness. I accepted that was the end of any expectation of being as good in fell races as before, certainly in shorter events and stopped entering many of the fell races.'

But being on the moors and fells is still her love, especially over the Covid-19 lockdown. She points out that she can be up on the moors within a mile, on foot, from leaving her door. 'Since no longer considering myself a fell runner, I have completed such events as LDWA 100 milers (taking about forty hours for the one hundred miles, compared to about fourteen and three-quarter hours for the 63-mile Fellsman Hike in 1983), Bullock Smithy, Three Rings of Shap, One Foot in the Gargrave and the Upper Wharfedale Three Peaks. Those entering these events include 'proper' fell runners, but also joggers/walkers and strong hikers, so times are more generous, refreshments are often available on route and route finding is usually not too difficult – a suitable way of gently declining into obscurity.'

When asked to give her finest race or achievement in the sport, Anne-Marie says that she finds it hard to differentiate between her proper fell races and her hiking achievements. 'As a true fell running activity, both of my Bob Graham Rounds are the pinnacle of my running, and I can still picture incidents on both outings.'

Suggestions are flowing now. 'Ros Coats and I were the first female couple to complete the Elite class of the Karrimor in 1978, though Anne Bland, with Pete, was the first lady to complete the Elite class in the same race. That really pleased me though our time was not as good as we had expected. On the first day, I had a fall and strained a muscle. Ros rethought our route to minimise the ascent/descent to make it easier for me, but the contouring round increased some of the distance.'

Blurring the edges of running/hiking, she then nominates winning the Jim Nelson trophy six times (once jointly with Jean Dawes) on the Fellsman Hike as ranking very high in her list of achievements. She adds, 'I was proud to complete the High Peak Marathon four times. It is one for the head bangers, setting off at midnight in early March to complete a circuit of the upper Derwent watershed. My first entry into this event was as a member of the Ladies of the Lakes team, though, when one lady dropped out, Pete Dawes was recruited at short notice to fill in. The other members were Jean Dawes and Janet Sutcliffe. We came 10th out of 31 finishers. The next year as Clayton Ladies (Linda Lord, Alex White, Pat Brown and myself) we finished 9th out of 13 finishers (and the only ladies' team) with 31 retirees. Gales, rain and sodden ground made for hard going. In 1982, I joined Clayton Z team (Will Grindley, Doug Brown and Don Talbot) to finish 4th out of 23 finishers. In 1983, another Clayton Ladies team, Wendy Dodds, Pat Brown, Ann Sayer (the latter not actually a Clayton member) and I finished 12th out of 27 finishers.'

Another proud moment came in 1980, when Will and Anne-Marie won the very first Haworth Hobble outright. 'That is overall, not just the first mixed couple. It did not have a high-class entry field in that first race, though we did beat George Brass and Eddie Hill and a couple of other Clayton teams. Will's map-reading skills gave us a real advantage. That and the fact that not many others had recced the whole route.'

Finally, Anne-Marie reminisces how, in 1980, Jean Dawes and Carol McNeill recruited her to join them on the Three Peaks Yacht Race. 'It was the first time I had ever been on a yacht. We set off in a gale, then Carol and I ran up Snowdon in the darkness. An entertaining event. We had two men as sailors and were considered outsiders but finished fourth.' Later she recalls that they, 'had to row our yacht through the Corran narrows, as the tide turned, to get ahead of the army team!'

Modesty overtakes Anne-Marie again when discussing setting records, as she says she was never a very fast runner and was not competitive enough to put the speed training in. 'I set a record in the Fellsman when I finished first lady and overall 14th in 14 hours and 48 minutes in 1983. In the same year, I completed the full route of the Welsh 1,000 metres race, from the beach at Aber to Snowdon summit. I can't remember whether there were other ladies in the race. Obviously, winning the first Haworth Hobble I set a record but that was easily beaten the following year. We ran on frozen snow, quite icy in places making it slow going.' Actually, there were five women in the results of the Welsh 1,000m race the year Anne-Marie mentions.

Anne-Marie Grindley concludes by commenting on her fiftieth birthday treat. 'In company with Will, we walked/jogged the BGR over four days, finishing with double toasted teacakes and tea in Keswick on my fiftieth birthday. We stayed with Joss Naylor's brother at his B&B in Wasdale, dropped into Grasmere for a B&B from Steel Fell with a final B&B in Threlkeld. Happy days.'

Having started competing on the fells in 1976, Anne-Marie says that given that a lot of fell running is competing against yourself, she is not sure that she has stopped yet. Anne-Marie contributed to getting women into clubs and into races, and also applied a detailed approach to endurance planning when setting up her extended BGR record.

The Fellrunner, in Autumn 1976, had a long piece by Peter Knott that spelled out in detail the 'rules' for fell racing for women, quoting from Rules 27, 31, and 47 of the WCC & RWA

(The Women's Cross-country and Race Walking Association). They were printed as a 'guide to promoters and competitors', and were handily summarised by Knott at the end of the article:

> This means that, over 10 miles, or its fell equivalent presumably, men and women can start together and run the same course, but not compete against each other i.e. separate result sheet etc. Over shorter events, a separate start time should be used.

This was presumably to satisfy the different male and female governing bodies [of athletics] of the time. It was these guidelines that allowed females and males to run together officially for the first time in the Spring of 1977.

CHAPTER 4

First official women's races

Breaking Rules to Achieve Change and Recognition.
Profiles: Pauline Stuart, Joan Lancaster, Ros Coats

'We just want to take part', was increasingly the call.

Many race organisers were at the forefront of rapid changes that took place in 1977, under pressure from the women who supplied the growing demand for races mentioned earlier. So, 1977 saw shorter women's races set up in parallel with some of the long classic Lakes fell races, like Ennerdale, Wasdale and Borrowdale. The Langdale fell race (organised by Dave Meek) also had a short women's race, up Pike o'Blisco that year, although the next year it changed to have all entrants traversing the full course.

The first official women's race (that is a women's race under AAA Laws) was held in that April, in Lancashire, at Pendle, made possible by changes in the AAA Laws.

There was a report in *The Fellrunner* (Spring 1977 issue) by Ben Redfern, which managed to include some casual sexism:

> At 1-30pm on 2 April occurred an event more momentous than votes for women or the Sex Discrimination Act, i.e. the first Pendle Fell Race for Ladies. In cold conditions with the going sticky, the field of twenty set off to tackle the same course that the men would run later. On the ascent pretty nineteen-year-old Kathryn Binns of Sale Harriers began to establish a good lead which she gradually increased up the

> Big End and glided home effortlessly in forty minutes thirty seconds, four minutes ahead of Blackburn's Hilary Mathews, with Gillian Pile of Sale in third place. The winner received the Tiger Lily Cup. Afterwards she said that she had found the race relatively easy and she would like to run in more fell races. The winning time was faster than the last hundred in the men's race, so watch out fellas or you may find yourselves holding the track-suits and carrying the drinks as I am sure ladies fell racing is here to stay.

The results were (full names were not given, and only the first ten listed): 1 K Binns (Sale) 40-37, 2 H Mathews (Blackburn) 44-58, 3 G Pile (Sale) 48-27, B Robinson (Bury) 48-45, 5 A Pendlebury (-) 49-52, 6 A M Grindley (Clayton) 50-11, 7 R Carthy (Sheff) 50-20, 8 S Lloyd (Walla) 50-31, 9 K Etherden (Rochdale) 51-40, 10 S Styan (Holmfirth) 52-16. It was the 22nd men's Pendle race that day, but with a separate and later start.

The Autumn 1977 issue of *The Fellrunner* summarised some of the races in that year, in a report by Peter Knott. He says that 'at least twelve events have been held, most of which have had good support from the ladies. Congratulations girls, you have confirmed our belief that there was a need and given the race organisers confidence for the future.'

The first fell race in Cumbria to officially accept women was on 22 May 1977. It was the well-established 9-mile Fairfield fell race, although (according to Bill Smith) there had in fact been an informal run over the course the previous year, when Margaret Belk (Airedale) had been first back. Bill Smith reported that in the first formal race, 'an unattached runner by the name of Pauline Cushnie (later to become Mrs Pauline Haworth) won the ladies' race from Brenda Robinson and Joan Glass'. Pauline Cushnie/Haworth subsequently became one of the first of the great female fell runners, and is now married to Kenny Stuart, who is also an icon of the sport.

Pauline Stuart

Pauline's was the only interview that took place in person, as we happened to be in the Lakes in one of the post-lockdown periods. We still had to meet outside, but sitting in the Stuarts' garden in the shadow of Blencathra was no hardship. Kenny Stuart left us to it, only being called on once for confirmation of a date. As always, Pauline was informative and entertaining.

It was a great start in fell racing from Pauline, who was born in Northampton in 1956, but raised in Southport. Her mother, Muriel Cushnie, was a Southport girl, who married a Northampton man, but the marriage broke up when Pauline was four years old. She went to Southport High School for Girls.

At the age of seventeen she left school to work the summer season for the YHA, at the Wasdale hostel, then began training as a nurse, which she pursued in Liverpool for two and a half years. 'I hated city living. I came back to the YHA, and went to work at Barrow House hostel where I met Pete Haworth, who was an assistant warden at Ambleside hostel. A year later we married then moved to Keswick and eventually became wardens at Llanbedr hostel, in Wales, and worked there for a year. In 1980 Pete applied successfully for the job of managing the Blencathra Centre in Threlkeld so we relocated back to the Lakes.'

Pauline was a keen fellwalker in her teens, spending most weekends travelling up to the Lakes from Southport before taking that summer job in Wasdale. 'It was during a walk on Yewbarrow that I came across Joss Naylor, rounding up sheep and running with his dogs, which inspired me to have a go at fell running. I started by walking for an hour or so over the fells then would turn round and run back to the hostel. As I became stronger, I ventured further and further away and in order to be back for 5pm I got faster and faster. I loved hurtling down the hills but also enjoyed the pain of running up them!'

The summer season of 1974 passed too quickly for Pauline's liking, and she swapped wardening for nursing, and the fells for the streets of Liverpool. Having got the running bug, she soon learned that it wasn't to be the same back in Liverpool. 'After just a couple of night-time excursions along the Docklands and a scary encounter in Sefton Park I was persuaded that cycling was a much safer option, although the dual carriageways between Southport and Liverpool were not without hazards!'

Nursing was abandoned basically because Pauline hated living in Liverpool. 'I spent nearly all my days off trying to hitch up to the Lakes. I had decided that was where I wanted to live. Moving and changing careers was a pretty daft decision really,' she recalls.

Within the YHA there was an enthusiastic group of fell runners. 'I was persuaded to enter the 1977 Fairfield Race. At the time I didn't realise it was the first time women were allowed to enter. I was surprised to win it as I had only been running a couple of months so had to walk a lot of the uphill but found the downhill quite easy and very enjoyable.'

Looking back on that particular race Pauline recalls that, 'a taunt of "you'd never make it round Fairfield" was enough to land me on the start line with some exceedingly fit looking individuals sporting Bolton vests and those of Sale Harriers, the majority of whom were from a background of road and track running. The start was a blur but maybe due to my past experience of descending, I ended up in front.'

Over the next two years she entered a few more races, mainly the short versions of the main Lakeland Horseshoe races. 'They were friendly affairs at first with maybe only six or so ladies running but they soon started to become more competitive with the likes of Jean Lochhead, Ros Coats, Sue Parkin and Rosie Naish coming on the scene. I realised that I would have to put some training in if I wanted to be competitive (I always preferred racing to training!), so by 1980 I felt more prepared to race and was able to win the championship.'

During that winning season Pauline ran the Kentmere race in

very poor conditions, with the women having been set off before the men, as was the way at the time. She recalls that she got to the section that traverses after Kentmere Pike before you go on to High Street. 'It was just deep virgin snow with this incredible gradient and I thought, "well I am not going anywhere". I stopped along with (as far as I can recall) Jean Lochhead, Véronique Marot and a few others and waited for the men to catch up. If you had slipped that would have been it really, as the slope was extremely steep with a slip meaning a fall of a few hundred feet. Mike Short from Horwich and Billy Bland were first on the scene and didn't even pause, just galloped along like a couple of mountain goats. We duly followed in their footsteps! I think most of the girls finished, all the times were slow and a lot of people dropped out that year. I wasn't going to drop out, I just didn't fancy going on to kill myself.'

Pauline also travelled up from Wales to run the Ennerdale race. 'I had never trained any longer than about ten miles, and just thought I'd give it a go. I was surprised to do so well on it. I enjoyed it and it suited me.'

There had been a mix-up over the championship scoring for women in 1980. It was a simple mistake, according to Pauline. 'It was something to do with Jean Lochhead being declared the victor using the previous points scheme of the best ten race results regardless of length. I think the 1979 championship was based on this, but then for 1980 it followed the same criteria as the men's championship. Someone corrected the suggestion (in *Compass Sport*) that Jean had won, because it was now scored on the best of three medium, three short, three long and one other. Because it was all very much in its infancy someone had got confused, I don't know who. We (the girls that were running) knew that we had to do the ten races and that was what I targeted. It wouldn't have been a problem if it hadn't been reported wrong.' She adds that she ran Borrowdale and won that. 'I knew that you had to do three long races, so I did three long races. I couldn't see the point of not doing so if that was what the rules asked for at the start of the season. To be honest there weren't that many women running then. I enjoyed doing the longer races to be fair. A good number wouldn't have wanted to do the longer races. That new format suited me nicely.'

Pauline then had a couple of years of injuries and operations. She had an operation on a bunion, which had become very painful, and had a heel spur operation as well. 'I had originally carried on and thought they would just go away. It took about four months really before it was OK to run on. I then didn't do much in 1982 and 1983. I came back towards the end of 1983 doing a few races.'

In those very early days her training was limited. Then she got a job at the doctor's surgery in Brundholme Terrace, in Keswick, while still living at the Blencathra Centre, which is where the longer training runs came in. She did that for four years. 'My training consisted of running in to work quite slowly then returning home via different routes depending on how energetic I was feeling, and what time of year it was. It was much quicker to run direct through the woods but far more rewarding to go over Latrigg or round Lonscale valley.'

She also comments on how things have changed. 'When it was dark at night I used to come back along the A66 road. But in the early 1980s there wasn't the traffic there is now. You could run along the A66 at 7.30 at night with a torch and back up the minor road to the Centre. You didn't have a fabulous lightweight head torch like you have now of course. You used to have a heavy hand torch with a poor beam!'

Pauline didn't really do that many long runs, but details one of them. 'Some weekends I would run from the Blencathra Centre across to Walla Crag, on to Watendlath, Rosthwaite and back along Cat Bells Terrace and through Brundholme Woods. Otherwise, I didn't do that much training. My training was racing. Probably a stupid way to do it but I wasn't much of a trainer. I was competitive though. I enjoyed the racing and the whole fell running scene. I was quite lucky because I came from a fell walking background. I had been walking on the fells from about eleven years old. I had an ability to get up and down hills.

Maybe a good power to weight ratio, I have no idea. If I had trained hard, I would maybe have got injured.'

Getting over the injuries, Pauline came back in 1984 to have a go at the British Fell Championships, managing to win it that year culminating with an impressive win at Ben Nevis and again in 1985, when she won ten out of ten of her championship counters, sealing it with her win at the Ben Nevis race. That full house of wins was no big deal, as Pauline explains. 'It wasn't really anything I thought about. They were just races that I went to that I enjoyed. I was competitive in the race, but it wasn't, "I really must go and win this race". I enjoyed winning but didn't set out with a racing mentality. It wasn't that important in those days. The training in 1984 was still simple, like it had been in 1979 and 1980.'

Pauline and Kenny Stuart swept all before them in 1984 and 1985, winning many doubles at races, and uniquely it is the only occasion that male and female British championships were BOTH retained in successive seasons.

In July 1984 Pauline went to the Snowdon race with Kenny, and also Blackstone Edge. 'We weren't a couple then at all. We got together at the end of that year though. Did it alter my training? I don't think so.' In 1985 Pauline married Kenny Stuart and they started a family when they were house-sitting for a couple who were away – at Brocklecrag, round the back of Skiddaw. It was a very remote spot just down from Dash Falls. Their son Matthew was born there, and their other children, Rosie and Emma, were born in their present house in Threlkeld. From that house out the back of Skiddaw she ran to work, or cycled. 'I carried on with this till I was about thirty weeks pregnant. I remember cycling back in deep snow and thinking I ought to stop work now.'

Pauline Stuart also showed the sort of determination that characterises winners. She told me the story of running the Ben Nevis race in 1984. 'I knew the steep, rocky course suited me. The main reason I was inspired to run such a fast time was because I overheard this well-known coach talking at the start.

"Ros Coats is here; Pauline isn't going to have it her own way. She never tries hard enough; she always looks as if she is out for a breeze." I thought damn you, I'll make sure I win this. I got really annoyed, and it fired me up. I was absolutely determined to win, and I beat the coach as well, much to his dismay. I showed them I could run really hard when I needed to.' Pauline set the course record for the Ben Nevis race that day which stood for thirty-four years before being broken by twenty-four seconds by Victoria Wilkinson in 2018.

It was the ninth Snowdon race on 21 July 1984, and although not a championship race it was by now attracting around four hundred athletes. Pauline Stuart set a new record in the women's race of 1-24-03, but perhaps surprisingly says it was not really her sort of race, as it was too much like a road race. 'Snowdon was a very fast race. I was no good at roads and didn't have natural speed, it wasn't the best for me. I preferred rocky and rough terrain. I didn't do a particularly good time. I think 80 minutes was my fastest [*1-20-29 in 1985*] but if you look at the record now it is something like 73 minutes. There is a big difference. My time wasn't that special.' Pauline won a pair of socks that time in 1984. 'Prizes were not that good, but it didn't matter to me. It wouldn't have bothered me to not win a prize at all. I am also not a trophy person, I haven't kept any. I was glad if I won a bar of chocolate.'

When asked to consider her career, back in February 2004 (for a profile published in *The Fellrunner*), she commented, 'looking back at my diaries confirms Kenny's view that I was very laidback about training (actually he used the word lazy, but I refute that!). For me running just happened to be the quickest, most convenient way to get to work, with the route through Brundholme Woods on the lower slopes of Latrigg always a delight. My mileage was low, around twenty-five to thirty miles a week, although my frequent racing schedule upped the tempo and miles a little more.'

Talking to Joss Naylor about Pauline he commented on her influence. 'Pauline worked hard. For a year or two she was practically unbeatable. It was good for our sport. Pauline is a lovely person, and I have got a lot of time for her. She made the other girls work too in races.'

When asked to assess her own abilities, Pauline replied, 'I guess I was good at climbing and descending, especially steep craggy fells, but not so good on the flat bits in between or the run out to the fell and back again. I didn't do any specific training but I suppose I raced a lot more than other people. My advice would be to be confident – if you are hesitant you fail!'

Like husband Kenny, Pauline tried road running but didn't take to it. She completed the Barnsley Marathon in just over three hours, and had PBs of 1 hour 24 minutes for the half marathon, and 1 hour 2 minutes for 10 miles. Pauline Stuart also ran at the Inter-Counties cross-country a couple of times, noting one time in the Keswick AC club newsletter:

> Boob of the year must go to the County Cross-country selectors who presented me, Gill and Daphne with knee length, size 40" chest county t-shirts for one year at the Inter-Counties. Try tucking those in your knickers!

What Pauline Stuart did have were great powers of recovery, as in the 1984 season she won the 17-mile Borrowdale race on a Saturday, and then won the Latrigg 3-mile race the next day, in a new course record. She was able to hold her own on short courses. 'I did a reasonable time at Butter Crags. It was steep and I was quite good at coming downhill. Anything that was steep and rough underfoot I could hold my own on.'

Her career may have been reasonably short, but she dominated the sport when at her peak. In the championship winning season of 1984 she ran twenty-eight races of distances varying from 23 miles down to 1.5 miles, and won twenty-four of them, setting fourteen course records in the process, a phenomenal achievement.

Like several other women I have spoken to in bringing this book together Pauline Stuart did not really consider herself a pioneer. 'No, not that I recall. I did it because I enjoyed it and thought it nothing grander than that. It took a while for the number of women to increase. Sometimes there might be just two of you. I judged my performance by the men that I used to run around with and whether I beat them or not.'

Pauline stopped competing for a combination of reasons. 'I had a knee injury from skiing in 1983. I had fallen and torn my meniscus. In 1985 I was going to get an operation on my foot. Then I became pregnant so I didn't have the operation and thought I would see if it settled down. By the time I had finished having babies my knee was a real problem. The meniscus had frayed and started to rub away on my femur. I then had two operations and they weren't that successful. I still have knee problems. It was a combination of injuries and having a family really. Matthew came along in 1986, Emma in 1988 and Rosie in 1991. I started to do a little bit later, but my knee prevented it. Had the knee operation gone right it may have been different. The knee often flares up still when I go walking.'

After having a family Pauline did child-minding for ten years prior to becoming a GP practice manager and then manager of Cumbria Medical Services, which she did for the last six years before retiring early following breast cancer. She concludes: 'I am reasonably healthy now but have been diagnosed as pre-diabetic, and I have had a few health scares. But I just take it as it comes.' Seemingly relaxed about what life brings, Pauline was an intense and very successful athlete at her peak, helping to bring up the standard of competition by her approach.

It might be of interest to look at details of some more of that year's races that included women. Some reports from both *The*

Fellrunner or *Stud Marks* follow. It shows the range of women that were running races already.

The Welsh 1,000m Peaks Race on 4 June 1977 was 'not new to the Ladies, who compete over a shorter course than the men and with the additional handicap of boots and rucksack regulations.' Anne Bland finished first in 2-42-18, with Carol Walkington second, exactly three minutes behind. The race's fifty-year anniversary booklet notes that Anne Davis enquired about entering the B Class, which was over the full course, and was 'surprised by the dismissive refusal to contemplate a woman doing this'. She entered anyway, using her initials. 'At the start, with her hood up in the rain, she looked much like the others.' Her disguise didn't fool a marshall on Carnedd Llewellyn, but she carried on to the finish, in 7-50-36. The next year the B Class was opened to women, but it was not until 1988 that the A Class was officially opened to women, at which point they were acknowledged in the results and awarded prizes at the presentation.

On 11 June the Crag Fell race was inaugurated in parallel with the Ennerdale race. 'Approximately four miles. There were eight starters with Joan Glass (Wrexham) winning from Anne Bland.' This women-only race ran for three years.

The 5.5-mile Burnmoor Chase race was held in July, in conjunction with the Wasdale fell race. Joan Glass set a furious pace on the climb but then blew up and had to retire, possibly due to the heat. The winner was Joan Lancaster from Whitehaven with Brenda Robinson 2nd, and Anne Bland 3rd. This short women's race was held for three years before women were allowed to run the full Wasdale course.

Also in July, at the Kinniside race, started three years previously, the organisers allowed women to run for the first time. Local runner Margaret Scrugham beat Joan Lancaster in the women's race, which was just up Dent Fell and back. The women ran the same course as the men at the Snowdon race, from Llanberis up the Llanberis path to the summit and back. 'Gillian Pile (Sale) had a two-minute lead over Joan Glass at the summit turn in a time of 66-40 but had to surrender the lead on the descent.' Glass won in 1-39-36, with the top five completed by Anne Salisbury, Anne Bland and Anne-Marie Grindley.

At the same time as the Borrowdale race (organised at the time by Chris Bland), a 5-mile women's Dale Head fell race was held, on 6 August. 'Eight competitors set off up Dale Head. Anne Bland (Pete's wife) was first back into the sports field but with Joan Lancaster in close pursuit. Finishing third in her fell racing debut was Billy Bland's wife Ann.' Ann Bland was something of a reluctant competitor, normally preferring to just run and not race, and recalled recently, 'I remember being knackered when I got to the flat again off the downhill, but got some encouragement from the other ladies and managed to finish third. I could run pretty well downhill though.' The last Dale Head race for women was in 1980, although confusingly six women ran the full Borrowdale course that year. Joan Lancaster finishing second at Dale Head was a really good performance, as she had only run her first couple of fell races in the two months prior to this.

Joan Lancaster

Joan was recovering from a fractured patella when I contacted her, so we agreed to an email conversation, so she could reply in her own good time. She was duly diligent in her responses, taking the time to correct a couple of misrepresentations I had allowed when collating her replies.

Joan Lancaster was born in 1944, in Carlisle. She was a keen athlete, doing cross-country at school, and competing at inter-school sports events. She also loved team sports, especially hockey and played for Cumberland in the late 1950s.

Before getting into fell running she enjoyed playing for the local tennis club in the summer. She also learned to ski in Glenshee, in the 1960s. 'Then I lived in British Columbia, Canada, in the early 1970s, where I skied every day. I also did mountain walking, mainly in the summer months. When back in the UK, I enjoyed a few Alpine skiing holidays, and also joined a walking club.'

Joan's boyfriend was a keen all-round club athlete, doing track, cross-country and fell running. 'At that time, in 1972, I had recently returned to live and work in Whitehaven. With the local walking group I was spending a lot of my spare time walking in the Lake District fells, especially the Western Fells. I completed a Mountain Leadership course to enable me to be "safe on the hills", as an individual walker and sometimes I led groups. My summer holidays were spent walking/climbing in Scotland and/or the Alps and I ventured on a winter mountaineering course later.'

In 1976, with a few other fell walking enthusiasts, she entered and completed the 4 x 3,000m peak marathon in the Lake District, finishing in 17 hours 55 minutes. 'I think it was two years later, in 1978, after I had done a few fell races, that I entered and completed the 4 x 3,000m peak marathon again, in 13 hours 55 minutes. It was a superb day. Carol Walkington (now Campbell) and I paced each other to achieve a great result in exactly 4 hours less than 1976.'

It was Joan's boyfriend who influenced her to try fell running. She says her first event was in June 1977, when she ran in the official Crag Fell race (at Ennerdale). 'At the time, I used to meet friends once each week for a 1 to 2 hour fell run/walk. Otherwise, I trained most days on the local roads in and around the hills of Whitehaven, running 3 to 6 miles.'

Joan found some ancient paperwork about the Chevy Chase race, in Northumberland, which shows that she ran in it the month before Crag Fell. She adds, 'it indicates that my friend, Anne Todd, and I ran in together, and included the message, "Congratulations on your very speedy traverse of the Chevy Chase. Your times of 4 hours 28 mins 30 secs were a record"!' Joan drily adds that she is sure that this joint record was broken in subsequent years, and then quotes the female winner in 2019 running it in 3-31-43. Neither *Stud Marks* nor *The Fellrunner* mention female athletes taking part in the Chevy Chase at this time.

Joan wasn't initially in an athletics club, but soon joined Cumberland Fell Runners. She found all race organisers to be extra encouraging to females. 'I was choosing to run as I loved spending a lot of my spare time in the mountains, but I never considered myself as a pioneer. For me, fell running was about having fun, keeping fit and healthy, with the freedom to be myself in the most beautiful natural world. Fell running sometimes felt like "heaven on earth". However, the local press would use headlines like "Women worthy Fellrunners".'

One article in particular read: 'The days of the "fell running widow" are rapidly becoming a thing of the past. Now, instead of waiting those patient hours for a husband or boyfriend to return from a race, the wives and girlfriends are donning vests and shorts and running shoes themselves!' Joan was headlined as a 'Trailblazer' in the local Whitehaven newspaper, after winning the inaugural women's Burnmoor Chase race, in Wasdale in 1977.

Joan regularly ran on the fells from 1977 to 1980. 'In 1980, I had a career change and went off to Leeds University for a year. From 1980 onwards, I continued to road run and entered lots of 10km, 10 mile, half marathon and full marathon events, including the Windermere marathon in 1982, the Cumbria Lakes marathon and the London marathon in 1983. I also ran the occasional fell race between 1981 and 1985.'

From 1981 onwards, Joan worked as a Health Promotion Specialist in the NHS and part of her role was promoting a healthy lifestyle. 'This gave me an opportunity to promote exercise, especially running as a positive fitness activity. I initiated a popular weekly running group for women in response to local fun runs and 10km runs.'

Joan has particularly happy memories of the spectacular Sierre-Zinal race in Switzerland, known as the *Race of the Five 4,000m Peaks*. 'You climb/run at the foot of the *Imperial Crown* composed of the Weisshorn (4,404m), the Zinalrothorn (4,221m), the Obergabelhorn (4,063m), the Matterhorn (4,478m) and the Dent Blanche (4,357m). At that time, I strongly believed in the philosophy of the event, which was (to quote the Sierre-Zinal race website): "the heart before the watch". As I walked most of the uphill parts and jogged/ran on the level/downhill bits, my times were steady.' In 1984 and 1985 she completed the course in 4-52-19 and 4-51-23 respectively.

Looking back, Joan feels that Joss Naylor's record on the fells is the most impressive of those she has witnessed. For her, those runners that had the most impact on the sport in the 1970s and 1980s, other than Joss, were Mike Short, Billy Bland, Jean Lochhead and Pauline Howarth.

She concluded our discussion by summing up her experience on the fells. 'For me, it was brilliant to be able to run in the fells alongside the early, like-minded, pioneers who had similar goals to have fun, enjoy the camaraderie and support each other. At the time, I never felt like we were running to create records, but on reflection we were creating records as early pioneers!'

Joan then digresses slightly to tell a story of visiting the Himalayas. 'I had a love for fells and mountains, locally, in the UK and all over the world, for adventure and exploration. My ambition to climb in the Himalayas was fulfilled in 1987, with the late, beloved Doug Scott. Doug, with other climbers, guided a few trekkers and myself up a 6,000 metre subsidiary peak of Makalu, (8,545 metres, fifth highest mountain in the world.) The fleeting glimpses of Mount Everest were a dream come true. I was reminded of the quote, "Dream Big because dreams do come true." This Himalayan journey was an enlightening adventure, which was a wonderful, spiritual experience. My life changed for ever, realising that life was, and continues to be, a journey of self-discovery. I loved meeting the happy, smiling, Nepalese mountain people. Some of their key values were the importance of their family, patience, trust, calmness, tolerance, simplicity, companionship and generosity, whilst always living in harmony with nature.'

Joan Lancaster returned to the Himalayas twice more in

the 1990s. 'Those visits helped to reinforce the craziness of the western, material world and the importance of love, care, compassion, courage, gratitude, support for family and friends and much more, while continuing to be at one with the world, the people and the natural world. These are some of my key values for life and living.' Joan Lancaster is someone whose experiences on the fells and in the mountains are a fine example of how to lead a rich and balanced life.

There was a women's race alongside the men's Ben Nevis race on 3 September 1977. 'There were half a dozen competitors in this unofficial ladies' race, and the winner was Joan Glass in a new ladies' record time of 2-27-00. Anne-Marie Grindley was second and Anne Bland third.' The report for the Hades Hill Race on 10 September just lists the first three finishers: Brenda Robinson 30-32, Gillian Pile 30-58, and Kath Etherden 34-48.

Similarly for the Pike o'Blisco race, a week later, 'run in conjunction with the men's Langdale race, Anne Bland and Brenda Robinson decided to share this one and finished together in 54-57. Third was Ann Bland (Keswick) in 57-26.' At the Eccles Pike race it was reported that '10 or 11 ladies started in this race which was won by Brenda Robinson from Heather Matthews (Blackburn) with Collett Chapman (Bolton) third.' According to the trophy this race had been going (with men only) since 1928, although not run every year.

The Moffat Chase, on 2 October, was 'a new event for both men and women. Both compete over the same tough [*15 mile*] course. The event attracted five in the ladies' race.' The first four to finish (in order) were: Ros Coats, Anne-Marie Grindley, Jean Dawes and Anne Bland. Ros Coats' winning time of 3-57-00 was noted as being 'a time faster than a third of the male competitors.' On the same day as the Moffat Chase, the Stoodley Pike race had 'a ladies' race over the same course as the men but with a separate start time, attracting a field of 10 or 11 and was won by Gillian Pile (Sale) in 23-54. Heather Matthews was second with Brenda Robinson in third.'

On 30 October *The Fellrunner* reported that at the Gale Fell Race, 'in the ladies event over the same course, Brenda Robinson (Bury) defeated Gillian Pile (Sale) by 32-35 to 34-08.' At Black Lane Ends 'there were also a few ladies competing over a short course (about 1.5 miles shorter), and the fastest among them was Brenda Robinson, though no other details are at hand at present.'

The Blisco Dash, on 19 November, had eight women competing, with Ros Coats winning comfortably, and The Copeland Chase, the next day, also had added a shorter course for women with Margaret Scrugham coming home first. Finally, for 1977, on the last day of the year, the Wansfell race was won by Ros Coats, from Brenda Robinson and Anne Pendlebury, with five finishers listed in the results.

Ros Coats

I was given the contact details for Ros Coats by a fellow fell runner and made my initial contact with her by email. She replied that she was very willing to help, saying, 'I need to dig out an old box which had some of my results in it, but first I have to find the box!' She seemed to enjoy the process of recalling the details of her career as she later added, 'thanks for getting me to do this – it has been a real trip down memory lane!'

Ros Coats certainly burst on to the scene, winning her first three races, all within three months. She was born at Langbank, Renfrewshire on 17 January 1950. She didn't do athletics at school as it was not available. 'I have always lived on smallholdings and as a youngster I spent a lot of time outdoors. We had a couple of paddocks, and I was luckily able to have a succession of ponies and horses on loan.'

Ros's introduction to hills was quite dramatic. 'It was in October 1969. Whilst doing a degree in Physics, I had agreed to accompany a friend on a Mountaineering Club weekend. I had never been up anything higher than about 600 feet, so I had no idea what I was letting myself in for when we were told we were to go along the Aonoch Eagach Ridge in Glen Coe. As I was a complete novice, I was totally overawed and scared. I would have stopped except I was not brave enough to go back along what we had just come over. I had no idea then that I would get to love the Ridge and go along it many times, including winter traverses; running along and back in the same outing; and doing it as part of my 12-hour Glen Coe round. The following day I was taken up Curved Ridge on the Buachaille. It was dark by the time we descended. Such an introduction was going to put me off forever or fire a deep and lasting passion.'

It was the latter. She started to go hill walking or rock climbing whenever she could. 'Early on, in Glen Etive, still feeling the newbie, I was happy to leave all the navigation to the experienced walkers in the group. However, when we got to the mountain top there was considerable discussion as they found they had gone up a neighbouring Munro by mistake! That prompted me to be responsible for my own navigation.'

Ros's introduction to actually running up a hill came in 1973. 'Up to then, wearing big boots and carrying climbing gear, we might "race" each other up the hill but it was a walk-march and running only happened on a downhill. I had gone out for a jog with my Norwegian brother-in-law in Bergen – a town with several steep little forested hills. We had jogged along the road to the foot of the hill then started up the track. I assumed we might turn at the first corner, but no. Maybe the second one? No. We kept on going ... right to the top! I didn't know it was possible to run up a hill. He told me later he was just as surprised. He had been waiting for me to say stop!'

The next step for her was orienteering. The first opportunity came in 1975 when she had a year at Jordanhill Teacher Training College. 'I ran right off the map on my first event, as I was used to reading the 1:50 000 scale of OS maps. But I enjoyed it and realised it would be an excellent way to improve my mountain navigation.'

Ros's main interest was still mountaineering, and the highlight of the year would be a trip to the Alps. But she got to hear about a new event – the Karrimor International Mountain Marathon. 'My climbing partners weren't so interested in it, but a friend from orienteering was happy to give it a go. It was the 1976 Galloway event, infamous for the continuous rain and boggy terrain. Unfortunately, John's strengths were football, basketball and circuit training, not long days in the hills in bad conditions. The final straw came at the overnight camp when he unpacked a soaking wet sleeping bag. We retired.'

The following year she arranged to do the Karrimor International Mountain Marathon in the Howgills with Anne Salisbury. Anne suggested they should get some long runs in and came up with the idea of entering a fell race, so they agreed to enter the Moffat Chase. 'In the end Anne couldn't make it, so it was with a fair amount of trepidation I found my way to the Moffat school to register. I really didn't know what to expect as I had never seen an actual fell race. Was it similar to a mountain marathon? What do people wear? Would I have the embarrassment of being left behind at the start in the middle of the main street if they all sprinted off? Do they take a straight-line route between checkpoints?'

However, everyone was very friendly and helpful. 'T-shirt and shorts with a top round the waist was OK. They started off at a modest jog. Relief! However, as we started to go uphill, I felt I was using more energy to stay back with them, so after debating with myself I decided to go at my own pace and do my own route and accept the consequences. I was constantly checking over my left shoulder to see if everyone else was taking a straight-line route to the next control. They weren't. The men had started forty-five minutes after us and caught me up on the steep climb on the way back; they were also friendly and encouraging, wanting to know who I was and where I had come from. It was a huge surprise to find I had won the ladies' race and by such a significant amount.'

Saying that she had never been particularly good at anything, it was a very new experience to have been so successful and Ros says she was eager to try again in case it was all some sort of fluke. 'By the time I had won the Blisco Dash (in November) and the Wansfell (December), it seemed as though I had found a niche and began to think what other races were available. The Ben Nevis race, being the highest, was an obvious attraction and as I only knew it from the climbing perspective, I was very grateful to Eddie Campbell and Roger Boswell for their encouragement and showing me the race route. The ladies started two minutes behind the men, so there was a lot of overtaking to be done. I was delighted on that first race to break 2 hours, finishing in 1 hour 53 minutes. I joined Lochaber AC, in spite of living more than a three-hour drive away. I remember on several occasions hitch-hiking there and back.'

Ben Lomond was another special race for Ros. Partly as she could see the hill from home and partly as she used it for training, sometimes running up and down it twice or parking about a mile before the start to include a bit of road.

When Ros started there were no other regular female runners in Scotland, but there was a small group consistently competing in England, often the partners of male fell runners. 'There were difficulties with a few race organisers not wanting to let women start or not including them in the results. I tried not to get involved though I did ask the Ben Nevis race committee to let us start with the men, pointing out that women can finish in the top half of the field. It all sounds a bit absurd nowadays with more and more women getting great results and even beating the men's records.'

Ros was part of the first female team to complete the Elite course at the KIMM, in 1978, with Anne-Marie Grindley. 'In theory we were a very good team, but unfortunately Anne-Marie hurt her ankle part way through, so though we finished thanks to her tenacity and generosity our result did not reflect what we were capable of. Running with a partner can be very rewarding when working successfully as a team, but immensely frustrating if the two are unbalanced or one gets injured. The injured one feels bad about letting the team down, they hurt and worry how much more damage is being done. The other one feels bad for even thinking of continuing, always hoping things aren't as severe as they look and also worries about further damage. Not a happy state of affairs.'

Ros had read all she could lay her hands on with regard to training but admits she didn't have half the knowledge that is around now. 'I ran because I enjoyed it and I ran on hills because I loved them. Latterly Malcolm (my husband) and I used to drive across Scotland once a week to take part in the interval sessions organised by Martin Hyman at the Meadows in Edinburgh. Those sessions certainly did make a difference. But I was hardly hill running then, it was orienteering training. Sue Harvey was my orienteering coach, and she was very supportive, in spite of my short comings. There were a number of occasions when I got an early morning orienteering start time, then went onto a fell race in the afternoon. Not the best preparation for either sport, but fun! I was hooked.'

In 1979 Ros ran her first road race, the Barnsley Marathon. She finished second woman in 3 hours and 4 minutes. She also won the Fell Running Championships in 1979 and 1980, but in those days there wasn't anything beyond that. 'I could try to improve my times and do more races, but with orienteering I had potentially more improvement to make and there were World Championships. I had started spending winters in Norway (at Kvitavatn) and was interested in the Ski Orienteering World Championships and then there was the 1984 Winter Olympics for Nordic Skiing.'

She also really enjoyed Mountain Marathons, doing the Swiss version with Miriam Rosen and a Norwegian one with Carol

McNeill. 'Latterly my regular partner was David Rosen; we were a competitive team and ran well together aiming to finish in the top ten in the Elite class. It caused a few comments when my husband Malcolm competed with David's wife Miriam in the A, whilst David and I did the Elite.'

Ros set a number of course records, one of which, the Cow Hill Race, still stands today. It is the oldest Scottish Hill Race record. 'The Cow Hill record – that is meant to be a secret! I did it as part of the Lochaber Three: Saturday was the Meall an t-Suidhe; Sunday was the Half Ben and Monday the Cow Hill. I do remember turning at the top and flying down, no holds barred. Luckily for me, it is not a particularly popular race or else the record would have been long since broken! But it is fun to know I still have one record left. Even more so as it is published in the Scottish Hill Running Calendar where my daughter (Neah) is named as the record holder for the Creag Bheag Race. Surely that cannot happen very often? (Both Neah and my son Donald have won the Scottish under 23 Hill Running Championships). I have told Neah she is not allowed to run the Cow Hill until someone else breaks the record then she has to try to get it back again!'

Ros was second to Pauline Haworth when Pauline set the Ben Nevis record in 1984. 'I was fit. My target that year had been skiing in the Winter Olympics, but I was not hill racing fit and was disappointed with my run. I think Pauline had been racing all season and it does make a difference.'

Ros was one of several female runners who have competed at the Three Peaks Yacht race. 'I did it twice. As I am no sailor, I had patches behind the ear to prevent seasickness. I asked to do all three hills, which made sense as I was the strongest. I could help the others by carrying their rucksacks or whatever.'

Ros's commitment to fell running continued to decline as life events took over. Marriage, rebuilding a ruined cottage, three children and the decision to home educate them all until they sat their Highers, meant little time for the hills. 'I consider myself very fortunate to have had the opportunity to home educate. It was a way of life which was incredibly rewarding. Nothing like the "school at home" scenario (or nightmare) experienced by many during lockdown.'

When daughter Neah was at university, she unexpectedly phoned home one day to say she was going to do a local hill race and wanted some advice. 'Malcolm and I were delighted to help, but then sometime afterwards we looked at each other and grinned. We both wanted to run again! Unbeknown to Neah, we turned up and entered. As we were not sure what sort of disaster might result, we hung right back at the start line. We completed it and started hill running once more! I don't think "comeback" is the correct term, as it implies back at the top. Very obviously that is not the case. But I still enjoyed it. My aim was to run the Ben Nevis at seventy but Covid put a stop to that. Will sixty-nine do?'

Ros plays down an outstanding global achievement. 'I had the dubious honour of competing in four different sports at World Championship level. These were Nordic Skiing, Ski Orienteering, Orienteering and Le Trec (which is orienteering on horseback).'

Ros is not alone in challenging me for my simplistic question about her finest achievements, and of presumably expecting an answer involving fell running. She says that, 'one doesn't really stop to think about it until old age creeps up, and then you have to admit that if you haven't done something earth-shattering by now it is not likely to happen. A bit sad but there it is. Lots of thoughts have passed through my mind. The following are perhaps fond (or strong) memories rather than finest achievements. After all, how do you measure achievements?'

She starts by telling her version of a story that has already appeared in this narrative, about a Mountain Marathon in Norway with Carol McNeill. 'One route choice was swimming across a lake or running round it. We chose to swim, not that I was an especially good swimmer, but Carol at that time was an outdoor education instructor, so I thought if I got into difficulties, she would be able to tow me across! However, part way across it was not going so well and I looked over to Carol to find that she wasn't doing much better than me. I began to see newspaper headlines, "Mountain marathoners drown . . ." It was very much a case of concentrate hard and keep on going. In fairness to us both it was the last leg of the second day, and we did win the class! And it probably clinched the deal with Rod Tuck for me to go out and work/ski there that winter.' She adds that a rowing boat was produced for later competitors.

Ros then chooses memories from different activities. 'In mountaineering: the day my partner and I climbed the four main ridges on Ben Nevis, up two and down two, then bivvied near the CIC hut. With some of my animals: riding my horse high up in Austria, mutual pleasure just the two of us together; winter hill walking with my faithful dog when she had to swim as I had to ford because the stepping stones were iced over. Skiing at Kvitavatn: usually on my own, hearing the swish-swish of the skis high up on the deserted tracks amongst the few small stunted trees, rocks, mountains, with everything covered in beautiful cold dry snow and magnificent sunrises and sunsets. Makes me glow just thinking of it.'

Then came a range of hill running memories. 'Winning the Ben Nevis seven times was an achievement. I always had a soft spot for the Moffat (my first hill race) and Ben Lomond (visible in the distance from home). I still have a race record (Cow Hill), albeit a very small race. I got a lot of satisfaction from some of the long-distance runs. In the Bob Graham Round I was so disappointed when I found we had made a mistake in the dark and lost time. I always meant to go back and re-do it. Doing Tranter's route with Charlie Ramsay in a group including Wendy Dodds. I had walked over it all before but at different times so was really chuffed to do it all in a oner. Also my own Glen Coe round in under 12 hours.'

Ros Coats/Evans talked about the work she had done and what that meant to her. 'I have been tutoring since Teacher Training in the 1970s. It is always a good feeling to help someone who has been struggling to get a good pass in a National exam. A

1 Kathleen Connochie training for the Ben Nevis race with Duncan MacIntyre, 1955.

2

3

2 Kathrine Switzer being hassled by the organisers of the Boston marathon, 1967.

3 On the start line of the Muncaster fell race, 1977. L–R: Jean Dawes, Maraline Baines, Audrey Orr, Peggy Walker, Gillian Naylor, Joan Glass, Joan Lancaster, Carol Walkington, Anne Bland, and Anne Todd.

4 L–R: Joan Glass, Anne Bland, Carol Walkington, Joan Lancaster, Peggy Walker, Jean Dawes at the Crag Fell race, 1977.

4

5

5 Joan Glass at Muncaster, with Bob Roberts, mid-1970s.
6 Ros Coats, Pendleton Hill, 1978.
7 Jean Dawes finishing her Bob Graham Round, 1977.

6

7

8 Anne-Marie Grindley at Muncaster, date not known.
9 Jean Lochhead at Pendle, 1978.

9

10

10 Carol Walkington at the Crag Fell race, 1978.
11 Anne and Pete Bland, KIMM, 1974.
12 L-R: Jean Lochhead, Brenda Robinson, Gillian Pile, Linda Lord, Anne-Marie Grindley, at Pendle, 1979.

13

13 Brenda Robinson at the Three Peaks race, 1979.
14 Carol McNeill with Wendy Dodds at the KIMM at Arran, 1980.

14

15

15 Vanessa Brindle at Fiendsdale, date not known.
16 Competing with Jean Dawes and Carol McNeill in the Three Peaks yacht race, 1980, Anne-Marie Grindley helps to row their trimaran through the Corran narrows.

17 L–R: Cath Whalley, Fiona Wild, Pauline Haworth, Carol McNeill, Ros Coats, Marguerite Pennel, and Joan Lancaster at the Wasdale race, 1981.

18 Fiona Wild at Ben Nevis, 1981.

18

19 Pauline Haworth on the way to winning the Ben Nevis race, 1984.

small achievement in the overall scheme of things but it can open doors for individuals.'

Finally, Ros added. 'Perhaps my finest achievement has been in raising three kids, all smarter than me and all able to think independently and not just follow the crowd. They have all been excellent company on the hills, sometimes helping me bag Munros. In fact, this year (2021) I have finally completed all the Munros. It only took fifty-two years.'

Ros Coats/Evans was very much a pioneer of fell and hill running in Scotland. Her racing is just one part of the very rounded life that she has led.

CHAPTER 5

An expanding race programme

Women Speak Up. Major Races Open Up and Others Have to Follow. The Cumberland Fell Runners Association. Profiles: Jean Lochhead, Sue Parkin, Norma Hughes

'It would appear that they aspire to compete over the long courses of the men's events.'

This was part of the feedback some leading female fell runners gave at the end of that 1977 season. The report summarised these comments (written by a male, in *The Fellrunner*) and added that, 'a constructive criticism concerns the lack of advanced publicity given to many of the events.' The informal review that was being reported on had been conducted by Brenda Robinson, Jean Dawes, Anne Bland, Kath Etherden and Hilary Matthews, and the report concluded that, 'they are most pleased at the extent to which their competitive aspirations have been received by us males in general and by the race organisers.' Well, they did get to run the full courses eventually, but only after even more campaigning.

One race that didn't seem particularly ready to encompass this trend was the Three Peaks. The race secretary (D. A. Croft) said the following in a letter published in *Athletics Weekly* on 20 November 1976.

> Fell running is now gaining increasing support from ladies, and I have received a number of enquiries. This matter has been considered by my committee, who take the view that the factors

> [the location, facilities and the provision of rescue and first-aid services] preclude extending the present race to include lady competitors. We and our sponsors would, however, be prepared to consider a separate race, provided that sufficient support was forthcoming.

He seemed to be offering a different date to the men's race, suggesting late April or early June, and asked interested women to write to him. They must have done so, because the first women's race took place in 1979, and was not separated from the men's.

The 1978 fell race programme expanded significantly and had a number of extra races that year that accepted female entrants. Going through the results in *The Fellrunner* shows twenty-nine races that year with female competitors, twenty-one being new (for women). However, there were still some issues. Six of them were shorter versions of the standard men's race, and another four had starts for the women that were either before or after the men, arguably disadvantaging them unnecessarily. These last four were Rossendale (five minutes before), Edale (ten minutes before), Stoodley Pike (ten minutes after) and Ben Nevis (starting the females 'just after' the men).

The year started well with the first female to be featured on the cover of *The Fellrunner*, for the Spring 1978 issue. 'Ros Coats (Clydesdale) winning the Wansfell Race for ladies at Ambleside on New Year's Eve', was the caption. The next individual female cover star was Carol Walkington eight years later, in 1986, with Anne and Pete Bland having shared the Summer 1979 cover, as they completed the Karrimor International Mountain Marathon.

Extracts from some of the race reports for the year give a feel for the racing scene, an idea of who was performing well, and any issues encountered – and also how the women's events were reported at that time. It is good to see that race numbers were high at several of the races that year. There were, for example: twenty-one women running at Fairfield, seventeen at Kentmere and Burnmoor Chase, sixteen at Pendle, fourteen at Rivington Pike, and eleven for the shorter Blisco Dash.

On 19 March 1978 the fifth Edale Skyline Race was held, incorporating the 'first official ladies' race' at that venue. Peter Knott's report noted that there were twelve finishers:

> The ladies, a class field of 13, set off 10 minutes before the men. It would be interesting to read their thoughts as the faster men passed them between Grindslow Knoll and Jaggers Clough, but I am sure the men find it a pleasant distraction. As far as I could tell Ros Coats led all the way from Grindslow Knoll to score a comfortable win from Kendal's Anne Bland.

The following week's race at Rivington Pike was witnessed by Bill Smith, with helpful comments on who was whose wife:

> There were fourteen competitors and Colin Robinson's wife, Brenda, assumed the lead on the final steep climb to the summit tower, with Sue Styan (Andy's wife) in second place and Gillian Pile lying third. Brenda increased her lead on the descent to finally beat Sue by 17 seconds, though Gillian was beaten into third place by Anne Pendlebury.

The history of Rivington Pike noted that: 'Chauvinism ensured that the ladies race should be separated from the men's race. It was decided to run a slightly shorter race for the ladies.' This was just a one-off though, as all athletes ran the same course together the next year.

The Pendle race, two weeks later, had sixteen competitors completing the same tough 3.75-mile course as the men. Jean Lochhead set a new women's record of 39-43, with Jean Haigh second and Ros Coats third.

The Fairfield Horseshoe race on 21 May had a piece of positive reporting about it in *The Fellrunner*: 'The Ladies Race produced a fantastic improvement in performances with the first seven faster than last year's winning time.' Jean Lochhead won, from Ros Coats and Janet Sutcliffe. The same weekend saw the Fellsman Hike taking place in good, clear weather. 'Jean Dawes turned in a gradely performance to set a new ladies record of 17 hours 35 minutes, having gone round with husband Pete.' The women's Crag Fell race (at the Ennerdale event) on 10 June had a healthy fourteen competitors, with Jean Lochhead winning from Janet Sutcliffe and Véronique Marot.

Jean Lochhead

Jean was a great choice of interviewee for this book, as she had previously written an article[12] expressing strong views on the fight for equality and recognition in women's track and cross-country. She answered my questions in depth, in between organising a series of orienteering events.

The Pendle race (mentioned above) was the first fell event Jean Lochhead had ever run, so she had started her fell career with three straight wins. She says: 'I was very fit after eleven years of hard training for track and field and cross-country, so didn't think I needed to do anything extra to compete in fell running.'

Jean was born in Huddersfield in 1946. She admits that she wasn't especially athletic at school. 'Because we were young ladies, we were only allowed to do short distances and whilst adequate I was never the best at sprinting but had a fair turn of speed at the end of a XC race.'

Before fell running Jean took to cycling and middle-distance track and cross-country racing, to international standard. An internet search shows that Jean competed in the International Cross-country Championships from 1967 to 1971; and the World Cross-country Championships in 1974, 1976 and 1984 (all for Wales). Jean points out that it was rather more than that. 'I competed in all the World Cross-country Champs except one in France (I was fit enough but upset one of the selectors), so

12. For her athletic club newsletter.

it was probably seventeen in total. I was in the Guinness Book of Records until it was revised to include only proper athletic records. Then the number of appearances for just being there was not one of them.'

Jean adds that the most memorable was her best one in 1973, in Waregem (Belgium), where she was sixth. 'You have to remember at that time the African women were not competing in cross-country or marathons.' However, it was good that women were (officially) competing right from the first International Championships in 1967, which was held in Wales. Jean adds, 'I am not sure that four home nations plus USA could be counted as a World Champs.'

On the track Jean was selected for Wales to run in the Commonwealth Games, in Christchurch, in 1974. She was 12th in the 1500m in 4-29.9, and 7th in the 800m heats in 2-09.84. 'There was the long flight to New Zealand and then two weeks of crashing boredom. I was self-employed at the time, studying, training hard and my life was very busy. To be suddenly left with an endless amount of time on my hands fried my brain and whilst I trained hard in New Zealand, I was in no condition by race day to do a good time. Going the day before would have been fine! I did not make the 800m final as I was told by an experienced official that the African women made up most of the other competitors and that 2-10 would get me to the final. By the time I realised they weren't that slow and had speeded up to get into a qualifying position that bird had flown. I could not gain enough ground, so missed out on the 800m final. I feel that 1974 was the emergence of the African women on to the athletics scene.'

Her move to running on the fells came later. 'I always enjoyed cross-country, and fell running was like cross-country all year round.' The first race she ran in was the Yorkshire Cross-country Championships at Bingley 'in about 1967', and she moved to the fells in 1978. Competitive from the start, Jean says she looked up to anyone who went faster than her. To be more competitive still she joined Longwood Harriers in 1967, it being her local club. 'Holmfirth Harriers did not have women's membership at that time, although I did some hard road training with them in the 1970s.'

Training time was never a problem as she never had, or wanted, a family. What she did have was an issue over equality for women in sport, which she detailed in a piece in the Holmfirth Harriers newsletter in the late 1980s, which included the following (slightly edited) paragraphs:

> In 1964 there were three Cross-country races per winter. The Yorkshire Women's Cross-country Championship, National Junior and the National Cross-country. These were all for 17+ seniors, no children's races in those days which you may find confusing as the National Junior was for competitors who had not won any other races. This meant that if you were any use at all you were soon down to two races a winter.
>
> To combat this situation the Northern Women's Cross-country League was formed in 1967. Shortly afterwards races for younger ladies and girls were incorporated. By the early 1970s more Cross-country races were available for all the age groups, however the iron grip of the governing body of Women's Athletics ensured that we never mixed with the opposite sex, never ran in road races with men and never ran more than the 1 mile distance, which was a feature of the Yorkshire Women's Track Championships.
>
> This state of affairs continued through the 1980s as the Women's Cross-country and Race Walking Association also fought to control Women's Fell racing without any conception about what was involved.

Jean Lochhead had her own brushes with the authorities. Once she was threatened with a ban after jumping into a men's race after a quarter of a mile. It was the Croxteth 10-mile road race. She adds: 'Véronique Marot nearly suffered the same fate after joining the male fell runners in the Ennerdale fell race. I did not feel like a pioneer at the time, but I can see now that I did push the limits of what was considered acceptable by both male and female organisers.' She concludes that discussion by saying that it is a shame that the women weren't as well organised then as they would be now. In some ways they just accepted that was the way it was.

Jean stopped competing in athletics (track and field, cross-country and fell races) 'when it was difficult to see the front of races', but by that time she had taken up orienteering seriously. This was around 1985.

Jean Lochhead's own assessment of her finest achievements in the sport don't come from the fells, or cross-country, or even standard summer track athletics. For her it is her British Indoor titles at Cosford at 1500m, and following that, winning the World Masters Urban Orienteering Championships in the W65 age group in Germany. 'Cosford would have been 1972 and 1973, which were my fastest years. The World Masters orienteering was in 2012, in Grosler (former East Germany).'

Jean's fell running career, although impressive, was actually fairly short. When asked which of her rivals impressed her, she replies obliquely. 'Fell running in my day was not the elite sport it is now. So that is difficult to answer as I moved on to orienteering before I could be impressed with others' achievements.'

Many FRA members may not be aware that Jean Lochhead part-designed the original FRA logo. 'The components were hills, bracken etc. I never thought it was important until I was asked to sign away the rights. Others had a hand in its design as well.'

Jean explains that she mainly trained on her own. 'We did not have qualified coaches in my day, so I made up the sessions. I used to train with Airedale and Spen Valley ladies, and they did the same intervals as me. It had a good ladies' section and we won National Relays and cross-country team titles.'

She comments on the more relaxed attitude to kit carrying in the early days. 'The one and only time I did Marsden to Edale we had a kit check at the start. I complied with everything and could have done without the woolly cycling shorts! I was passed by a chap on the way down to Edale who was wearing shorts and a singlet. Maybe there wasn't a rule then that you had to wear full battledress all the way round. I believe kit checks today are far more strictly enforced.'

Jean Lochhead reckons her orienteering navigation is passable. 'For walking and cycling I just look at the OS map on my phone although I do always take a paper map.'

Jean Lochhead won the first Three Peaks race for women in 1979 with a fantastic time of 3-43-12. 'The time would have been faster had I not climbed too early and got on to Simon Fell and straight into a headwind all along the top to the summit of Ingleborough. I ran the Three Peaks about five times for fun. The thing that sticks out in my mind is what a long way it is down from Ingleborough. One time, whilst crossing a deep bog between Pen-y-Gent and Whernside I thought, "I have not noticed that boulder there before", and leapt on to it and my foot went through a dead sheep!'

Jean hit the ground running in the 1980 season. Despite winning many races, she didn't win the Championships. 'I thought I had won it, but there were two lists of Championship races in circulation and the woman who did win had used a different list to me and pointed this out. The FRA Committee discussed it and asked if I was bothered about conceding the FRA Champs. I never considered fell running that important, so I did not dispute the matter. Fell running was not as prestigious then as it is now.' It has not been possible at this distance to find out how two lists could have been in circulation, or who produced the two lists.

In some ways Jean Lochhead's running career mirrors that of male fell legend John Wild. They both won the Inter-Counties cross-country title, ran track and cross-country to international level before turning to the fells, were the top fell runners for a couple of years, and also tried a marathon in later years. For Jean it was the Berlin Marathon, which she ran twice, winning in 1982 (in 2-43-56, as a v35) and coming second in 1983. 'I had not been chosen to run for GB since 1973, and possibly as a result of running the Stafford 20 in under two hours I was chosen to go to the Berlin Marathon and I got to wear a GB vest again in 1982. I was chosen for GB the following year, finished second and that was my last marathon.'

Jean Lochhead adds that she was very fortunate to have no serious injuries in about fifty-five years of running, although she had to have a hip replacement in 2017, but is still orienteering regularly. She concludes with: 'Women today who can enter any open race with men are astounded to hear of the restrictions we had to face and also the limited number of races that women could compete in.' Jean Lochhead was a brilliant all-round runner who deserves more credit than she seems to get.

The women were still running the Burnmoor Chase on Wasdale race day (8 July 1978). 'Orienteer Sue Parkin (nee Banner) scored a truly decisive victory over her nearest rivals – by over six minutes – with seventeen competitors taking part.' Joan Lancaster and Anne Bland completed the top three that day.

Sue Parkin

Contact with Sue came through another interviewee passing a message on, illustrating a nice web of contacts that was being established. She admitted that she might be a bit fuzzy on some of the details. 'It is all a bit vague now I'm afraid. I still have a few really good friends from those days, but otherwise I am out of touch with the fell running scene. It was wonderful while it lasted though!'

Sue Parkin was born on 17 November 1952 in Whitehaven. Mostly she worked as a teacher of modern languages at secondary level, then later in early years and education at a college. She also had what she calls 'short deviations' to Outward Bound, the police and nursery-age care and education.

At her school there was little on offer regarding athletics, as she explains. 'Harry Jarrett was in the same year, and I knew he was a successful runner, but the circuit on which he competed was a world I knew nothing of. I think (hope) that nowadays schools are better at forging contacts with local sports scenes.' Sue says she has a vague recollection of being entered in the Cumbria cross-country championship and of turning in a mediocre performance. 'Mostly I played hockey, with matches two or three times a week. I later ran in hockey boots until chronic bruising forced me to take a long rest and investigate other footwear!', she chuckles.

Through her mother, who worked with some of the founders of West Cumberland Orienteering Club (WCOC), Sue was introduced to orienteering, which she immediately loved. 'I enjoyed early success, largely because the number of female competitors was small.'

Sue was first mixed team (with husband Mike) to finish the KIMM 'A' class in 1977 and 1978. Sue says memories of those two events are all a bit vague now. 'The 1977 Karrimor was in the Howgills and I remember a long leg where we seemed to be the only ones going that way. I kept worrying about it, but amazingly we popped out ahead of the field. The 1978 Karrimor was in Peebles and we missed the last control and had to go back.'

'I think my first fell race was at the Wasdale Horseshoe [*in July 1978, noted above*], which I was aware of only because organiser Danny Hughes was a fellow WCOC member. A short course up to Illgill Head was provided for women. Looking back that looks rather patronising, but I didn't question it at the time. The idea of being able to do the full course seemed preposterous.' Sue had actually run another race in May that year, the women's Duddon race, which at the time was also shorter than the men's course. She hit the ground running, because she won both those first two races, against some very good female runners.

Looking back on those times Sue feels that, 'male competitors were overwhelmingly encouraging and respectful, even if officialdom was sometimes less accepting. Joss Naylor was already becoming a celebrity and I was in awe of his achievements. I also think there was a strong camaraderie between the few female fell runners at that time. I was just happy to take what was on offer. But today's women have others like Ros Evans to thank for challenging the status quo.'

Sue adds that, 'Orienteering became my main sport and it offered opportunities to train and travel, not available to me elsewhere.' Later Holmfirth Harriers was her first athletic club which offered great training on the road and fells, and great camaraderie. Sue acknowledges the help with training she had over the years. 'The structure of my training came mainly from Martin Hyman with whom I corresponded for years via the orienteering squad. He was massively supportive even though the long-distance nature of the relationship had its limitations.' Sometimes Sue trained at Holmfirth with Wendy Dodds and other runners. This was even though they were with different clubs, and it would normally be LSD (long slow distance training).

Orienteering remained her main focus, even though she loved running on the fells. 1982 was the only year she targeted the FRA championships. It is strangely not something that stirs big memories for her. 'Sorry, I remember little about it apart from two of us (my friend Richard White and I) from Holmfirth trekking up to do the Ben Lomond race and it being a lovely day.' At the end of the season Sue had 72 points to Linda Lord's 61, so a pretty solid win. Sue had many good performances on the fells, setting several records at her peak.

Sue Parkin comments that the Lake District Mountain Trial (LDMT) was her idea of a perfect day out, as it played to her strengths. 'Orienteering meant I was a confident navigator but growing up in Cumbria meant I did not feel intimidated about being alone on the fells, which some perfectly competent women still do.' The event certainly must have suited her, as she competed in the LDMT nine times and won it eight times, across the years from 1981 to 2000.

Later on, Sue Parkin became the course planner for the LDMT for a good number of years, which added pressure on herself. 'I was intimidated by the sense of responsibility when asked to plan the courses. This came entirely from within as both the organisers and competitors were overwhelmingly positive. I loved everything about the planning and recceing, but found the seeking permissions from landowners and recruiting sufficient reliable checkpoint marshals tiresome. I believe the role has since been split and the use of manned checkpoints reduced. Now that we have become more prone to extreme weather events a race like LDMT can also demand high stakes decisions.'

Sue Parkin was British Orienteering Champion in 1970, 1977 and 1980. However, her orienteering highlight was something quite different. 'I guess my outstanding result was posting the fastest time on the first leg of the World Champs relay in Switzerland. I'd been last out of the start area and scarcely seen another competitor thereafter, so it was a surprise to us all!'

Eventually she drifted out of both orienteering and fell running when they became difficult to combine with family life. 'My husband Mike's job took him away from home a lot including at weekends. Gradually supporting our children's enthusiasms took precedence for us.'

Despite the drift Sue Parkin did compete for many years. For example, to choose one other random race result, she was second to Wendy Dodds at Langdale in 2000. 'Wendy did indeed beat me. She took better lines and I recall catching up with her twice. In later years any races I did were usually in the course of my bid to get fit enough to do the Lake District Mountain Trial and the results were nothing to shout about', she says modestly. Then adds, 'I am not sure I have a particular claim to longevity. There are others who have lasted longer.'

She admits she is no longer part of the sport, but ends with a really upbeat comment. 'I still have a few really good friends from those days, but otherwise I am out of touch with the fell running scene. It was wonderful while it lasted though!' Sue Parkin is one of the many women who have enjoyed the friendship that the fell running community offers, who also made sure that she put something back into the sport, a common theme in this book.

The Ben Nevis race was held on 2 September 1978 on a mild and overcast day, and *The Fellrunner* report highlights the difficulty separate starts could engender. 'Setting off just after the fellers, the ladies were hampered by so many breathless male bodies cluttering the narrow tourist path. Some fast times were recorded nevertheless, none more so than that of Lochaber's latest and greatest recruit, Ros Coats. Ros completed the course in the incredible time of 1-53-29 to win by a street.' Anne Bland and Bridget Hogge came in very close to each other in second and third respectively, with nine women listed in the results. The Ben Nevis book calls this, 'the first time an official ladies event was run', but later contradicts this when saying that fourteen women had been entered for the cancelled 1980 race, which it called 'the first official ladies race'.

A week later women ran in the Lake District Mountain Trial for the first time since 1968. In awful conditions Ros Coats won from Anne Salisbury and Bridget Hogge. Twenty women competed that day.

There was also confirmation that the Three Peaks race was indeed coming in line:

> At the recent Three Peaks Race Association AGM it was decided that there would be a Ladies Race in the 1979 event, covering the full distance with a common start time but separate result list, prizes, etc.

Not being able to claim experience of a previous race, females had to prove that they had 'completed 2 category A events of at least twelve miles in the last two years'.

At the end of 1978 Roger Boswell announced that there would be a women's race in (all three of) the Lochaber Three events in July 1979. These were the Melantee, Half Ben and Cow Hill races, which are all held over one long weekend. This was good news because Scottish races seemed slow to come on board with inviting women to compete.

One of the biggest catalysts in the expansion of races in the 1970s, some of which have been noted already, was the Cumberland Fell Runners Association (CFRA), who became very much involved in encouraging women runners. It wasn't a running club but a self-described group of like-minded volunteers who give up their free time to organise fell races.

Their first race was the Ennerdale Horseshoe, which was first held in 1968. CFRA went on to have a roster of nine fell races and one road race at their peak. Although not involved right at the start, Danny Hughes soon became an integral part of the CFRA. Eventually the whole family were involved in fell race organisation, as his wife Norma recently recalled. 'I think we first got involved with helping to organise in 1971, as we certainly helped to plan the first Wasdale race in 1972 and continued for the next twenty years!'

Norma Hughes

Contact with Norma Hughes was made via her son Dave, and a Facebook connection. Norma and I originally carried out a phone interview and I followed that up with some further questions by email. Norma had not been an active fell runner, but was a central part of the developing scene in the 1970s.

Danny Hughes was working at BNFL when he first started getting involved in fell running. He and Norma had lived in Gosforth, near Wasdale, since 1968. They had a young family by then, sons David and Johnny, who didn't run themselves but eventually helped on checkpoints, and their daughter Rachel – who always helped on registration.

Norma adds: 'Rachel has done one or two fell races, but I was never a runner myself. I was very much involved in the organisation though. I always typed out the results, in the days before computers of course. We did split times for the Ennerdale and Wasdale, so it was a lot of typing.'

Although she wasn't involved with the first two or three races at Ennerdale, Norma vividly remembers the first Wasdale Race in 1972. It was thought that because the Ennerdale race was so successful maybe CFRA should try organising a Wasdale race. 'That was the other nearest valley to us. They were both natural courses to run, around the mountain tops flanking the valley. They were also walking routes. Normally registration was outdoors, although we used the Scout hut at Ennerdale for changing and registration and eventually bought a couple of tents.'

The first Northern Counties Championship Fell Race was organised by CFRA in 1979, from Honister Slate Quarry, moving down into Buttermere Village in 1984.

Before that, in 1977, CFRA had instigated four women-only races. They were Crag Fell, run at the same time as the Ennerdale Horseshoe Race; the Burnmoor Chase, run with the Wasdale race; Kinniside, where the women ran up Dent Fell; and Muncaster, where the women ran a shorter version of the Muncaster Luck race from its instigation in 1977. Crag Fell ran for five years, Burnmoor Chase for four, after which time the women were invited to do the full Ennerdale or Wasdale races instead. At Kinniside the women ran the full course from 1980 onwards, and at Muncaster they ran the full course from 1981. Also, the Copeland Chase was started by CFRA in 1975 and accepted women from 1977 onwards.

Kinniside, which was attached to Cleator Moor Sports, was always held the day after the Wasdale race. Muncaster took place on the day after the Ennerdale race. The Muncaster race is called the Muncaster Luck, after an incident in history, as Norma Hughes recounts. 'One of the kings was found on Muncaster Fell – I think it was Henry VI. He was fleeing from the battle of Hexham and was found wandering on the fell, and they brought him down and fed and watered him at Muncaster Castle. He gave them a little glass bowl which is called the Muncaster Luck. As long as that remained intact there would always be an heir at Muncaster.'

Norma adds that as far as she can recall, 'in the 1970s I think the ladies were quite happy at having a shorter race to compete in and hadn't really considered running with the men in the long races. It wasn't until Véronique Marot ran unofficially in the Ennerdale race in 1979 that some of them started to run with the men in the long race. In 1980 some ladies ran in the Horseshoe, but the short ladies' race continued until 1981.'

Not surprisingly, Norma Hughes remembers the Marot incident well, straight away pointing out that Véronique always seemed to compete in white elbow length gloves. Norma takes up the story. 'There was a bit of a discussion, or argument shall we say, with Danny that day. Marot ran unofficially in the end. We had never had a woman before who wanted to run in the long race. We had the (shorter) ladies' races. It was very sexist, wasn't it! But sexism didn't really come into it at the time, that was just the way it had always been. Danny was usually ahead of his time with his fell race initiatives. He was the one in the end who said that they should be allowed to run. It was Joe Long who was one of the main organisers at the time. He ran the Scout Camp at Ennerdale, where they started from. Joe started the Ennerdale race, in 1968.

CFRA was not a competing club at all. It was Danny Hughes who decided that the time had come for people to be able to compete, and it was suggested that a new club was needed. Cumberland Fell Runners (CFR) came into being in December 1986. 'It was another of Danny's ideas – as there wasn't a fell running club in the western fells at the time. Both he and Joss ran for Kendal. It quickly became popular, and a group of runners met at our house in Gosforth each week for training during the summer and at Whitehaven Sports Centre in the winter.'

As there were already races up Ben Nevis and Snowdon, CFRA decided to add Scafell Pike to their list of races. 'The race still takes place and a few years ago my son Dave organised the race on the day for Richard Eastman, who wasn't able to be there, and I ended up once more on registration. There were quite a good number of runners in the early days, but it has never taken off in the same way as the other two races.' Women were invited to compete right from the start, as was the norm by then. That first race in 1986 was reported on in *The Fellrunner* by CFR runner Alex Smith. The eighty entries included one lady – Helene Diamantides. For the next year it was advertised as the European Communities Scafell Pike Race and was won by Italian Battista Scanzi. There were eleven female entrants, led home by Clare Crofts (DPFR).

By now Danny Hughes was heavily into the international scene, having run in several Swiss and Italian races. For the World Mountain Running Trophy in 1988, which was held in Keswick, Danny was the main organiser, and by that time people saw it as equality of racing opportunities. Norma recalls, 'the first World Trophy was actually held in Italy in 1986 following several planning meetings with the Italians to form the International Committee for Mountain Running. Danny did write a history [*unpublished*] of international mountain running a couple of years before he died in 2009, after I had said to him "really, you are the only one who knows all the details of how it was set up."'

Finally, on CFRA, Norma Hughes notes that 'they were instrumental in writing *Safety of Fell Races*, following the death of Bob English in the Ennerdale, and also introduced the tally system for checkpoints. When Danny was Chairman of the FRA, he also introduced insurance for fell races.' Danny Hughes certainly paved the way for many advances in the sport, including safety procedures which formed the starting point for all FRA safety requirements up to the present.

CHAPTER 6

A women's fell running championship

Taking on Committee Posts in the Sport.
The First Women's Championships.
Still Some Unofficial Entries.
Profile: Véronique Marot

'Deeds not words' was the order of the day.

This is also the title of a book on women's rights, written by Helen Pankhurst – great-granddaughter of suffragette leader Emmeline Pankhurst. Things had begun to shape-up in 1978, with two good examples of females taking initiatives to further their aims.

First, Anne-Marie Grindley was elected to the FRA Committee. She was soon adopted onto the sub-committee charged with the task of negotiation with the AAA (Amateur Athletic Association) over a sensible arrangement for managing the sport of fell running.

Secondly, the notes of the FRA Committee activities show that, 'a Ladies Fell Runner of the Year competition was also discussed briefly at both meetings, the outcome of which was that Carol Walkington would like to hold a brief meeting with as many ladies as possible an hour before the 1979 AGM at Pendle next April to discuss the scheme proposed by Tommy Orr and other pertinent matters with a view to establishing a 1979 competition (if this is generally favoured).'

Many businesses, and sports' governing bodies, have been tardy in appointing females to top positions in their structure and the FRA has been no different. The Chair and *The Fellrunner* editor posts are arguably the most influential FRA committee posts. Madeleine Watson was the first female Chair of the organisation, taking on the post in 2012. Britta Sendlhofer had become the first female editor of *The Fellrunner* in 2007.

Discussing the organising of the meeting noted above, Carol Walkington says she is afraid she can't remember the details other than it being different to what was in place for the men. Tommy Orr's list had about ten races, but few of them were the same as the men's championship list, and neither was his points system.

Carol Walkington suggested some changes. 'My suggestion was to follow the same format as the men's allowing for some differences in the actual races due to lack of races available on the calendar. Ladies' races were gradually being included on top of the original 1977 ones offered and it was agreed by the ladies to follow the same format as the men. Of course, at the time our choices were limited but there were enough races available to allow missing some and still being in contention.'

The women's championship scheme had been fine-tuned, and was in place for the first time for the 1979 season. Sources differ, so it is not clear exactly what format was used for the first women's championships. The FRA not having a full set of committee minutes archived has made that level of detail hard to ascertain.

There were a good number of women running in most of the races now, although without the peak high numbers of 1978. For example, the Lake District Mountain Trial had sixteen finishers, from nineteen who started of the twenty-one who entered. There were also sixteen new races for women to choose from including Carnethy, Rivington Pike (using the full course), and the Three Peaks. Off-setting that was the fact that there were no entrants for the Kinniside race, and only one for each of the new Melantee and Half Nevis events. There was still a reluctance to let females run full distance courses from several race organisers, examples being Gisborough Moors, Duddon, Muncaster Luck and the Lake District Mountain Trial.

A few races from the year give a feel for the events of that year.

At the Manx Mountain Marathon the women normally started at halfway, and in June the female fell runners were still starting from Ogwen for the Welsh 1,000m race, which Jean Lochhead won. At the end of April women ran the Three Peaks Race for the first time, on a misty and windy day, with light drizzle. Bill Smith reported briefly on this auspicious occasion. 'There were eleven starters, of whom three retired. Jean Lochhead was first back in 3-43-12, ahead of Bridget Hogge (4-03-27), Joan Glass (4-07-25) and Brenda Robinson (4-09-42).'

As has been previously noted, Véronique Marot applied to run over the same course as the men at the Ennerdale race, in June, but was refused entry. She ran unofficially, to the consternation of the race organiser, Danny Hughes. The next year, women were allowed to compete over the full route, with five finishing of the seven that started.

Anthony Kay, who ran that day in 1979, gives an even-handed view. 'This was a week before my twenty-first birthday, so I was eligible to run the Junior race on Crag Fell, the same course that women were supposed to run. There was no way I could have taken on the full Ennerdale course at that time, so I was happy about that, unlike Ms Marot. I remember that all the talk after the race was about this dreadful woman who had defied the organisers by running the full course. Although many people there thought that what she had done was dreadful, I think there were also many who supported her.' Véronique Marot went on to run some superb fell and mountain races, and also twice set the British record for the marathon.

Véronique Marot

I introduced myself to Véronique via a cheeky message to her work email account, which some detective work had uncovered. We subsequently did two phone interviews and a couple of follow-up email conversations, which were quite difficult to co-ordinate as she was often switching between the UK and France.

Brought up in France, Véronique Marot passed her baccalaureate and then did a two-year training course in Paris as a trilingual secretary (in French, German and English). This was at her father's request because he wanted her to have a 'trade'. Véronique had been born in Compiègne, France, in 1955. Part of the second year of her course included three months of work experience, and she chose to do hers in Watford, England. This was in April 1976, and she never went back. She then went to York University to study history, from 1977 to 1980.

Véronique had started running in 1972 at age sixteen, because her PE teacher had noticed that she was the only one to ever run all of the weekly half mile 'race' round the school. Véronique was entered in the French equivalent of the county schools championship, and finished high enough for the winner of that race to suggest she should join her club. 'As soon as I joined her club I stole her boyfriend, but that is another story. For three years I trained about twice a week and competed in cross-country and on the track. Then, in the summer of 1975, someone convinced me that all this running would give me bulging muscles, and so I stopped for two years.'

She makes a couple of revealing comments about her parents' level of interest in her sport and her welfare. 'I had joined Compiègne Athletic Club, which they were fine with. However, I was supposed to be home for dinner at 7pm every night. Training started at 6pm and I then had to cycle home which meant that I would often be home after 7pm. Sometimes there would be a note saying "your dinner is in the bin"!'

Her parents may not have been interested in her running, but they were incredibly egalitarian. 'When I was about eight, I became the leader of a group of four girls in my class. There was a group of four boys also in my class with their own leader. To annoy me that boy came up to my father and said to him that I wasn't ladylike and that I would hit him and his mates (which I was indeed doing). We had little fights in the playground. My father said to him 'you have my permission to hit her back'. In his mind girls and boys were clearly equal.

I think that gave me some of my determination to do what I wanted to do in life.'

Véronique resumed running at university in 1977. She wanted to compete in the French National Championship marathon in June 1981. The French Athletic Federation would not let her, even though at the time she was ranked third in France with a time of 2-46. 'The Federation told me on the phone that, in their opinion, the London Marathon (where I had got my qualifying time) was short. This is very funny because the person who measured the London Marathon, John Disley, and co-founder of that race, was a qualified measurer. In fact, at the time, French marathons were notoriously all over the place, distance-wise, often about 400m short. When they turned me down, just before I was due to leave in October on a ten-month Grand Tour of the Americas with my husband, I vowed that I would apply for British Nationality on my return in order to try and compete for Great Britain. I duly applied for British nationality in the autumn of 1982, but only in a laidback way. Then in June 1983 I wrote to the Home Office stating that I had just been selected to represent GB in an international marathon in Szeged, Hungary, on the strength of my 1983 London Marathon placing (sixth British Woman) and was hoping to compete the following year at the Marathon distance in the Olympics, so would they please review my application as a matter of urgency. I got a phone call within a week to say that the Home Secretary had approved my application. It was a bit like Zola Budd's application in 1984, though more low-key. At the World Championships in 1987, at Rome airport, I met the head of the French Athletic Federation who apologised profusely in a typical French way: "France's loss is Britain's gain". It just made sense, as I was living in Britain, racing against British athletes, with stiffer competition than I would have had in France.'

Her university had also been instrumental in introducing her to the fells. It was a very small university at that time, and her immediate friends had a have-a-go attitude. The university cross-country club was also very small, four women and about eight men. 'One evening in October 1978, after training, in a Fulford pub where rehydration was the norm amongst the training group, someone mentioned the forthcoming Barnsley Marathon to be held in late November and we all decided it would be a great idea to enter. Though none of us had raced the distance before or trained for it, we all finished it. I did 3 hours 55 minutes, which included a tussle with a policeman who wanted to remove my training partner and best friend from the race because he thought she looked ill! I won the tussle (she did want to carry on) and we duly finished together.' Rosie Naish was one of the four women in the university cross-country club, and Sarah Haines was one of the others, so Véronique had good training and teammates.

Someone suggested fell running, so they all went off to do fell races. Maybe Ennerdale, Kentmere or Fairfield would be mentioned, and off they would all go. 'I did the 1978 Ennerdale race as my first fell race, but it was the short version, the same as the Junior men ran [*Crag Fell*]. I came third in 43-26. That race was maybe 5 miles or a bit more. The next day I went rock climbing, so clearly wasn't very tired. I remember thinking it is ridiculous, coming all the way from York to the Lakes, and right over the far side at Ennerdale, to run up and down a hill. I felt pissed off, with us doing so little and the men doing 23 miles. So, I said to the group in the minibus taking us back to York, "Next year I will run the men's race". Women were about to be permitted to run the Three Peaks race (the same distance as Ennerdale), or was it only up and down Ingleborough, which was 9 miles. I think Rosie Naish and I did that short race in 1978, but the following year the full Three Peaks was open to women.' In 1978 Véronique did indeed run the women's Ingleborough race, which was the same as the Junior race, with Rosie Naish. It was just up and down the one peak.

Véronique eventually ran the Three Peaks race in 1980. Her diary records how it went: 'I was leading most of the way and I knew Sue Parkin was fitter and better at descending. She overtook me after Ingleborough. I was second in 3-42-40.' Her problem was that she wasn't fell-fit. 'That undid me at the Three Peaks. I had natural endurance but hadn't trained on proper hills. The only hill in York is by the library, and apparently I used to amuse other students as I ran up and down that library hill, often in the pouring rain.'

She reckons that she tried to effect change by having a 'thou shall not stop me' attitude. 'A bit like Kathrine Switzer, perhaps. I was going to do it whatever they say. I would not be put off. It wasn't a feminist, striking a blow for women, kind of action though. I was more doing it because someone had to start the ball rolling. Even at Ennerdale (in 1979) some female athletes wanted to stop me running the full course. Seriously. I remember it very well. I was very pissed off by the attitude of some of the women about it. As a woman you could already run Kentmere, which is 12 miles.' She is not shown in the results for her (unofficial) 1979 Ennerdale effort, but Véronique recalls that her time was about 5 hours.

Véronique's commitment to the UK fell scene was greatest in the 1980 season. She did Fairfield, the Three Peaks, Gisborough Moors, Kentmere, and Ennerdale to come fifteenth in the British Championships. She also did the Lyke Wake Walk, which is 44 miles, and says she ran the last 7 miles as she was bored with walking.

She then tells a story that ties in with one that Wendy Dodds mentioned. 'My navigation was (and still is) absolutely appalling. I am renowned for leading an entire pack of women in a race astray. It was Gisborough in April 1980. It was a 7-mile race from the town onto the North York Moors and back down. Most of the field ended up doing an extra 6 miles, apart from some local women who knew the route and didn't get lost. Also, Rosie [Naish] and I did the KIMM in 1978 (Peebles), 1979 and 1980, and each time we got hopelessly lost and had to wait for men to come along with compasses to rescue us.'

Véronique went back to the Ennerdale race again in 1981, but the weather was awful, and she dropped out. She had a marathon to run shortly after, the national championships at Sandbach. Her diary reads: 'Weather was appalling so I only did one-third of the course. Felt very stiff afterwards. It seemed the right thing to drop out.' The marathon was a week after. 'I don't know what I was doing! I did 2-50-02 in that marathon on a very hot day, in second place behind Julie Barleycorn.'

Véronique met Brian Scobie in the winter of 1982 when she got a temporary job as a secretary at Leeds University (possibly proving her father right about doing that secretarial course back in 1974) and re-joined the Leeds University lunchtime training group. Brian was a lecturer at Leeds University and part of that lunchtime training group which included both students and university employees. Brian kept telling her that she should challenge herself more and would often run away from her forcing her to speed up into uncomfortable territory in order not to get lost. 'He tried to get me to basically be a bit more focused, and not do as many races. I wasn't really into training hard. I had been injured when I met him, and he couldn't believe that I had run 2-46 for the marathon. I proved him wrong by doing 2-42 in the 1983 London Marathon.'

Brian thought it was a good idea for her to do mountain races, so she told him she was going to go off and run some. 'It was Noel Tamini, a Swiss editor of a monthly fell running magazine called Spiridon (after the first winner of the 1896 Olympic marathon) who suggested I should do the prestigious Sierre-Zinal race. I think he must have heard of me via fell running and also maybe because I was French and the magazine was published in French. He offered me his chalet to stay in. I also ran Sierre-Montana and broke the record there by three minutes. Karel Lismont won the men's race. It is uphill on a road all the way, so a lot of road runners do it. I prefer the uphill only races that Europeans often put on.'

When she first ran the Sierre-Zinal race in 1984, she had been at altitude for two weeks already to acclimatise. 'You need that training to do well at Sierre-Zinal. It is tough if you are not used to the altitude. I was incredibly arrogant at the time. That first time I told the race organiser I would not only win but break the record by at least six minutes. It is quite a dangerous course, you can so easily twist an ankle.' She set a new record of 3-12-08, knocking over seven minutes off the previous record.

She went back in 1985 and took another five minutes off the record, two weeks after winning Thion-Grande Dixence, another mountain race finishing at the Grande Dixence dam. Returning again in 1987, she was very fit and getting ready for the World Championships in Rome [*for the marathon*]. 'I had been training in Davos for a few weeks, and I knew I was incredibly fit. It broke my heart that I couldn't break three hours at that year's Sierre-Zinal, but it was very wet and I didn't want to take any chances on the downhill and on the rocks by the Weisshorn Hotel. I had to slow deliberately and that is why.' She won the race in 3-01-57, a record that wasn't beaten until Angela Mudge ran 2-56-41 in 2001.

Whilst she was there that year the Davos organisers offered her a place in the 67km race and some accommodation. 'I warned them that it was too long and we did a compromise. I would run 26 miles (42km) and walk the rest. When I ran the first part a runner nicknamed Little Mo from Clitheroe complained that she had followed me, and it had ruined her race when I slowed to a walk. What a cheek! There is always someone in a long race who goes too fast in the early part. Everyone should do their own race. I did finish, but I did have a massage at the rest station at 26 miles. I jogged the last bit so it didn't look like I was walking. I was able to run hard the next day.'

Véronique says, 'I pretty much stopped fell running, in England, in 1981. It is not really the thing to be doing if you are trying to be an international marathon runner.' Having said that, she was very good at mixing her events. She won at least ten marathons, had been running them in 'the fell years', and came second in New York in the same year as winning Sierre-Zinal for the first time. She ran 2-28-04, in a new British Record in the 1985 Chicago Marathon, the same year as the second Sierre-Zinal win. She reckons that her time in Chicago should have been a low 2-27, if the wind in the last 5 miles had not impeded her progress. This confidence was due to spending four weeks training and racing at altitude in the constant company of Tim Johnston (2nd in the 1967 World Cross and 8th in the 1968 Mexico Olympic marathon), who had accompanied her to the Valais and, because he was fourteen years older, was the perfect running companion being just a bit faster to push her on the fells. She again broke the British record with a time of 2-25-56 at the London Marathon in 1989, which was only beaten by Paula Radcliffe in 2002.

She says she doesn't follow the fell scene, and never did really. 'I did it as a hobby, rather than seriously. Even the Swiss races were a way of getting fit rather than an end in itself.'

If you have seen Véronique run, or in photos, she is often wearing long white gloves, as she explains. 'The white gloves were because Rosie Naish and I were running together and we trained together. Rosie was incredibly blonde and I was dark haired so we thought it would be fun to have gloves on and be a bit more ladylike. They were long ball-gown gloves too. Rosie wore black gloves and I wore white.'

Véronique went back to the sport to take part in The World Masters Mountain Running Championships in Switzerland for her 'sort of fiftieth birthday celebration', in 2006. It was an uphill only race, at Saillon-Ovronnaz. She was a very creditable fifth place in her race. It was to be her last mountain event.

When her mother died in 2018, Véronique wanted to keep the French family house, as it had been in the family since the 1850s. She decided to commute between France and England, to look after her sisters, who needed disability support. She has now decided to move to Compiègne full-time.

She concludes by outlining her current situation. 'I have had a knee injury – a muscle that tightens up. I have not run for a year, but I still keep fit. I try to do 18 to 20 miles a week walking.' Véronique Marot was someone who insisted on her right to run long races, who also became an incredible fell, mountain and road runner.

The take-up for the new women's events at the Lochaber Three at the end of July 1979 was poor. Roger Boswell reported ironically on the poor treatment of the one entrant for the Half Nevis race, which is part of the event. 'Ros Coats was the only female on show, she ran with the fellers, but the scrupulous recorders wrote her time down on a separate sheet and conveniently lost it. It was roughly 66 minutes.'

Roger Boswell was not one to mince his words, as his report in *The Fellrunner* on the Creagh Dubh race on 4 August shows. He was not going to let the situation pass un-noted:

> Twenty-nine runners toed the start for this race, but one was obliged to wait outside the ground, and join in unofficially as the pack left the grass track to go up the hill. Her name was Morag McCleod of Lochaber AC. The reason she didn't start, or finish, with the rest was because of the antiquated rules governing hill running, which the fastidious organisers religiously enforced. Women will not compete in the same race as men. Morag enjoyed her run, nevertheless, even though she didn't get a time. If ever the women are to gain their rightful place on the hills of Scotland, the first thing we must do is ... [*he finishes with an unpleasant suggestion of what to do with the officials concerned*]

It was nice to see a long report appear on the Ben Nevis Race of that year, this time with some more measured analysis by Roger Boswell:

> The anticipated battle between Lochaber's Ros Coats and Airedale's Jean Lochhead did not materialise, as Jean did not run. Ros did win, but she had to work hard for that victory. She

> soon forged ahead of the field of nine and had a big lead halfway up the hill, but then had to contend with dizziness and stomach cramp. At the top she had only a slender 30-second lead over Joan Glass. Ros picked up somewhat going down the scree to the red burn, where she again had a good lead. Just as well, because she felt exhausted after climbing out of the burn on to the tourist path. She managed to hold out enough to win, with Joan Glass a good second.

Strangely, the Ben Nevis Race book doesn't mention these women competing in the race, which Bill Smith describes as 'now run officially under SWAAA rules'. The Ben Nevis Race book claims that the abandoned (because of the weather) 1980 event included '14 women taking part in the first official women's race' and lists the first winner (in the appendix) as Ros Coats from the 1981 race.

Ros Coats had written a page-long analysis of the way female runners were treated by the Ben Race organisers, including 'after the [1978] prize giving several of us discussed our thoughts with the organisers – we wouldn't mind paying the entrance fee and can manage without showers – but please could the race be made official. Also, could we start, if not with the men, then one or two minutes ahead of them? (I must have had to overtake nearly three hundred men, whereas the dozen or so ladies would be no problem for the men to pass).' Things had not improved in a year, and the women's record was quoted wrongly; they started two minutes after the men again, had men's certificates, and no prizes. Ros finished by asking for 'some of the basic courtesies that other race organisers provide without fuss'.

To succeed in those first women's fell championships you had best cover as many of the races as possible. Ros Coats did just that, having an outstanding season, winning 214 points. Her races included six wins (Ben Nevis, Mountain Trial, Langdale, Moffat Chase, Blisco Dash and Wansfell) and four second places (Edale, Pendle, Fairfield and Ben Lomond).

The championship runner-up, Jean Lochhead, had 198 points

(including setting a new course record at Fairfield, by nearly three minutes). The rest of the top ten that initial season, with their points in brackets, were: 3 Bridget Hogge (182), 4 Anne-Marie Grindley (168), 5 Linda Lord (157), 6 Pauline Haworth (154), 7 Joan Glass (128), 8 Anne Bland (114), 9 Jean Dawes (105) and 10 Cath Whalley (92). That is as good a list of female fell running pioneers as you could ask for.

Females were now seeking committee positions as their influence increased. Jean Lochhead became caretaker Treasurer for the FRA after a resignation, and Sue Styan was also now on the FRA Committee. They had also been taking on what became known as the Big Rounds.

CHAPTER 7

Big rounds

The First Bob Graham Rounds and then 58 Peaks in 24 Hours. Profiles: Jean Dawes, Wendy Dodds

'Her courage and willpower, which she possesses in abundance, kept her going', neatly sums up how new challenges were being tackled.

Away from the racing scene women had been testing themselves over some classic endurance challenges. Back in 1976 Jean Dawes had been the first to have a crack at the Bob Graham Round, which at the time of her attempt had only had forty-eight successful men's completions.

Jean Dawes' BGR attempt took place from midnight 31 July 1976. It is recorded in detail by Fred Rogerson in the brilliant resource that is his loose-leaf 'publication' entitled *History and Records of Notable Fell Walks, 1864–1972, Within the Lake District* (henceforth referred to as *Notable Walks*). Even he starts by calling her 'a housewife with three children', before giving an interesting account of the effort, a much-reduced version of which appears here:

> Prior to the start Jean expressed her intention of completing the round irrespective of time taken. Never more than a few minutes adrift of the scheduled times it was after leaving the last summit, Robinson, that her body demanded sleep. From Newlands valley, with darkness upon us, the steep descent of Robinson was under constant observation. Torches were observed descending the

ridge but very slowly. They became stationary for what seemed to be ages and then downward movement for a short distance, then stationary again. Several thoughts crossed my mind but with time slipping away the hoped for successful attempt by the first women was not now possible.

At Honister Hause, even though she appeared tired, Jean was full of determination. On her arrival in Newlands valley we learned of the trouble. Jean was asleep on her feet and fighting sleep, she continued along the road to Keswick.

After finishing Jean departed from Keswick and was soon fast asleep in the caravanette. She slept [*some more, at Fred's house*] until 9.30am when she was up and assisting Margaret, my wife, make breakfast, seemingly little the worse for the previous day's endeavour. No blisters, swollen ankles or stiffness.

Jean Dawes had taken 24 hours 50 minutes, and said at the time that she was hoping that if she could get fit enough she could try again in June 1977.

Jean Dawes

Contact was established with Jean via a tentative maybe-correct phone number. Thankfully it was her number and she willingly agreed to be interviewed via email. She commented, 'you have certainly stirred some memories. I hope I can get my thoughts into order, but it's going to take a little while.'

Born Jean Tatham, on 16 February 1941 in Kendal, Jean Dawes didn't have much interest in sport when she was younger. She attended a girl's only high school and played hockey, tennis and netball. Both her parents were rock climbers, and they had camping holidays in Langdale and enjoyed many holidays at Seathwaite Farm, Borrowdale.

She married Pete Dawes in Windermere in 1962. 'Pete had previously run at school and in the Junior Guides Races. During his National Service he ran for the RAF team in Germany, and when demobbed he wanted to get back to running on the fells, so he joined Kendal Athletic Club and started entering the local races. He persuaded me to go running with him on the fells and I joined Kendal too.'

Jean says that she then entered her first (and last) cross-country race. 'I think I was actually last in the race! I was on my knees, it was so fast.' She went back to the fells and was doing longer walks with Pete and getting more competitive, especially on the downhills.

By the early seventies they had three children, and many summer weekends were spent driving to events and meeting up with other wives, partners and children. 'Pete was also training for the Bob Graham Round, which he completed in 1974. The support and camaraderie of so many friends willing to give time and effort, running through the night, carrying drinks and waterproofs was outstanding.' Jean also did a lot of supporting, which she admits was mostly brewing tea at checkpoints and transporting pacers to the next section.

Jean had met Lizzie Emery, wife of Carl Emery, and Carl and Pete were discussing entering the Karrimor International Mountain Marathon in Ennerdale in 1975. 'Liz and I said, "we can do that" and entered our first mountain event. My navigation was non-existent in the beginning, it was a case of learn or get lost.'

In 1975 Pete was looking for another challenge and decided to run the Pennine Way. He and Jean spent a lot of time driving north, learning the route and road crossings. 'In July he started off from Kirk Yetholm and headed south, and arrived in Edale in 3 days 1 hour 46 minutes and broke Joss Naylor's record. The help he received from his team of pacers was fantastic, with Fred and Margaret Rogerson organising brews and food.'

The following year, in May 1976, Jean competed in her second event, which was the Fellsman Hike, and the following month made her first attempt on the Bob Graham Round. Pete had decided that Jean should have a go at the BGR. 'Training during the week was running along the back lanes above Ulverston, sometimes with a head torch. Then weekend runs in the fells, with my lovely grandparents looking after the children. I was enjoying running on the fells and doing longer routes but I wasn't fast enough. In the 1976 BGR I was falling asleep as I trudged from Newlands to Keswick and ran out of time.' It had taken over twenty-four hours, but encouraged by Pete, Fred and Margaret, and many of her friends, Jean agreed to have another go in 1977.

Dawes did come back to the Bob Graham Round in 1977, setting out on a clockwise round at 8am on 25 June. An impressive list of pacers was lined up, with Chris Bland agreeing to start things off along with Pete Dawes. They had rain and mist on Skiddaw, but husband Pete's navigation was up to the mark. They descended Halls Ridge to a welcome cup of tea at Threlkeld.

Boyd Millen and Steve Tosh led off up Clough Head into more mist, gathering more runners as they went. Jean Dawes commented that she had the chance to 'catch up with all the news from Joan [Lancaster] and Anne-Marie [Grindley]. Boyd says "save your breath for running" or words to that effect'. There were drinks at Grisedale Tarn, before misty ascents of Fairfield and Seat Sandal.

They reached Dunmail Raise for tea and stew, Jean feeling she shouldn't get too comfortable at support points. The support party still seemed to be growing, and the weather was now dry but windy. More food was consumed at Stake Pass. It was cold on Bowfell, and Dawes took on salt tablets and worked through Roman Halenko's supply of butterscotch. Dawes had huge self-doubts halfway round, thinking of packing up at Wasdale, but didn't want to let her supporters down. She recalled 'Broad Stand, wet in places – *slape* you might say. Chris and I up first. Chris counting heads as they appear over the rock edge. Rough descent of Scafell and the rest of the team catches up. Chris leads us down a beautiful scree run. We sit and remove stones from our shoes. Then down to Brackenclose Lane for our supper.'

At 9.58pm they were off up Yewbarrow. She was now feeling tired and lost the pacers temporarily in the dark, and then dropped and broke her torch on Kirk Fell. A short sit down to mend the torch and she nearly fell asleep before moving on. They met Pete Dawes coming up from Beck Head, and took some tea with a drop of brandy before hitting Gable.

Soup and tea were taken at Honister at 4.05am and she set off with Bill Smith leading the way over the last three peaks. Eventually they came over the rock steps of Robinson and down to the river path, with just the road home to do. There was not much running, but an attempted sprint up the main street to finish in 23 hours 27 minutes, which included a total rest time of 1 hour 23 minutes. The first women's sub-24 Bob Graham Round was in the bag. Jean was the sixty-ninth BGR completer. Her own report (in *Notable Walks*) ends with:

> What can you say about a day like that – a day spent with friends in high places – I've been lucky to have had such support and encouragement. My grateful thanks. It was an unforgettable day.

Like many BGR efforts it was supported by friends old and new. It is good to see that Jean had Carol Walkington helping on the hill, as well as Joan Lancaster and Anne-Marie Grindley, and Janet Sutcliffe on road support. All top fell running females backing a colleague.

Jean was happy with that successful BGR (in 23-27), but she never pursued any of the other big rounds.

Jean says that the concept of being a pioneer never crossed her mind. 'I had been going on the fells since primary school in the 1940s. Running in the hills is an adventure, and now that I had made a conscious effort to get faster I was enjoying it even more. I don't think my main objective was ever to break any records. Every event has always been a personal challenge. It is always satisfying to know that the training has been successful in getting me to the finish, without me having to lie down halfway round. Physical endurance is only half the task, the other half is mental endurance, determination to get to the finishing line when you're knackered.'

Jean says her racing days are over. 'I am doing more long treks especially in Scotland which I love, despite the midges. I am still running, plodding up and running down.' Looking back, she adds that she always considered Ben Nevis her happiest race, 'even though slogging up to the summit was hard work and my time was nothing special. I loved the long run down and I got my official (pink) certificate. Earlier, three of us ladies had run unofficially, joining the race at Achintee.'

In order to ascertain in which years she had run the Ben Nevis race Jean went through all her certificates and found the following. 'I have a certificate for The Ben from 1978 and 1979, but I didn't run in what I think was the first official run for women in 1977 as we were moving house in that first week in September from Ulverston to Kendal.'

Having moved to Kendal in 1977, Pete joined the Mountain Rescue Team, and the Climbing and Caving Club, and they now had three teenagers. 'We still entered a few events, the Fellsman Hike, the Three Peaks and Vaux Mountain Trial, and a group of us went camping to run the Sierre-Zinal Race in Switzerland in August 1978, with members from Horwich, Clayton-le-Moors, and Kendal.' Jean set a record for the Fellsman Hike of 17 hours 35 minutes in 1978.

She also competed in the Three Peaks Yacht Race, in 1978, as a result of the publicity about female fell runners. 'Anne-Marie Grindley, Carol McNeill and I were invited on a free trip, a bit of an adventure, sailing in a catamaran from Barmouth, Wales, to Fort William, Scotland. We had a sailing crew of two and three female runners, who had to run up Snowdon, Scafell and Ben Nevis en route. It was an interesting cruise, rough weather from Barmouth, becalmed in Liverpool Bay, becalmed again in Loch Linnhe and rowing up the Loch to Corpach to finish fourth out of twenty-two teams.'

Jean also did some cyclo-cross, but admits she wasn't really competing, as she hadn't done any training. 'It was a random suggestion by Pete. He had two cyclo-cross bikes and said, "why don't you have a go at the Three Peaks Cyclo-cross?". So I did, but I stopped halfway down Whernside to have a cup of tea with Linda Lord, one of the Clayton-le-Moors runners I hadn't seen for ages. I came in as second lady, but I think there were only two of us. In first place was Brenda Atkinson who went to America as part of the British Team, but it was a fun day out.'

Looking back, Jean recalls that she did a lot of camping in Glen Brittle, and running on the Cuillin with Pete. 'For some reason I never got up Sgurr nan Gillean, but my favourite part of the Cuillin Ridge was abseiling off the In Pin [Inaccessible Pinnacle]'.

Jean Dawes gave back to the sport by being on the committee for both the Bob Graham Club and the Lake District Mountain Trial Association.

She finished by reflecting that our conversation had certainly stirred some great memories. 'All this was forty-five years ago! I have been rooting through old files and have found certificates for races I didn't know I'd run. I am still planning long walks and did the West Highland Way solo in 2019.' Jean Dawes was truly a pioneer, particularly for so determinedly showing the way for others on the Bob Graham Round.

Just like the 4-minute mile, once Roger Bannister had shown the way, the feat by Jean Dawes (of completing the Bob Graham Round in under 24 hours) was soon repeated. Anne-Marie Grindley became the second woman to join the Bob Graham Club in June 1978. 'Ladies: may I recommend the Bob Graham Round to you – all those lovely men waiting on you hand and foot! Not only have I never been so pampered, never have I been so bossed about so much', was a memorable comment from her at the time. Both Jean and Anne-Marie were described as housewives in a report in *The Fellrunner.*

Anne-Marie had really good weather and was up on schedule all day, despite missing a pacer as she went through a road crossing earlier than planned. Returning to the Moot Hall, she knocked nearly two and a half hours off Jean Dawes' time. Just like Jean, Anne-Marie had her husband, Will, for company, except that he did the whole round. Incidentally, Jean and Pete Dawes were also part of the support team on the fells. A short extract from Anne-Marie's own report (in *Notable Walks*) gives a feel for this second women's completion:

> As we ran up the first gentle inclines along the road from Keswick John Haworth shouted 'you'll regret it later'. I appreciated John's concern even if I did appear to disregard it. We women fell runners are made of sterner stuff.
>
> The sunny weather was infectious and the whole proceedings had an air of lightness. We had a marvellous tea party at the top of Rossett Gill. The fates were smiling kindly on me that weekend with various crises smoothed out by my helpers without worry to me. It was the most enjoyable day on the fells that I have ever had, due to our wonderful companions.

Anne-Marie finished in 21 hours 5 minutes, and had taken a total rest time of 1 hour 36 minutes on the round. Anne-Marie and Will Grindley became the 98th and 99th members of the Bob Graham Club, respectively.

Men had been repeating Bob Graham's 1932 achievement since Alan Heaton became the second under 24 hours in 1960. Soon 42 peaks wasn't enough and the new challenge was to increase the number of peaks visited whilst still getting round in under 24 hours. By 1979 three men had seven times increased the total and it now stood at an incredible 72 peaks – a mark Joss Naylor set in 1975. It was not long before a woman first had the ambition to increase the woman's total. This was now known as the Lake District 24 Hour Fell Record, and it was directly in Anne-Marie Grindley's sights.

One monumental weekend in June 1979 Anne-Marie planned to inaugurate the initial women's fell record with an audacious effort that is described in an early version of the Bob Graham Round booklet:[13]

> On the same June weekend of Anne-Marie's attempt, a large group of runners also assembled at the Moot Hall, including Ros Coats, who was after a fast round, and Roger Baumeister, who wanted two [*i.e. a double BGR*]. The main risk was to the support teams rather than the runners: in the midst of a fuel crisis, nearly all of Cumbria's filling stations had run dry. In two parallel challenges, cars were nursed to the roadside stops while the runners traversed the fells.
>
> Anne-Marie completed a round of 58 peaks, just as Ros Coats finished her Bob Graham in a time of 20 hours and 31 minutes (despite going astray between Blencathra and Great Calva). Ros had set the fastest women's Bob Graham time by over half an hour.

Ros Coats was the third female to complete the Bob Graham Round, and she said at the time: 'It gave me tremendous satisfaction. The comradeship from the helpers and pacers is an incredible experience.'

In just one weekend Ros and Anne-Marie had set two remarkable records, which lasted until 1988 and 1994 respectively. They both showed what women are capable of in such endurance events. For the record Roger Baumeister completed his double BGR in a remarkable 46 hours 34 minutes. Wendy Dodds had made an unsuccessful attempt to complete the Bob Graham Round in 1978, her failure due mainly to insufficient preparation. Wendy mounted her own second attempt in 1979, when her 23 hours 30 minutes circuit resulted in her becoming the Club's fourth lady member.

---

13. *42 Peaks: The Story of the Bob Graham Round*, Hayloft, 2012.

Wendy Dodds

Wendy and I had a long and very interesting phone interview, fitting in with her Covid-19 work. She also happily chased up details of the times and events that we discussed and always came back with some more background details.

Wendy Dodds was born in Tynemouth in 1950. She retired from her job as a consultant physician in 2011. Although retired, she went back to work as an NHS returner when the Covid pandemic struck, but says she, 'had hoops to jump through because I had rescinded my licence to practise five or six years beforehand. They had called back people three years after they had rescinded their licence. Having jumped the hoops I was re-employed from 1 May 2020. This has been a non-clinical role. We all thought this [*Covid-19*] was going to be over in six months. Recently I have started vaccinating.'

At school Wendy didn't do athletics, but she did every team sport available, including hockey and netball. 'The individual sport I did was swimming. I was a junior international swimmer. I took it to triathlon in the 1980s and did quite a lot. I was third in the national long course, fourth in the short course, and third in the Grand Prix series, so I used to do about a dozen triathlons a year for a while. My big regret was that I turned down an opportunity to do a mega team event with Sarah Springman. It was to run from London to Dover in a relay, swim the channel and then cycle on to Paris. I felt my cycling wasn't good enough to participate, so I didn't join up. I even got invited to write a book on triathlon in the *Teach Yourself* series, but turned that down because my cycling knowledge and skills were way down.'

Wendy did quite a bit of road running, but it overlapped with her fell running time. She came to fell running through mountain marathons. She was part of the first women's team to complete the KIMM, with Val Pacey/Finch, in 1972 at Tibbie Shiels (in Selkirk, just east of Moffat). 'Two women had competed the year before but didn't finish. In 1972 there was a mixed team finish for the first time and also Val and I were the first women's team to finish. We were students together. I just moved on from there.'

Wendy Dodds went to university in Birmingham, to do medicine (taking a year out to do a physiology degree, en route). 'I continued to swim and started orienteering. My swimming was on the wane. I started fell running after I left university and was doing mountain marathons by then.'

No one in particular influenced Wendy to try fell running. 'It was just one of those things I found out about. I had an attempt at the BGR in 1978. The Moffat Chase that year was my first proper fell race, although I had done the Aboyne Highland Games race earlier that summer. I was working in Aberdeen at the time and happened to be able to get off on a Wednesday afternoon and I heard there was this race at Aboyne. I just drove west to enter. I can't remember if I was the only woman or whether there might have been one other who was a tourist at the games.' Wendy says that she didn't have to ask anyone, she just turned up and entered. 'Actually, it was quite a long race, about six miles I think, on a very hot afternoon. I had read about having electrolyte drinks, so I mixed my own version, which was far too concentrated and had the reverse effect. Moffat was relatively local. I had been at a meeting in Edinburgh the day before and they had a doctors' 5km which I ran in, around some playing fields.' Not ideal preparation, then.

Wendy hadn't done that much running, but had done a lot of mountain walking. She used to go at weekends into the Cairngorms in 1977 and 1978 and walk round the ridges without realising they were Munros. 'In 1978 Chris Brasher invited me to join him on one of his many attempts at the BGR. I think it was quite late in the year. I used to run and walk and jog on the hills, really only as mountain marathon training.'

Coming from an orienteering background she had navigation skills before she did any mountain marathons or fell races. 'But I was never a good fine navigator,' she says. 'My fine navigation was not that good, but for fell races and mountain marathons it is not fine navigation, it is more about your route choice. For about two decades I looked after the British Orienteering squad, so I would go to a lot of squad weekends and do nav training with them. It was always a bit of a joke as I wasn't at their standard.'

At this time Wendy was in an Orienteering club and the Nordic Ski Club of Scotland, but not an athletic club. 'It was the Nordic Cross-country Ski Club and it wasn't until I moved to West Yorkshire, to work in Leeds in 1979 and 1980, that I joined an athletic club. It was Jean Lochhead that said, "you must join Airedale and Spen" [ASVAC]. Having joined Jean said, "Oh I never train with Airedale, I am second-claim to Holmfirth". Because Jean lived near Holmfirth that is where she trained. So, I joined them second-claim, as did Sue Parkin.'

Wendy Dodds calls out Danny Hughes as a race organiser who refused to start women together with the men. 'I remember arriving for the NCAA race and it was advertised to start at 11am. I got there to find that the women were starting at 10.45am and raced to the start line. Before racing up Dale Head a wall collapsed and I had blood all down me. Neil Shuttleworth got a great photo of it later in the race, all down my left thigh.'

Wendy points out that she wasn't really a pioneer. 'Although there was a handful of us, I was after the time that they had to run unofficially. It didn't cross my mind to try to make change happen, not in the early days. Later on, I was pushing for veteran classes, but early on I just turned up and ran.'

The long races were the ones that suited Wendy, particularly the long Lakeland ones. 'Very early on I raced at Ennerdale and Wasdale. I remember before my first Three Peaks Yacht Race running Ennerdale and doing some recceing the day after. I am not a good sailor, but I have done several all-women yacht-peak races.'

Wendy finds it very difficult to identify her best performances. Admittedly she has a pretty wide choice. 'I am very pleased that in 1990 I was able to be first woman at Langdale. The worst thing about that race was that I made a bit of a navigation error coming down after Blisco. If I hadn't done that I might have been very close to a very good record. I just had a really good day that time. I was pleased to go back ten years later and win it again, to my surprise. That was because a lot of people went wrong, including Sue Parkin. It was quite funny running down off Blisco and towards the end Sue Parkin, Kate Beaty and I were all together. Sue and I were running from the cattle grid and I am looking over my shoulder. Sue said, "Kate is miles behind". I wasn't worried about Kate, it was Sue. Sue let me win that day and I said, "you could have won that. Why did you let me win?" She said, "morally you had won, as twice we met when I had gone a bit AWOL". Another group of runners ended up going very wrong and found themselves at Cockley Beck and had to hitch a lift back to Langdale.'

Recalling a bad experience one day running the Winter Hill race, Wendy says she never went back because of what happened. 'We were in the finish funnel which was about a hundred metres long. My strength was downhill running, and I must have overtaken this guy at some stage in the last bit of the race. Running down the funnel he came up behind me and literally pushed me to the ground and I went face down into the mud.' Unacceptable behaviour, whatever your age, sex or competitive feelings.

Wendy says she hasn't set any important race records really. 'There was a race at Kielder that I set a record for. It was called something like the Kielder Border Race, I am not sure. There may have been one of two others that I held for short periods.'

Her training wasn't very organised because it had to be focused round her work. In those days junior doctors used to work at least 80 hours a week. 'It was as and when really,' she says. 'I would go for a run on my way home from work. In Aberdeen you are so far north that you have very long days in summer. I remember running in the forest at 10pm sometimes, still in daylight. When I wasn't working at weekends I would get out for long days on the hills. It was time on my feet.' She admits that she probably did not train hard enough. 'It is a very fine balance between being at peak performance and overtraining. I was always on the upward part of the curve somewhere.'

Wendy was fortunate on the injury front over her career. 'I had a ruptured plantar fascia once. In the early days I had quite a lot of ankle injuries, but that was one of my few actual running injuries. Most of my injuries have been doing other activities. I was running with two friends between Christmas and New Year. We had been on Cartmel Fell and were almost back at the cars. I leapt over a ditch and didn›t quite make the other side. My foot was across the ditch so was forced the wrong way. I knew intuitively what had happened. It is a rare injury for runners, as it usually occurs in jumpers.' She also tells the story of an earlier injury she had which happened during one of Dave Woodhead's races. It was on the Stanbury Splash. 'On the return my heel went down a rabbit hole or divot in the ground and I had what turned out to be a partial rupture of the medial belly of the gastrocnemius (the main calf muscle). I got to the finish but had to walk backwards up the hills. A spectator found a fence post which I could use as a walking stick. One of my then teammates gave me an extra thermal top, so I walked back to the finish ... and I wasn't last. I was out for several weeks. For the plantar fascia rupture I had to have at least three months off. The first race after that was the Anniversary Waltz. I had done loads of gym stuff and it perturbed my club mates when I moved ahead of them during the race having not run for so long.'

Wendy liked to do the KIMM but had good reasons to miss it on two occasions. 'I missed 1978 as I was working in New Zealand for a year. The one other one I missed was the year Steve Birkinshaw was doing *SAS Are You Tough Enough* [a 2002 TV programme]. I was also doing that. He did the Langholm KIMM that year, but I chose to miss it in order to do some more specific preparation for going to Namibia the next month to take part in the SAS challenge.'

Wendy Dodds has been a very prolific racer over the whole of her career. 'I have done thirty-seven Three Peaks races, more than any other woman, but far below the men's record of forty-eight by Dave Scott. In my sixties, on one occasion in this race I sprinted past a man on the run in, not knowing he was first MV60 Ken Taylor, so was first overall O60.' She also has multiple v50 British titles, and several V50, V55, V60 and V65 English titles at the Championships.

One record Wendy Dodds did set was the women's record for Haworth Hobble in 1991 with Sarah Rowell. 'We did a lot of recceing, separately and together, to get good lines, paying particular attention to routes in and out of Haworth, which were not well defined back then. I was running as a member of Clayton le Moors, with members always coming out to support in large numbers at this event, so we got a lot of encouragement, though I felt embarrassed as Sarah was not very well known on the fells at that time, yet she was an Olympic Marathon runner, with a very good time at London under her belt and I was hanging on to her 'coat tails'. Of the numerous 'Hobbles' that I have done, I ate less on that one than any other, perhaps that was why it was the fastest!'

Prompted by something being discussed, Wendy gave a response that probably shows how she has continued to challenge herself over the years. 'I get a lot more enjoyment going for something that I don't know if I can do than going for something that I know is achievable.'

CHAPTER 8

Consolidation

The 1980s: Race Fields Increase. More Events Open Up. Contrived Short Courses in Terminal Decline. Profile: Fiona Wild

'We just did the standard Wasdale race', said one athlete, making the decision for herself.

More races were being forced to open up, as the second British Fell Championships took place in 1980. The year was notable for a race record being set that still stands, for a few new races allowing women to run (Chew Valley Skyline, Otley Chevin), and some good size fields, such as Great Hambledon (27), the Mountain Trial (21) and Rivington Pike (19). However, women were still running shorter courses than men in several major races, such as the Lake District Mountain Trial, or separate short races, like Crag Fell. In an article on Ros Coats in *Compass Sport* she spoke out strongly on the problems faced by women on the fells, including race start arrangements and not being able to run the same distances.

The 1980 season got off to a bad start with the cancellation of the Carnethy Hill race on 23 February, due to dense fog right down to the start. A cross-country race was held instead, in which nine women ran, and which Anne Bland won.

On 2 March the inaugural Chew Valley Skyline took place, which soon became an important early season race. Women ran the same 13-mile course in conjunction with the men, and were led home by Sue Parkin. Four weeks later though, the Edale Skyline race (on 30 March) was using a shorter 14-mile women's course to the men's 21 miles. Then, in contrast, on 7 April Wendy Dodds was the winner of the first official women's race to be held over the full course (30 miles) at the Manx Mountain Marathon.

The next weekend Wendy Dodds was one of seventeen women who ran the Gisborough Moors women's race, which was around 7 miles to the men's 12.5 miles. It didn't go totally as planned (for her and others), as Wendy's report in *The Fellrunner* records:

> I shoved the 1" OS map of the course in my pocket. [After a hard week's training] my only aim was to finish the course feeling tired. I was at the back of a second group as we reached open moorland. I came upon two runners stopped at a junction, with the front bunch out of sight. Out came the map, with only contours and place names showing up clearly. We dropped down ... but there had been a major error and we were 3 miles off course. We were now joined by the front group *returning* from Commondale and those catching up from behind. 2.5 miles along the road and we re-joined the course. At Percy Rigg I had used up the 75 minutes that I had allowed myself for the race (I had a 2pm assignation in Stockton). Hitched a lift from the marshals returning from Sleddale to the finish, arriving before any of the other women who were by now overdue.

Eventually only five athletes stayed properly on course, some taking well over two hours to finish.

Nine women ran the 23-mile Three Peaks race. Bill Smith describes the action in *Stud Marks on the Summits*: 'Véronique Marot was three minutes ahead of Sue Parkin on Whernside but the Yorkshire girl closed rapidly on the descent so that she was only one minute adrift at the Hill Inn, and then forged ahead going up Ingleborough to arrive at the summit with a two-minute lead.' That lead stretched to over seven minutes by the end, with Joan Glass closing Marot down rapidly in the last few miles.

In May Ros Coats showed impressive stamina to win the

9-mile Ben Lomond race from Wendy Dodds. Ros had taken part in the Scottish Orienteering Championships at Dunblane that same morning. Meanwhile, one week later the inaugural Goatfell race had just the one competitor, so numbers could still be low for events that encouraged women. Women were still offered a shorter course at the Welsh 1,000m race at the end of the month. In June there was one female entrant in the new Otley Chevin race, and later in the month they were still being offered the 3.3-mile Crag Fell race at Ennerdale. Commendably, women were also offered the full 23-mile Ennerdale race if they preferred, which was the first time they had been officially allowed to do that. Five finished out of the seven starters who had 'voted with their feet' to do the full distance, on a rainy and misty day. Pauline Haworth won in 4-37-47, from Joan Glass and Janet Sutcliffe, with Véronique Marot in fourth.

The Skiddaw race, in early July, had a strong field and Pauline Haworth beat Sue Parkin by forty-four seconds at the end of this tough 9-miler. Just days later Pauline Haworth was running in the Wasdale race. There had been no entrants for the shorter women's Burnmoor Chase that day so Pauline and Janet Sutcliffe ran the full 21 miles with the men. Impressive stamina, and recovery, and another marker for women to be allowed to run full distance races on the fells. Pauline explains. 'We (Janet and I) turned up for a race and Janet especially was into longer races and I was up for it too. I had already done the Ennerdale earlier that year. I can't particularly remember it [Wasdale]. I wasn't bothered. I would run anything. The Wasdale organisers realised it was silly to use the short 4.5-mile course for women, as Ennerdale had already changed that year.'

At Ingleborough the next week there was a bit of a glitch with the organisation. Sue Styan came in in 5th place, not an especially long time after winner Jean Lochhead, only to find that the timekeeper had gone home, so got no official time. Pauline Haworth was now on a roll, as Peter Knott reported on the Snowdon race: 'Eight ladies braved the elements and again the previous fastest time was broken, together with local runner

Joan Glass's domination of the race, by Pauline Haworth of Keswick in a time (85-18) which placed her amongst the [176] men. Locals Joan and Bridget Hogge had to be content with 2nd (90-48) and 3rd (93-05).'

Roger Boswell reported on the Lochaber Three. 'Bridget Hogge was a clear winner of the ladies' Melantee, while Ros Coats walked off with the Half Nevis, with Caroline Britten 2nd and Bridget Hogge 3rd. Bridget said she wasn't feeling any after effects from the Melantee race – who's she trying to kid? Ros stuck around to clean up in the Cow Hill.' All *Stud Marks on the Summits* says about the latter result is: 'Ros Coats was the fastest lady in 21-38.' It is a shame there isn't more detail as that initial Cow Hill race record has never been beaten, and is currently the longest standing women's fell race record.

At the Borrowdale race on 2 August there were two races on offer to the women. The fourth, and last, 5-mile Dale Head race took place that afternoon, with Ros Coats beating Bridget Hogge, from Anne Bland. Meanwhile, six women were entered for the first time in the full 17-mile Borrowdale race, running with the men. Once again, it was a triumph for Pauline Haworth, who won in an excellent 3-50-45, with Carol McNeill and Janet Sutcliffe 2nd and 3rd respectively.

Janet Sutcliffe was someone who was very much there or thereabouts in the early days, and always seemed to know when a new race was available to try. She was often on the start line when races first allowed women to compete in them. Born in Cannock (Staffordshire) she lived and worked in North West Cumbria. Before taking to the fells she had been a good squash and tennis player, at county standard at hockey and athletics, and a very good orienteer. She came to the fells through walking events, including winning the Fellsman Hike in 1975 and 1976.

In her profile in *Stud Marks on the Summits*, Janet commented on her approach to fell running. 'I dabble in fell racing as I have done in other sports. I would say that my first love, though, is still walking the fells – long days out. I do not enter many fell races and those I do are mainly longer ones because they provide more variety.'

She was very determined and ran well into her veteran years. She did a twenty-seven-hour solo unsupported Bob Graham Round, 'not wanting to trouble anyone'. Janet was the fourth woman to receive the award for completing fifteen Mountain Trials, going on to complete seventeen in all. At the World Masters Championships in Keswick in 2005 she achieved a Bronze medal in her age category, despite not feeling well on the day. Sadly, Janet Sutcliffe passed away in 2007, aged sixty-seven.

The 1980 season rolled on and included two major disappointments. In August there were no takers when the Burnsall race offered to take female entries, and the Ben Nevis race (which had at last accepted female entrants semi-officially) had to be cancelled on the day because of the weather. Better news of the Lake District Mountain Trial, which was held in Borrowdale, and had twenty-one female entrants. The women still had a shorter course though, taking in Dalehead Tarn, Base Brown, Glaramara and Sergeant's Crag and back via Langstrath. The first three were probably the top runners of that year, with Ros Coats securing a hat-trick at the event, winning from Bridget Hogge and Pauline Haworth this time.

In October three women entered the Butter Crag race, which had started as an amateur event the year before, with Pauline Haworth winning in 17-36. Later this race and the Grasmere Guides race became the same (amateur) event. One other new event started that year, more as a hiking than a running event. As Rob Grillo notes,[14] the first Haworth Hobble 'saw sixty-four teams set off from Haworth in snowy conditions, nine teams dropping out before the finish. The winners were mixed team Will and Anne-Marie Grindley from Clayton-le-Moors Harriers, ahead of two further Clayton duos.'

14. *Staying the Distance: The Story of Distance Running in Keighley & District*, self-published, 1999.

At the end of the 1980 season, when the championship title scores were totted up, Pauline Haworth was the second British Champion. The 1980 calendar spells out the criteria which applied to the men's championships: 'A runner's ten best positions in Category A races will count for points with the proviso that at least three of the ten are short, at least three medium and at least three long distance races. The winner will be awarded 22 points, the second 19 points, the third 18 points and so on.' Then, the twist, which muddied the situation: 'The basis for determining the [female] winners will be similar but not identical to the method used to decide the [male] Fell Runner of the Year.' [The 1979 Calendar had not had information about how the women's championships were to be conducted.]

Pauline Haworth had had some exceptional results that year. Her ten scoring results included six wins and four seconds, giving her 208 points. Bridget Hogge was second, her 195 points coming from three wins, three seconds and four thirds. Doing the maths on these numbers confirms a scoring system of 22 points for a win, and 19 points for second, etc. Strangely, there were less females scoring this year than the first year – sixty-eight compared to eighty-three. At this time there weren't the restricted fifteen races to choose from for women, as evidenced by the first three on the list showing that they had won a total of sixteen different races in their scoring lists. For the record the remainder of the top six that year were: Jean Lochhead (third with 171 points), Linda Lord (167), Ros Coats (151) and Gillian Pile (127).

There was a really embarrassing (for the FRA) twist to this story, that was revealed in a note in *The Fellrunner* magazine (August 1981). 'Last year's ladies' championship [*i.e. 1980*] caused some problems, and no doubt, some amusement, with no clear-cut decision about who won. Readers of *Compass Sport* [magazine] would have seen Jean Lochhead heralded as the Lady Fell Runner of the Year, while those at the FRA dinner saw Pauline Haworth presented with the trophy. The mix-up arose because it wasn't clear which races counted towards the ladies' championships. It was eventually decided that the 'green sheet' of qualifying races should be the guide and Pauline, on this basis, came out a clear winner'.

Perhaps in an attempt to tighten things up, there was another change of the championship format the next year. In *Stud Marks* it was noted that for 1981 'the Ladies championship was run on the same lines as the men's using the same 15 events nominated by the FRA, with the exception of Burnsall, which had no ladies event and was therefore replaced by Thieveley Pike. However, points were awarded for only the first ten places, with 11 for 1st, 9 for 2nd, and so on down to for 10th.' It was still an individual's best ten results, three long, three medium, three short, plus one of the individual's choosing, and the 1981 FRA Calendar confirmed the fifteen chosen races.

There were still shorter women's courses at some events in 1981 (such as the Welsh 1,000m event, and the Mountain Trial), but things were improving, with more new races being available for women to enter, such as a new women's Wasdale race replacing the Burnmoor Chase, Mytholmroyd adding a women's race in its third year, Muncaster Luck allowing women in its fifth year. Four years after the first Pendle race for women, twenty-two entered this year, to be led home by Ros Coats.

Similarly, in May, the Fairfield race had a classy field of twenty female competitors. The race report, which included an awkward remark about one of the athletes being 'attractive', noted that, 'an excellent performance [by Jean Ramsden] placed her third behind the more experienced fell runners from Lochaber, Ros Coats and Fiona Wild'.

In June the Ennerdale event had women running the full event, plus an optional shorter Crag Fell Race (for the last time). Ros Coats won the former, and Ali Crabb the latter. A week later, at Butter Crag, Ros Coats led the women home in spite of a bad fall on the descent.

The Lochaber Three race series was still struggling to attract female entrants. None was reported for Cow Hill [although Fiona Wild did run the race], and just two for the Half Nevis. Four results were recorded for Melantee on the Saturday, with Ros Coats beating Fiona Wild (the same positions as they achieved the next day at the Half Nevis). They were described in the published race report as 'Lochaber's lovely ladies'.

At the Thieveley Pike race the race reporter noted that: 'Sue Parkin staggered lots of the fellas by finishing 36th. It is really about time that the male runners accepted that being bettered by females such as Sue, and Ros Coats, is nothing to be ashamed of, and stopped making a fuss about it when it happens.'

At the FRA EGM, in November 1981, 'there was discussion on the fact that some of the women's courses were different from those of the men.'

Comments accompanying the points table for the Women's Championship results indicate that take-up for their events wasn't particularly strong yet:

> Overall, the 15 champs events there was an average of 8 ladies finishing. Overall, only 42 ladies scored in the champs events. In all but 3 of the events it was only necessary to finish in order to score points (awarded to first 10 finishers). Only three ladies completed events at all three distances (long, medium and short).

It ends with a positive spin though, noting that Ros Coats, Fiona Wild and Pauline Haworth, who were the only athletes who did a full complement of ten championship scoring races, 'ran superbly, demonstrating that the toughest fell race is well within the capability of the gentle sex'.

Ros Coats won the title for the second time (with 110 points), followed by Fiona Wild (90), Pauline Haworth (72), Carol McNeill (21), Rosie Naish (20) and Gillian Pile (18). With the best ten races to score and 11 points for a win, that means that Ros Coats had a full house of wins in all her scoring ten races across the three distances, a really impressive season.

Fiona Wild

I was discussing details of some old photos of fell races on Facebook at one point and I realised it was Roger Wild that I was talking with. This prompted a request to interview his wife Fiona, which was readily accepted. She soon came back, saying she was enjoying trawling through her memories.

Fiona Wild now makes little of her achieving second place in the Championships. 'I don't remember being very aware of the Championships', she says. Fiona Wild was born, as Fiona Hinde, in May 1951 in Bulawayo, Southern Rhodesia [now Zimbabwe]. She had no real interest in athletics at school, despite doing some high jump in primary school. A PE teacher obviously missed her potential, once telling her she, 'should have been able to run faster. I guess because I was tall.'

Before trying fell running Fiona was predominantly doing hill walking and rock climbing. 'I regularly jogged up the glen where I lived, to then swim in a pool of the river. So, in a way my first running was on the hill.' Her husband-to-be, Roger Wild, commented about the jogging, "That's not *running*!". 'So, then he showed me some real running – Beinn Bhan, in Glen Loy – in my gym shoes!'

Roger Wild always encouraged her running, and he also did a lot of racing/running around this time. 'He did the Ben Race in 1979 and 1981. He became an international mountain guide in 1992 through the International Federation of Mountain Guides Associations.'

Fiona's father, John Hinde, was also a significant influence. A passionate mountaineer all his life, he passed on his passion for the hills to her. The mountain of Ben Nevis, and the race up and down it, had history in Fiona's family. John Hinde ran the Ben Race in 1978, aged fifty. 'He was not a runner but was hill-fit. He worked with Outward Bound (at Loch Eil). I still have his certificate, showing a time of 2 hours 48 minutes 45 seconds. Although not a runner, he did a bit of jogging – and lots of hills!

He loved every minute of the descent and "felt like singing", his diary records', Fiona adds.

As she gained more experience Fiona did try some cross-country. 'I did do the district cross-country just for fast, short experience, and tried the Scottish cross-country once. I came sixteenth, without any specific training.' Fishing in her training diary she finds a reference to that race. It was at Falkirk, in February 1982. 'I did the North District cross-country races over the winter, just for a short, quick blast. There were very few women running. In fact, we ran with the Senior Girls to make up numbers. Perhaps the courses were shorter for that very reason. I really don't know, and to be honest they meant very little to me. Running round fields was certainly not my thing.'

By then Fiona had competed in the Karrimor International Mountain Marathon, in October 1979. It was held in the Rhinogs, and she reckons it was probably her first official event, but adds, 'I was at the start for the Ben Nevis Race 1980 – but it was cancelled due to the weather. So, I think my first fell race was the Blisco Dash in November 1980. I won that.'

By this time, she was regularly running in the hills, doing the Munros for instance, and had had a few trips to the Lake District. Then the Wilds moved up to Thurso in 1982, so the big hills were rather distant. 'I did keep very active, doing more local runs and races, and with memorable trips to Skye and other Highland mountain regions.'

The Wilds started a family there, with Finlay born on 8 September 1984, a week after the record breaking Ben Race of that year. 'We then moved back south to Kingussie in 1985, and my second son, Alex, was born in 1986. I still ran but didn't do many races.'

Finlay has turned out to be a bit of a runner, with multiple Ben Nevis wins and some very impressive Fastest Known Times (FKTs) and fell race records to his name. When Fiona was a few months pregnant, in May 1984, she had ten days of climbing and walking in the Cuillin of Skye. 'The highlight of this trip was the classic Dubhs Ridge which rises from Loch Coruisk and takes in the peaks Sgurr Dubh Beag and Sgurr Dubh Mor. Finlay, in utero, has no memory of this, but I like to think it instilled some awareness of the joy of moving in the mountains.'

Fiona explains that their children had early introductions to sport. 'The boys spent their early years in Kingussie with the Cairngorms on the doorstep, so it was in their enthusiasm for skiing that I first appreciated that they were keen to be in the hills. Finlay's initiation into running was probably during our time in Kingussie. There were plenty of fun runs. The local Highland Games would include a children's race to accompany the adult hill race. The same happened at orienteering events.'

After they moved to Fort William, the Nevis Range was their new winter sports venue. Finlay continued with skiing whilst Alex became an accomplished snowboarder. 'Our first family trip to the Chamonix area was in 1989, when the boys were three and four. These annual visits continued for a few years. There was a lot of walking through the high meadows, and a few trips up to spend the night in Alpine huts. There was a period when the boys were about six and seven that their bike riding speed was similar to my running speed, and so we had a few outings together, I remember, along the forest tracks of Glen Nevis. This phase didn't last long as they could soon go much faster than I could. There was definitely there a strong "mountain" influence in the family, with us all passionate about the hills.'

Fiona was a member of Lochaber Athletic Club when she was competing, and she acknowledges that clubmate Ros Coats [now Evans] was definitely an inspiration.

Training was logged in a diary. 'When I was doing a lot of races, mainly in 1981, I would run six days out of seven on a variety of terrain. I kept a note of my mileage in 1981 and the average was about 36 miles per week. My navigation was all right though I tended to stay within my comfort zone, and didn't venture into the hills alone if visibility was poor.'

Going back to her introduction to running, Fiona points out that her very first introduction to running any sort of distance was actually in an event abroad. 'It was the Karrimor Internasjonale

Fjellmaraton 1978 [in the July] – in the "Trim class" (i.e. very easy!). It was based at Kvitåvatn, Norway. I eventually did three KIMMs: in the Rhinogs, Arran, and Langdale [in 1979, 1980 and 1981 respectively], and also some orienteering, but not very competitively.'

Reflecting on those early days Fiona says she wasn't aware of any issues with race organisers. 'I have never felt like a pioneer, although I was very aware of being almost the only local woman doing hill racing. Now dozens compete in the Ben Race every year. However, I was aware that women were not officially permitted to run the Ben Nevis Race. My husband did the race in 1979 and I noticed Ros Coats setting off behind the men. When I saw Ros that day, I remember thinking I could give that a go!'

Fiona Wild only competed on the fells for five or six years. 'After the boys were born I had little time for the regular training needed for racing, though I did continue to run through my thirties and forties, local fun runs and the like.'

Fiona is not alone among the early women fell runners in not really wanting to identify specific top performances. 'I never really thought about races in terms of "finest" or "achievement". I don't think I was very competitive. I ran within my comfort zone of effort, not even really pushing. I remember my husband telling me to put an effort in at the start to get ahead if possible. I never did that – not my style. I just enjoyed the running, and if I did well, so much the more satisfying.'

She then relented and listed several memorable events. 'My most satisfying race has to be the Ben Nevis Race of 1981. My time on that day was 1 hour 49 minutes 19 seconds.' She explains why it was satisfying. 'I was happy with my time, and position. I was pleased that all three of us, Ros, myself and Pauline, came within Ros's previous time. It was my most local race, and for various reasons, a favourite. The windows of my classroom in Lochaber High School, where I was a teacher, faced directly towards the Ben. I spent a lot of time looking!' She also adds that her son Finlay has recently told her that, 'he used my 1981

Ben Race time as a benchmark to try to beat in his first attempt on the race, in 2006. He beat it well!'

She adds that the Blisco race in 1980 was fun too. 'I have a vivid memory of getting a tip from dear Peter Brooks as we milled around at the start. Indicating Pauline [Haworth], he said, "She's the one to watch!" She certainly was that day – and for the rest of my racing days.'

'The other races I most enjoyed, and have clearest memories of, are Fairfield, I loved its route, and the Marsden to Edale Trog. The Trog was memorable for the freezing conditions underfoot, and clear weather that allowed unusually fast running through the groughs. I enjoyed the Ennerdale race in 1981 too. It was the longest I did. It was marred of course by the death of Bob English in the race that day. I was contacted by the police when I got home. I had been at Bob's last checkpoint at about the same time. "Had I noticed anything?" I hadn't known Bob and could not help.'

Fiona mentions that Pauline Haworth and Ros Coats were the two athletes she was most impressed with, looking back. 'Pauline came along in 1984 and broke Ros's previous Ben Nevis record by a minute. That record lasted for thirty-four years. That has to be a magnificent effort. That aside, Ros was consistently remarkable throughout my racing career. I was never aware of records, as such, but I'm sure she held many over those years, and possibly still does.'

Fiona had to travel quite a bit to race. 'Apart from the Ben, all the races I did would involve a fair amount of travel since most of them were in the Lakes, and some in Wales. I had an understanding head teacher at the time who would allow me the occasional Friday or Monday off.'

Her main rivals were Pauline and Ros. 'Undoubtedly it was them, both very experienced, and winning races I had not even heard of. Pauline was usually on my tail, or I on hers! If all three of us were running, Ros was always out there in front.'

Fiona mentions a memory from one particular Grasmere race, in 1981. 'The only time I overtook Ros was in the very short

Butter Crag Race. I was a few steps behind her on the descent, she stumbled, and for a few moments I was ahead of her. She still beat me by three or four seconds!'

Fiona admits to having no particular memories of her win at the Three Peaks in October 1981. 'No, I have no recall of this, though I did enjoy the course. I see I was just under four hours. I didn't know the other female competitor.' It was Anne-Marie Grindley, who she beat by over thirty minutes.

She adds that a win at the Ben Nevis race eluded her. 'I was second to Ros Coats in 1981 but inside the previous record. Ros, Pauline and myself were all within Ros's previous record, and NO, I never won! Indeed, I won very few other races either.'

Fiona has supported Finlay Wild all through his running career, including on his big rounds. 'I was there at the end of his solo Ramsay, and Rigby rounds, but not on the hill giving any support.'

Fiona Wild concludes by saying that her racing days were short-lived, 'but were totally absorbing, and I thank you for inviting me to record these thoughts!' It is rather pleasing that so many women that were interviewed for this book have commented on how much they have enjoyed being asked to review their running careers.

Early in the 1982 season Sue Parkin set out her stall for what was to prove to be a brilliant year for her. Having already won the two Skyline races at Chew Valley and Edale, she crushed it at the 12-mile Kentmere Horseshoe race. *The Fellrunner* reported that in dry, fast conditions, 'Sue Parkin set new standards for the ladies with a 1-46-46 time, taking 4.5 minutes off Ros Coats' 1981 time and finishing nearly 8 minutes in front of Pauline Haworth'.

On 23 May Sue also romped to victory at Fairfield. The race organiser noted: 'The ladies' winning time of 1-30-46 is one second outside the record set by Jean Lochhead in 1979, BUT this year the ladies had to run round the start field with the men, so Sue Parkin's time must be acknowledged as the record for future events'. Then in June Sue won the Ennerdale race, over the full distance, which was the only distance offered from this year on. Meanwhile, in Scotland, two races – Cairngorm and Mamore – recorded just one female entrant between them, a fact lamented by the organisers. At Wasdale, in July, Sue was rueing the lack of challengers she was facing at some races, as she ran well to finish in sixty-ninth place overall.

At Snowdon, while John Wild was showing a clean pair of trainers to a triple Italian challenge, a new record was being set in the women's race. The race was dominated by Rosie Naish. Reaching the summit in a new record fastest time (54-20) she crossed the line in 1-24-10. Joan Glass was second, coming back from an injury.

In August it was the centennial Burnsall Classic race, and the first time women had been allowed to run in it. Carol Haigh won in 17-53 (at the age of sixteen), from Carol McNeill. The Lake District Mountain Trial (still shorter for women) that year was held in storm force winds and horizontal rain. The organiser noted: 'In the absence of Sue Parkin, Ros Coats again ran off with the women's race, although Angela Carson and Carol McNeill both made good starts. The size of the women's field [eighteen] was very good compared with (say) the Ben Nevis Race. Keep on coming. It won't always be as tough as this.'

The 1982 British Championships were poorly reported in *The Fellrunner*. It just says, '40 scored but only 7 of these finished 3 or more championship events.' Sue Parkin won with 72 points, followed by Linda Lord (61), Rosie Naish (50), Fiona Wild (33) and Carol Haigh (24).

In the 1983 season there were still small female fields in many of the fell races, although fifteen entered the Kentmere Horseshoe in early April in gale force winds and white-out conditions, 'all suitably clad and twelve completed the course, headed by Sue Parkin, Ros Coats and Wendy Dodds.'

The Three Peaks organiser appealed for more women to run in future years, with just six being recorded in the results that year. In May the race organiser for the NCAA championships race, Danny Hughes, used his race report to make the same point. 'The ladies were short on numbers – only four deeming it worthwhile competing in an event which offered championship points for the taking. Are we flogging a dead horse here?'

While John Wild and Kenny Stuart were knocking pieces off each other in the men's race at the Fairfield Horseshoe at the end of May, 'fourteen ladies competed with no retirements, but thirteen non-starters. They gave the men something to chase as they started half an hour in advance but next year it is proposed that everyone will start at 2pm.' Two positive advances there.

In June, at the Holcombe Tower race, the number of female entries was up to eleven. Colette Harkin beat Brenda Robinson, and 'the freshly crowned Miss Ramsbottom presented the prizes'.

At Burnsall, in August, John Wild and Kenny Stuart were challenging each other again (it was very much THEIR season), with Wild flying down taking risks Stuart wasn't prepared to take, like leapfrogging a wall, to set a new course record. Going quite unnoticed at the time was a course record that Carol Haigh (who was still only seventeen) set that day, which lasted until it was beaten by Victoria Wilkinson in 2018. John Wild's record still stands.

Two items noted in the FRA Committee minutes were: Pauline Haworth being elected to the committee, and membership numbers reaching 1950, including eighty-six women. Pauline recalls that, 'someone asked me to go on committee. They wanted a woman on there, so I said yes. I was co-opted I think.' She says that she had no particular agenda to pursue at committee.

The 1983 Fell Championships table listed forty-seven women scoring points within the year, as against 162 men scoring points. Kevan Shand's report noted: 'a fine victory for long distance traveller Angela Carson. It wasn't until Burnsall [*where she was second*] that she overtook Carol Walkington, who had led for most of the season. Carol did well finishing second after four years off to raise a family.' Angela had scored 91 points to Carol's 85. The others in the top six were: Wendy Dodds (43), Gillian Wilkinson (41), Sue Parkin (36) and A. Sexton (32).

CHAPTER 9

Running abroad

International Fell/Mountain Running. Sierre-Zinal.
Snowdon International Race. A World Cup.
Profile: Brenda Robinson

'The Committee on the whole was in favour of attracting foreign competition.'

Back in November 1974 at the FRA Committee meeting there had been a discussion about international fell running, but it was pointed out at the end of the discussion that any invitations could not be made by the FRA as it had no money to do so and was not a promoting body. More positively, the committee minutes noted:

> George Broderick suggested that since British fell runners had been invited to take part in a race in Switzerland in 1974, a reciprocal arrangement to be made by the FRA to invite foreign competition to a specific event in Britain so as to foster international fell running and to make fell running an internationally recognised sport.

Earlier still there had been a report by Alan Lamb on the 1973 Pikes Peak race (held in Colorado, USA) in the Autumn 1973 issue of *The Fellrunner.* He noted that the women's race was to the summit only, and that 'Joan Ullyot's winning time of 3-24-44 broke the previous record set by Donnci Messenger of Belle Vue, Colorado, by four minutes.' There may be some confusion here, as the results (on the web) show no females running the ascent-only event that year, and Ullyet as the winner of the full (up and down) marathon in a time of 5-28-00. Traditionally, the Ascent takes place on Saturday (slightly longer than a half-marathon, at 13.3 miles), and the round-trip marathon on the Sunday after (the full Pikes Peak is 26.8 miles with a climb of 7,500 feet, all at altitude). Women first entered the Marathon in 1959 (as a one off) and then from 1971 onwards. The Ascent is more complicated, with a first women's entry in 1936, then 1959, 1961 to 1964, and most years from 1970 onwards. Angela Mudge, in 2003, is the only UK athlete (male or female) to have won either of the Pikes Peak events.

A race receiving more attention than Pikes Peak from UK fell and mountain runners was the Sierre-Zinal race, in Switzerland. Furthermore, it also accepted female entrants right from its inception in 1974. Instigator Jean-Claude Pont aimed 'to showcase and celebrate the breathtaking Anniviers mountainscape that had enthralled him since childhood. The race would be named, not just Sierre-Zinal, but the *Race of the Five 4,000m Peaks*.' It is a 31km race which starts in the valley bottom at Sierre and finishes in the Alpine village of Zinal. It has an elevation of 2,200m and finishes with a 1,100m descent into Zinal. Despite its current reputation of being a European race to win, it has always had its non-elite side, as the website explains:

> A new 'Tourist' category was created – unique to Sierre-Zinal, as it was designed for runners 'whose sole aim is to get together, push their physical limits and measure them against a challenging trail.' Runners in the 'Tourist' category receive a certificate with their final running time but with no ranking. Personal excellence and goals of camaraderie, fun, appreciation of nature and physical challenges are most valued. In brief, the philosophy of 'the heart before the watch' wins!

The Christmas 1978 issue of *The Fellrunner* has a report by Brenda Robinson on Sierre-Zinal and another race abroad she competed in. Brenda was one of the first women from the UK to venture abroad to race. She was not the first to run Sierre-Zinal though. At the second running of the race in 1975 Margaret Thompson finished in 338th place in 4-25-32.

Brenda noted: 'The 1978 Sierre-Zinal race again attracted many British athletes, and it was particularly pleasing to see our women fell runners out there and doing so well.' The results showed a win for Moser of Switzerland, with Brenda Robinson 2nd, Anne Bland 7th, Jean Dawes 10th and Carol Walkington 15th, with 43 women completing the race. Brenda Robinson had come 6th in the Sierre-Zinal race the year before and improved by four positions and well over thirty minutes between the 1977 and the 1978 races.

Brenda Robinson

I originally contacted Brenda when I was writing a piece for Cumbria magazine on early women fell runners in the Lakes, and I wanted to quote from something she had written (in The Fellrunner*) and to ask about photos. This later morphed into a full email interview, as she was a pivotal person whose story I wanted to tell from those early days.*

Brenda Robinson was born Brenda Bailey, and married Colin Robinson in 1964. She was born in Bury, Lancashire, and had a career including being a Civil Servant, a Careers Officer and a Lecturer in Further Education.

She attended Bury Convent Grammar School where they had an annual sports day, which included the egg and spoon race, the sack race and 100 yards sprint. Being quite fast, her PE mistress referred her to Father Joseph Coulthard of St Bede's College Manchester, who coached several women athletes. In August 1959 Brenda joined Bury AC. 'I trained with Father Coulthard at White City (Manchester) on Sunday mornings for about eighteen months. I was selected for my first international at Easter 1960, representing the English Catholic Schools in the European Schools Championships. I went to do the high jump, but competed in a sprint relay team and won a medal. The next year I won the 220 yards sprint in the Lancashire Schools Championships and represented Lancs in the English Schools Champs.'

Leaving school in 1961, Brenda concentrated on her athletics. She was women's Captain at Bury and competed in events from 100 yards to 880 yards on the track, and also did throws and jumps at track league events. 'I represented Lancashire and the North of England in track events. On the country I usually placed in the County and North of England Championships and in 1963 I was fifth in the National Cross-country Championships. The following year I finished third and Bury were first team. Sadly, there was no international cross-country for women until 1967.'

By 1967, following the birth and tragic death of her first child, she was not as fit either physically or mentally as previously – so decided to run the Irish trials for the Cross-country International, as her mother was Irish. 'I finished second at Santry Stadium, Dublin, and was selected for the Irish team. The first women's International was on Barry Island, Wales where I finished twelfth. The following year I was non-travelling reserve when the International was in Maryland, USA!' Her second son, Kristian, was born in September 1968.

Brenda had been with husband Colin to all the events he competed in and had seen him win the Three Peaks race in 1969. As previously noted, she had *nearly* been at the founding of the FRA, so it was a natural progression to running on the fells for her. By the time women were allowed to race officially she had been competing in different types of running for nearly twenty years. 'Having been reasonable at cross-country I enjoyed the trail type courses, and of course the environment. I trained mainly on paths and trails, and I can see the moors and my highest hill, Knowl Hill (at 1,300 feet), from my kitchen window. I didn't train specifically for the fells other than doing hill reps, but I also did a Mountain Leadership course to improve my navigation skills. I enjoyed the camaraderie at the fell races I had been to with the men and had met most of the early women racers there with their husbands and partners.'

Brenda particularly admired Jean Dawes, for being the first woman to have the courage to complete the Bob Graham Round. 'The men I admired were my Colin and Ricky Wilde. Colin held the UK record for 2,000 metres on the track and Ricky the World record for 3,000 metres indoors. Both were accomplished fell runners and I admired their versatility in athletics and their ability.'

The first race to accept women officially was Pendle, in 1977, which was organised by Clayton-le-Moors Harriers, and Brenda Robinson was entered. 'There was a small field for the women's race, and it felt exciting to be doing something different. I did the Pendle about five times, and I always forgot how steep it was going up Pendle End – until I got there. I did feel like a pioneer leading the way for other women, but women's fell racing gradually became the norm and numbers grew. I don't feel I made any major changes for women other than by taking part. In the early days there were no women on the FRA committee, so we didn't have a voice.'

Brenda feels that the race organisers in the early days were supportive of the women. 'I never came across anyone objecting. We had to start separately from the men, which was usually half an hour in front of their race.'

She raced on the fells regularly until the early 1980s. She then moved into Further Education which took up more time and so she took to the roads. 'In 1982 I was second in the Manchester Piccadilly Marathon in 3 hours 3 minutes, and I did the London Marathon a bit slower in 1986.'

Reflecting on her time on the fells, Brenda Robinson offers two top memories. 'I was pleased with my eight wins in the Gale Fell Race at Littleborough between 1977 and 1985, and I was also well pleased with my run in the first women's Three Peaks race in 1979.'

Brenda gives some details on why this was such a memorable experience, and which could have ended badly. 'We started in

Horton in front of the men and had climbed Pen-y-Ghent and were on the way towards Ribblehead via the bedstead route. I was in the leading group when the men started to catch up with us. We were all heading for a stile, and a queue was forming. To the right was a wire fence that I thought I could climb through. I left the track and jumped onto a rock in the middle of a wet patch. The rock turned out to be a dead sheep in the middle of a bog. As I sank down into the mud the girls ran on, and the leading men glanced at me and continued running. I am five feet tall and as I sank further the bog was up to my waist and I couldn't move. I shouted but there was no one around except the runners and I couldn't expect them to stop. Some of the men did eventually shout advice like "lean forward and swim out", but I was well and truly stuck and still going down. Someone in the race must have told the next spectators he passed, and a man eventually came running back to me. He lay on the ground and held out his hands which I was able to reach, and it took some time to wriggle out and get free of the mud. I hope I thanked him. Amazingly, my shoes didn't come off and I was able to finish the race coming in fourth. I stayed calm during the experience because there were people around even if they were not stopping. Afterwards I did have a few anxieties about it all.' It seems astonishing that so many athletes failed to offer any help in this desperate situation. There are many examples of other occasions where runners have given up their race to help out a fellow competitor who is in trouble. That is the norm, and the true ethos of the sport.

Brenda recalls another strange experience she had in the early days of women's racing. 'Running in the Black Lane Ends fell race, organised by Harry Walker, I was running behind my friend Hilary Mathews of Blackburn Harriers. We approached a cattle grid shortly after the start and Hilary fell down into it. Her size 3 feet had gone between the bars, and she was well and truly stuck. Having pulled her out we were chasing the field when a pig started to run after her and chased her down a hill. Fortunately, she outran it!'

Brenda Robinson was one of the pioneers of the international race scene. She competed at the prestigious Sierre-Zinal race in 1977, 1978 and 1979. 'The first race there was in 1974, and the following year Jeff Norman went over and won. Several of the male fell runners then went to do the race each year, usually as part of their holiday. We enjoyed Swiss holidays, so I wrote to John Claude Pont asking for details for the 1977 race. We stayed on a package holiday near Chamonix and drove over for the weekend. John Claude was kind enough to move out of his apartment and let us stay there. I didn't know what to expect from the race and after an hour of climbing through trees burst out onto a plateau with the mountains all around, which was absolutely breathtaking. After that it was a trail race and I looked at the floor all the time so as not to fall down the mountainside. I ran for quite a way on a narrow part of the trail behind a cow and her calf and I couldn't get past them. I finished sixth, got a wooden trophy and was impressed by the after-race celebrations. The following year I finished second and got a heavy metal sculpture. We camped at Zinal and so were able to get it home. In 1979 I had to drop out with altitude sickness, but won the Marathon De Cretes in the Vosges a week or so later.'

Brenda reviewed her attitude to long and short races. 'The longest race I have done in the Lakes would be the Kentmere Horseshoe. I did do a 23km trail race in the Lakeland Trails series over the Garburn Pass. The hardest run I did was the Karrimor International Mountain Marathon in October 1977. It was in the Howgills and my partner was a GB orienteer, Kath Etherden. We did OK but I struggled with my kitchen sink back-pack over the 30 miles! Colin and I did the Saunders Mountain Marathon in June 1978 around Ambleside and finished second in our category over the 24-mile course. I enjoyed the shorter fell races, as coming from athletics generally I liked the racing aspect rather than the endurance. Plus, I wasn't able to go over the courses with having a small boy and working full time.'

Brenda (and Colin) have always been very active in the club

athletics scene. Brenda stayed with Bury AC until 1997 and then joined Rochdale Harriers. 'I was Club Secretary for a few years and in 2002 set up a Women's Group in the club. I did this for over five years and was a UK Athletics Level 2 coach. Now I give advice when asked.'

She then explained how the naming of the Brenda and Colin Robinson Race came about. 'In the Rochdale area there are charity races organised by Andy O'Sullivan. We have been timekeepers, takers of entries and recorders of finishers for over twenty-five years hence one of his races was named after us.'

Since becoming a Veteran at thirty-five, Brenda has been very active in Masters Athletics, competing in track and cross-country events. 'I was selected for the English Masters team for the Home International cross-country in Dublin 2010 (2nd team silver medal, V60) and Dublin 2015 (2nd team silver medal, V65), and have been reserve several times.' She has competed at the World Masters Mountain Running Championships five times, with a best position of 5th in Poland (in 2010, V65), and twice at the European Masters Mountain Championships, with a best of 4th in Spain (in 2010, V65). She says she has really enjoyed being part of the England team in the cross-country internationals.

Brenda concludes: 'I most enjoyed the World and European Masters Mountain races for the scenery and the friendship. It's good meeting people who we have raced against and picking up the conversation where it was left off. That happens in the fell running fraternity too.' Brenda Robinson has had a long and successful career, particularly on the fells and mountains, and over the country, and has also selflessly given back to the sport when and where she could.

From early on, the Snowdon race had encouraged international entries (from men). In 1980 an Italian (Pezzoli) won, and five other Italians finished in the top fifteen, with the race report saying that 'a significant continental challenge in the form of a crack Italian team added spice to the fifth annual Snowdon race'.

The enthusiasm for racing abroad, and to invite international runners to UK races, was there. However, efforts to formalise things were very drawn out, and nothing much happened for a couple of years. In December 1982 *The Fellrunner* had an article by Andy Styan on fell running in the USA, and a listing of races organised by CIME (Coupe Internationale de la Montagne). In July 1983 Welsh and English teams (but male only) travelled to Verona for an international 9-mile hill race, and the FRA also formed a World Championship sub-committee, as they wished to be involved.

In 1984 negotiations were taking place with regard to a possible World Cup (of mountain running), with a venue of Val d'Aosta and a 15 September date suggested, to include men's long, men's short, women's and junior races. That plan bit the dust and was replaced by an invitation event for Senior Men on 30 September in Zogno, Bergamo. The day beforehand, at a meeting of officials, an International Mountain Racing Committee was formed with Angelo de Biasi (Italy) as Chairman and Danny Hughes (FRA) as Secretary. The plan was to work towards worldwide membership of the committee and to convince the International Association of Athletics Federation (IAAF) to authorise world championship events.

It seems that that the IAAF rebuffed the FRA and the Italian equivalent (CNCM), who had been planning the World Cup. The IAAF were 'reluctant to see it launched as such until an established international competitive forum is evident'. FRA and CNCM came under the auspices of the IAAF, via their parent bodies, and were obliged to be guided by them.

Whilst all this was going on the Reebok International Mountain Challenge was set up (by Danny Hughes) for three dates in May 1985, incorporating the Buttermere Sailbeck race (on the 12th), the Grasmere Dash, over the Guides course (16th), and the Fairfield Horseshoe race (19th). This initiative did not meet with universal approval, with the FRA committee reporting a 'lively discussion on the move away from evolutionary to revolutionary progress with the advent of the Reebok Challenge. An invitation to an international match in autumn has been received.' As it turned out, the Reebok Challenge was a damp squib as far as it being an international event. There were no international entries in the first two races, and just a few Italians racing at Fairfield.

As well as trying to facilitate international competition, Danny Hughes was also trying to help individual runners get to races abroad. In 1985 he arranged for Kenny Stuart and Pauline Haworth to go to Lenzerheide in Switzerland, for an uphill-only race. Kenny Stuart wrote an extended piece on the race for his club newsletter, which shows the extent athletes were willing to go to in order to get good international competition:

> Pauline Haworth decided to go along and pay her own fare. Pauline and I caught the 7am train from Oxenholme on Friday 5 July and with Jack Maitland flew from Heathrow to Zurich airport. After getting the tube into Zurich City, a further 1.5 hour train journey followed to bring us, via long, flat, narrow valleys to a large town called Chur. We were met here by 'Parpon' the race organiser and after driving up the mountains to Lenzerheide at 4,500 feet above sea level we settled down in our accommodation, a superb guest house/hotel with private bathrooms and even a 'mini-bar' fridge in the rooms.
>
> Race day dawned very cool and misty – more like the Lakes than Switzerland! As the race began at 10am we didn't have to wait long before the suffering started. But the last mile incidentally comprising the only 'fell' of the race. After a slow start Pauline came through strongly to finish 5th lady.

Pauline shares her own memory of the race. 'It was like a sprint. I remember getting mown over at the start and falling in a ditch. That was just awful. I didn't enjoy it at all.'

FRA's *The Fellrunner* magazine in its 1985 and 1986 issues carried much coverage of issues in the sport, including the whole amateur versus professional issue. This discussion, together with international race activities and the introduction of sponsors, was creating cracks – as evidenced by a resignation from the FRA committee and a vote of no confidence in the FRA Chair at the time.

Eventually though, the first World Cup in Mountain Running was arranged (and immediately became known as the World Trophy), and it took place in San Vigilio de Marebbe, Italy, on 21 and 22 September 1985. *The Fellrunner* reported:

> The first running of this event attracted teams from ten nations, with there being races for ladies, juniors and two races for the senior men. England, Scotland and Wales all sent representatives who were to experience friendly hospitality, superb scenery and 3-star hotel accommodation. The junior, ladies and senior men's short races were run on the Saturday and consisted of two laps of varying lengths in the hills around the village. According to Jon Broxap, the ladies race was won by an anorexic 16-year-old from West Germany.

The winner was Olivia Gruener, who led the twenty-six women home in a time of 26-20 for the 6km course. The only UK runners present were Pauline Haworth (running for England, in 9th) and Angela Carson (Wales, 15th).

Pauline Haworth gives her take on that race, which London Marathon founders Chris Brasher and John Disley had paid for her to go out to, as the AAAs funding couldn't be stretched to include her. 'Unfortunately, I was pregnant, but didn't know it. I came ninth, but felt dreadful. I was sick on the way; it was a long bus journey from the airport and I had to stop the bus, which was really embarrassing. I thought "this isn't like me", as I am rarely sick. On the morning of the race I was throwing up on the start line, but ran anyway and ninth wasn't bad really. I was sick again at night, and again on the way back. I thought actually,

I wonder if I am pregnant. When I got back, I had a pregnancy test and found I was seven weeks pregnant. With each child I have had morning sickness from six to thirteen weeks. It just happened to coincide with that first big international trip.'

Angela Carson also commented on it being a very friendly event, but that the Welsh team had kit issues. 'The village was so proud to be the host to the first ever World Mountain Running event that it ensured we had a truly memorable trip. In those days the Welsh team did not even get provided with any running kit. I was asked to take a red vest along and I was given a badge that I had to sew onto it before the race.' Kenny Stuart won his race to become the first World Champion, and no doubt would credit a part of his success to the pre-race massage that Angela delivered, in her informal role as the team's physiotherapist.

Following the first World Trophy in 1985, the FRA were invited to organise a second one in England in 1986, which they declined, mostly on the grounds of cost – the Italians admitting to having spent £42,000 hosting the first. There was also a groundswell of feeling that this international perspective was only relevant to the real elite of the sport.

Meanwhile, individual athletes had continued to travel to their favourite races abroad. On 11 August 1985 Véronique Marot had taken six minutes off her course record of the previous year and finished sixty-sixth overall at the ever-popular Sierre-Zinal race. This was just one of many outstanding female performances that began to be recorded in international mountain races.

CHAPTER 10

Record breaking

Records Fall, Great Racers and Champions Emerge: Carol Haigh and Pauline Haworth. Profiles: Vanessa Brindle, Christine Menhennet

'Pauline finished exactly a minute under the old record.'

The 1984 fell season was notable for two things: Pauline Haworth dominating the British Championships, winning ten championship races to secure a win with a full house of 120 points; and a course record breaking spree, by both Pauline Haworth and Carol Haigh, a couple of which haven't been beaten to this day, and two others of which lasted over thirty years. The rise in quality and commitment shown in the women's races was shown by the standard of these records. There were still some events that set shorter courses for women, such as the early season Edale Skyline.

The first record to go was at Fairfield on 20 May, with Pauline Haworth beating a good quality field by seven minutes, to win in 1-29-59. The same day Sue Parkin knocked 6-23 off the record at the Kinder Downfall race.

In May every year since 1863 the Hallam Chase has taken place in Sheffield. Malcolm Patterson recalls being at the 1984 version of the race. 'The old codgers on the organising committee refused to allow women, (it is a 4-mile cross-country!), so five Dark Peak ladies staged a protest run.' The DPFR club records noted the event thus: 'This race was a male preserve until May 1984, when Dark Peak Ladies who were declined entry conducted a parallel 'training run'. On reaching the halfway point at Stannington

Church gate the official responsible for daubing competitors with paint as proof of arrival refused to afford Dark Peak ladies the same attention. Nevertheless, through our action the point was made and the determination of Dark Peak Ladies opened up the race for women in the future.'

At Saddleworth in June Carol Haigh beat her own record by over two minutes, with Pauline Haworth chasing hard and also getting inside the old record. This record was only beaten in 2015. Three weeks later Carol also beat her own record at the James Blakeley race, finishing in nineteenth place overall. On the first day in July the Skiddaw race report noted, 'the ladies – whose start time was transferred to the men's event so they could get more competitive urge! With only 4 runners, saw "history" made with Pauline Haworth breaking 80 minutes plus her own record (80-08).' Obviously in cracking form, Pauline proceeded to set a new record (1-24-03) at the Snowdon race three weeks later.

The records came thick and fast now: by Bridget Hogge at Moel Siabod; Pauline Haworth, with a mighty impressive weekend double of Borrowdale and Latrigg; and Carol Haigh at Pendleton – all within a four-week period. Carol's 36-36 is still the course record for the Pendleton race, one of the longest-standing female records.

On 1 September Pauline Haworth set about taking the Ben Nevis record from Ros Coats. Alan Bocking reported on how the race panned out. 'Pauline Haworth got a good start to immediately open up a gap on Ros Coats and reach the summit first. The lead that Pauline had was stretched to two and a half minutes by the finish.' It was an outstanding record (1-43-25), that was only beaten by Victoria Wilkinson in 2018, by twenty-four seconds, an awesome timespan for such a popular race. Even more amazing, if you know what the Ben race can do to your feet if you descend hard, is the fact that Pauline had to drop out of the Sedbergh Hills race just two weeks earlier with blisters. Pauline explains. 'It was a hot day. My feet blister easily. I knew the Ben race was hard so that is why I dropped out at Sedbergh. Actually, at the Ben I didn't like the road at the beginning and end of the race. If it had gone just from bottom of the hill and back I could have done extremely well!'

Pauline hadn't finished her record setting, though. Just two weeks later, she romped home at the Three Shires race, knocking minutes off the existing record, and coming forty-first in a very large field. Not to be outdone, the very next week Carol Haigh set a record at Lantern Pike that has still not been beaten. Another week on and Carol knocked nearly three minutes off the record at Thieveley Pike. Even in November records were still falling, to Pauline at Dunnerdale, and to Angela Carson at Winter Hill.

An amazing season. Pauline's dominance in the championships has already been mentioned. She won with 120 points. 2nd and 3rd were Gillian Wilkinson (77 points), and Bridget Hogge (75), with Linda Lord 4th with 70 points. Strangely, despite her record haul, Carol Haigh was only in 10th place, having not competed at enough championship races to be higher in the table.

The 1985 season once again saw Pauline in fine form, winning at both Benson Knott and the Carnethy Five in February, and sweeping to a second British Championship win. Early in the year the Edale Skyline race still insisted on having two distances, one for women (14 miles) and another for the men (21 miles).

The first Championship race was at Kentmere in April, where: 'Pauline [Haworth] was closely challenged by Angela Carson, with a much improved Vanessa Brindle a further two minutes behind her.' These were three of the in-form athletes of that year, and two of them subsequently topped the championships table at the end of the season.

The report on the Three Peaks explained the effect of a recent change in the course there. 'Vanessa Brindle won the ladies' race from a record entry of eighteen, with a time of 3 hours 38 minutes, which must be worth two or three minutes less than Sue Parkin's 1980 race record, set before the Selgill diversion was introduced.'

Vanessa Brindle

Having been given Tony Peacock's email, I sent him a request for an interview with his wife, Vanessa. On returning from a trip to Scotland (for them) we agreed to schedule a chat over the phone. Vanessa was pleased to speak about her fell running days and especially the early days when she says women runners were looked upon with some suspicion. On seeing the transcript she agreed that it summed up accurately her experiences in fell running.

Vanessa Brindle was becoming a force to be reckoned with, as these results showed, despite only having been running for a couple of years. Vanessa was born in Manchester in 1952. She did no athletics at school and left at sixteen to go to work at Burnley General Hospital. She did a lot of walking before trying fell running.

Vanessa's boyfriend (and later husband) Tony Peacock used to go to fell races and Vanessa got bored watching. 'My first race was at Coniston, in 1982, because we were staying at the Fell and Rock hut and a friend of ours was doing the Coniston fell race and he said come along, and if you are struggling you can tuck in with me. I was following Ann Bland (Keswick) because I didn't have a clue where I was going, and I ended up third lady. I don't really remember a lot about it, but didn't enjoy the coming down. I had started training in the evenings with Clayton-le-Moors by then, I am not sure from which year, but probably for about twelve months before then. I was not really aware of who was good at that time. My main worry was getting round and not getting lost.'

At that time in medium to long races there weren't many women running. 'One of two of the (male) race organisers were a bit anti-women, I think because they felt women would cause them a problem. They didn't give any prizes to the women either. I think some of the ROs thought we couldn't do it, to be honest.'

Vanessa also noted that when she started running there weren't many rules. 'You just set off and did the race. There wasn't a kit check or anything, but that obviously changed.'

She didn't feel she was in any way a trailblazer, partly because she knew the men that were running and just used to stick with them. 'It didn't enter my head about pioneering or anything. CLM had some females by then, but there was no great move to encourage more. If people did come along they were made welcome, but in a sense you managed it or you didn't.'

As for her training, Vanessa usually used to go out three times in the week and then would have a long run at the weekend with Tony and his friends, usually about 15 miles. In the week she would go up to about 8 miles on one of her runs. 'There wasn't any structure to my training and diet as it didn't exist, certainly not in Clayton. I did some training with the Clayton ladies, but it was mainly on my own or with my (now husband) Tony or the Clayton men, who were always there if I needed them on races or to give me encouragement!'

She managed to stress her body though. She suffered a stress fracture on her foot, which just meant a matter of a few weeks off training. 'I think I was training for a marathon when the first one came on. I was running to and from work and would often go out at lunchtime. I think I basically overdid it. I was not advised by anyone on my training, which is probably why I got the stress fractures. I was doing quite a lot on the road. Someone from the club said that I would lose my climbing ability, so I was doing some fell running as well.'

Vanessa says her navigation skills were not brilliant. 'Sometimes for the more difficult races we used to go round the course beforehand. I remember once in the Ennerdale race I wasn't sure where I was and there was someone behind and I waited for him.' Assessing her own skill set, Vanesa says she managed well enough with both short and long races, but was better on good running terrain, and admits she wasn't very good at descending.

Commenting on the fact that she won just one English Championship, and never won the British Championship,

Vanessa explains the situation. 'I didn't want to get too involved with competing for the British Champs. Fitting in the ten races was a big commitment and I couldn't always get the time off work to race. Generally, it was nine-to-five work, but we had on-call and late shifts sometimes.'

She started doing mountain marathons because husband Tony had done them before, and he still liked to do them, so it seemed a natural progression for her. 'We enjoyed the Saunders more than the Karrimor because the weather was better, and it was a bit more relaxed. There was one particular time in a Karrimor when we finished seventeenth overall and they were packing up as we came in. It felt like after the Lord Mayor's Show, we had just done a good run and yet virtually everyone had gone home.'

Vanessa did a Bob Graham Round in 21-51 in 1985. 'It was a lovely day, but I had issues with my knee towards the end, basically because I hadn't done enough specific training for it. Clayton-le-Moors members traditionally did it anticlockwise which is what we did too.'

Vanessa was selected in 1987 for the World Trophy, and again the following year, which was in Keswick. She added a couple of comments on the international scene at the time. 'I enjoyed the events I ran in, but there was another one I could have gone to and it was difficult with work as they were short-staffed. Work told me I couldn't have the time off. I can't remember who the team manager was, but they couldn't understand me not getting time off work and were a bit off with me, to be honest. There was a good camaraderie at these races.'

Vanessa set race records at the Three Shires in 1985, and the Three Peaks in 1985, 1987, 1988, and 1989. She admits that she isn't really one for remembering her times or any records. 'I just used to think that it was a thing about how you were on the day. I was pleased to do what I did and enjoy it really. I would say that I enjoyed the experience and the friendship and the bond that you got with people through fell running. Even if we meet them now, even after not seeing them for say ten years, you immediately feel that you know them well and there is still a bond between you.'

She was disappointed with her Three Peaks record, though, thinking she could have beaten it. 'After I set that record, on another year I was going really well and just near the viaduct I had veered off the path as it was better running, and a farmer had left some barbed wire on the ground and I got my foot in it. I finished but I think I was on for a better time than the record I had previously set.'

Looking back, Vanessa admits that she used to look up to Linda Lord. 'She was in our club, she inspired me quite a bit and she is still running now. I trained with her at times.'

Vanessa also makes a point that no one else I spoke to specifically mentioned. 'There was generally no specific ladies' clothing and the only fell shoes were made by Walsh, unlike today!' That is indeed so different now, with the range and cost of kit having increased manyfold. Some athletes still wear, and swear by, Walsh fell shoes.

Vanessa stopped running in 2008 because of her knees. 'We do mainly cycling now, as even walking bothers my knees coming down a hill.' Vanessa Brindle/Peacock somewhat plays down her own achievements (which were considerable) and I hope they have been suitably highlighted here.

The aforementioned Reebok International Mountain Challenge took place over a week in May 1985 and was singularly lacking in drama on the women's side. In all three races Pauline Haworth won from Wendy Dodds. Organiser Sue Courchee commented on the increase in numbers at Fairfield, which was the last of these three races. The results showed fifteen women, with

Pauline winning and Wendy in eighth place, so presumably you had to enter the Reebok Challenge specifically to score in that event.

On 29 June Carol Haigh set a new record at the Eldwick Gala fell race, 17-36 against her own 18-05 from the year before. That is another of her records that has never been beaten, although it is shown as 17-45 on the FRA website record listing. Carol finished an impressive ninth place overall in the race. In July Pauline Haworth won the Snowdon race in a new record of 1-20-19. She had previously won the race in 1981 and 1984. She now had three wins at the race, setting a new record each time, a remarkable achievement.

The FRA Committee news from August 1985 noted a significant revision to the Championship plans for the next year. The British Championships was now to be four from six races, with one each having to be from the Long, Medium and Short races on offer. This was because an English Championships was being introduced, which would comprise seven from nine races, with two from each category. There was a different selection of races for each championship.

The report on the 1985 British Championships noted, somewhat disparagingly, 'Pauline Haworth did not have much competition in retaining her title, although Angela Carson did record four wins when Pauline wasn't running.' Unfortunately, not enough women were yet doing enough of the events that counted to make the competition more interesting. The leading five scores were: Pauline Haworth 108, Angela Carson 101, A. Soper 66, A. Wright 24, J. Smith 22.

1986 was another year of records being set across a range of fell races, with Carol Haigh at the forefront of the action. Chronologically, she set new records at the Wrekin, Snowdon (knocking a chunk off Pauline Haworth's record), Barnoldswick and Eccles Pike. In an interview a year later she counted twelve records she had set that year, although not all got reported in *The Fellrunner.* Also getting in on the act were Angela Carson with records at Moel Eilio (after a race-long battle with Gillian

Wilkinson) and Wasdale, while Jacky Smith joined in with a record at Pen-y-Ghent.

In the 1986 British Championships Angela Carson came out on top, by a clear 10 points from Diane Ellerton. It was the first year for separate national Championships. The English Championship was won by Carol Haigh – with the same number of points as Diane Ellerton (48), with Jacky Smith third with 42 points. Angela Carson won the Welsh, with Ann Curtis winning the Scottish version.

Carol Haigh started off the 1987 season as she had finished the last, setting new records at Criffel and Rossendale. Carol also set the Rivington Pike record, which she still holds. Vanessa Brindle had a purple patch in the early and middle parts of the season. She set a record of 4-21-31 for the Ennerdale race. She had an early lead in the British Championships, before going on to win the English Championship title. Later in the season Sarah Haines set a new mark at the Buttermere Horseshoe, before Clare Crofts did the same at Langdale in the October. There was a new champion in the British Championships, with Jacky Smith just holding off Angela Carson by 5 points.

Jacky Smith gives an account of her early days of running, and of joining Dark Peak Fell Runners, in the club's booklet *Ten years of Dark Peak Fell Runners (1976–1986)*. It gives a feel for what it was like for her as a beginner and how she saw other (club) runners:

> My running was tentative and surreptitious – sneaking out alone and in the dark, when friends were safely ensconced in smoky atmospheres exercising only their right arms. I jogged around Endcliffe Park and Hunters Bar from October to Christmas (1983). Other runners began saying 'hello'; I really must be progressing! So, I went further, up to Porter Clough then venturing over to Burbage and Stanage Edge; this was great – I thought I'd invented fell running! But a colleague at work told me about fell races and I was proffered a form for the Edale Skyline.

> When the race started I went off like a shot, chasing after Bridget Hogge, intent on not getting lost. At the top of Grindslow Knoll she left me – disappearing into the murk never to be seen again. Twice round the Knoll in the mist and I thankfully met other runners – and slowly my drained confidence returned. I stuck in and was determined not to be last.

Jacky carried on her solitary runs and then was told about the friendliness and excitement of weekly runs with Dark Peak. She rose to the challenge and rocked up, in September 1984:

> I arrived promptly at 6.15pm. Not a soul. Was it the right 'Sportsman'? Then another car arrived and parked as far away as possible. The stealthy movements, gently rocking car and the occasional arm appearing over the dashboard indicated in-car changing (I presumed). I changed and sat huddled and nervous and wondering what happened next. Then at 6.25pm the whole world turned up, and fit people in strange brown, purple and yellow vests were jogging up and down and looking fit and fast. I ventured out to a chorus of welcomes. Then it struck 6.30 I was suddenly standing alone, everyone was off, rocketing down the road, then down the narrow boulder-strewn footpath, overtaking on precipices, and all talking and laughing at the same time! Eventually I reached the 'Sportsman' again with such a feeling of elation; I had completed a real Dark Peak run, and it had been worth every bit of my anxiety! I felt I could conquer anything.

There was another new race in Scotland that August. The Arrochar Alps was 15 miles long with 7,874 feet of climbing. It was a tough course, devised by Andy Dytch and Bobby Shields, starting at sea level and taking in four summits of over three thousand feet, with Billy Bland complaining he had to walk too much! Christine Menhennet was the first woman home, setting the inaugural course record of 4-09-26, which lasted twenty-three years.

Christine Menhennet

Christine was one of a couple of the pioneers who actually approached me, presumably as one of the other pioneers had suggested she did, saying she would be happy to try and be of help if required. She mused that 'such a book is long overdue'. She certainly could help, as she gave a new slant on the scene in Scotland that might not have been covered otherwise.

At her peak Christine Menhennet held several course records, including at the Glen Rosa Horseshoe, Glentrool and Corrieyairick Pass. 'Most records were only briefly held', she adds, 'but the record run that I enjoyed most, and which stood for the longest was the 1987 Arrochar Alps Race (there was no duck boarding over the bog in those days!). Her record was broken by Andrea Priestly in 2010 by three minutes and the current record is held by Jasmin Paris. My other favourite record was a win in 1999, in the 25-mile Great Wilderness Challenge (3 hours 21 minutes 36 seconds), broken I think in 2006 by Claire Gordon.'

Christine Menhennet was born in Bolton, Lancashire, on 15 October 1956, her maiden name being Taylor. Christine's school in Bolton didn't go in for track and field athletics but were big on team sports, according to Christine. 'I was in the school teams for lacrosse, netball, tennis and rounders but I wasn't a star, I was more of a good team player.'

She was brought up in a hill walking family. 'Don't sit down, you'll get stiff' was her dad's favourite instruction to Christine and her sister. 'As anorak-clad pre-teens, we struggled through wind and mist up numerous rocky Welsh and Lakeland peaks, when we would much rather have been at the beach. Without a doubt, I owe my love of mountains and adventure to my parents' early encouragement and passion for the outdoors. Kendal Mint Cake was a diet staple in my childhood!'

Christine also dinghy-sailed competitively as a teenager, crewing on Enterprises at various championship events. She enjoyed squash at University, and jogged to keep fit for that, including a very occasional run up Winter Hill not far from the house she grew up in. 'Little did I know that this kind of running was "a thing"!', she chuckles.

Whilst a student, she spent one summer working as a barmaid in the Clachaig Inn, in Glencoe. This allowed her to go daytime walking and climbing in the hills, her childhood reluctance having long since faded. 'Working behind the bar in the evenings, I gobbled up stories of derring-do from the punters, including many a famous climber and I eventually moved up to Glasgow after my postgrad course, in order to be close to mountains and with mountain people.'

She says she was a child of the marathon boom. 'Once I had moved to Glasgow I went from jogging round parks for fun, to training for the big one. I joined Bellahouston Harriers and ran several marathons including Glasgow, Lochaber, Snowdon, Windermere and Moscow (where black bread and lukewarm pear juice were the *en route* refreshments!) Like many, I had no idea how to train but bashed out the miles on the roads of Glasgow's southside, did the occasional half marathon and went to boxing circuits in a slightly dodgy gym.'

After she got married, her then husband took to ice climbing in the winter. 'However, I didn't find dark blue ice, mouthfuls of spindrift and freezing ledges much fun and preferred to live, so running became an increasingly important pastime for me in winter months.'

Back in the early eighties, Ali Coghill, a good friend of Christine's, worked at the Inverclyde Sports Training Centre in Largs as a rackets coach and sailor. 'She phoned me one time in a state of hyper excitement. "You would love this event", she babbled, "the Scottish Island Peaks Race (SIPR) – you could combine your marathon running and mountain skills, an all women team – next year – come to this year's prize-giving with me – you'd love it!" Through her work, Ali had been involved in marshalling the race in the inaugural year. We went to that prize-giving, Tom Weir was the guest speaker, and I was equally excited by it all. Wearing my favourite, figure-hugging purple frock, swigging gin and I think, smoking (can't believe I admit to that!), I told the lean, mean Lakeland running machine next to me, that I was going to do the SIPR race the following year! He looked at me in amused disbelief and said kindly: "Well here's a few tips!". The following year, 1984, after a winter of hard training and only one hill race at Carnethy, Ali and I had pulled together an all women team skippered by Southampton sailor Steph Merry. My running partner was fellow Clachaig barmaid, runner, climber and lifelong friend Lesley Kirkwood. Thanks to my dad's trust and generosity, we were sailing his 26-foot Contessa, *Alma Viva*; she was more of a cruiser yacht than a racer, but the perfect boat for our adventure. Light winds and calm seas prevailed that year, allowing us much needed recovery time, recuperating on a diet of pasta and paradise cake. We completed, in respectable rather than spectacular times and we were by no means last! That was the start of a passion that was to last for the next three and a half decades!'

Christine took part in several SIPRs and calls it the race of four smells. 'The fresh pungent scent of bluebells carpeting the birch woods at Knock on Mull; the garlicky tang of the ditch running alongside the road into Craighouse on Jura; the exotic scent of azaleas as you ran through the castle grounds of Brodick and the ever-worsening smell of damp, sweaty thermals each time you returned to the boat!'

By the time of the first SIPR, Christine had put in many miles and hours both in the hills and on roads to ensure she could cope with the rigours of this multi-day event. 'I felt I'd really arrived when I bought my first pair of Walsh PB Racers and wore thermal Helly Hansen tights under my shorts for the first time – that was the look back then!' Christine's early running days were also influenced by fellow Clydesdale Harrier Bobby Shields (former Ben Nevis and West Highland Way record holder) and his brother Jimmy, who were quietly supportive and encouraging. 'I was also encouraged by Carnethy's Robin Morris (now sadly passed) who was involved in the organisation of several races including the Carnethy, Glamaig and Pentland Skyline races and was always hugely encouraging of all the female competitors, both fast and slow, and similarly by Denis Bell (of Haddington) whose boundless enthusiasm was infectious and inclusive.' Others she admired included fellow competitors Ann Curtis and Helene Diamantides as well as Lake District legends Pauline Haworth and Joss Naylor.

Bellahouston Harriers was Christine's first club, but she soon moved to Clydesdale Harriers. She was encouraged to do so by Bobby Shields and his wife, and there met two other early lady hill runners, Shelagh King and Marjorie Small, both of whom are still running to this day. 'Then, once I began to succeed at hill running, I moved to Westerlands Cross-country Club as first claim club; they had several strong female hill runners and we could form a competitive team. I've been a member of the Westies ever since, have been ladies' Captain and was on the committee for many years.'

Looking back, Christine only recalls one race which she was almost prevented from taking part in due to being female, and that was the 1985 Mamore Hill Race. 'I insisted that I was going to run and was told that I did so at my own risk and that official safety measures wouldn't apply to me as they had no permit for women. I ran, it was a rugged and misty event, and I finished in a respectable time of 2 hours 21 minutes. I can't be sure, but I think one of the organisers' wives saw the unfairness of the situation and I was, in the end, given a certificate – which says:

> Presented to Christine Taylor of Bellahouston and certifies that 'he' took part in the Mamore Hill Race of 1985

She also recalls being told at various races that women would have to change, 'in a sheepfold, behind that wall, or in the car and that there were no showers for women – but none of that really bothered me. I did, however, get a bit fed up with winning cake stands and quiche dishes when the guys won malt whisky! Later, as women's times improved, I was keen to encourage race organisers to increase the value of women's prizes. I understood that the depth of prizes might not be as great – reflective of the fewer numbers competing, but felt that good times and equal effort should be fairly rewarded.'

She relays a story about one year being the only female competitor in the Glen Rosa Horseshoe race. She looked at the women's trophy sitting on the table, when an unknown, slightly disgruntled male competitor said to her before the start of the race, 'Well you don't need to really try do you!' 'That was a red rag to a bull, and I tried very hard indeed finishing well up the field in 2 hours 51 minutes 8 seconds and welcoming him across the finishing line long after I had finished!'

Like several others spoken to, Christine had no feeling then (or indeed now) that she was being something of a pioneer. 'Not really. It felt the most natural thing in the world to me, to be running in the hills. By the very fact that the percentage of women participants was low – frequently 10 per cent or less, you were aware that you were doing something that most women didn't do. I just didn't understand why more women didn't want to!'

She does accept that she was active in small ways in making changes happen, running off a list of those occurrences, including:

'I was part of the SHRA committee for several years, encouraging greater participation by women, trying to influence prize values and race organisers' support for women participants in general, and devising a set of early guidelines for hill race organisers.

One year Helene Diamantides and I commissioned and presented to the SIPR organisers a trophy for the first female running team in the event, in the hope that recognition would encourage female participation. We called it the Molls of Kintyre trophy, based on the fact that we had competed dressed in fishnet tights and feather boas that year!

As Lady Captain of Westies I always made sure that slower women and mums were included in relay events – we usually tried to ensure a mum's team complete with childcare.

With the help of Haddington runner and good pal Denis Bell, in the early 90s, I organised a Come and Try event in the Kilpatrick Hills and actively encouraged women to come along.

I also assisted my fell running buddy, Lesley Kirkwood, in the making of her college project video *Friends in High Places*, in which we filmed women taking part in a snowy Carnethy Hill Race and interviewed women as to why they ran in the hills and what it meant to them.'

Christine ran on the hills for thirty-three years. She stopped doing so when trying to stay race fit, rather than running-for-fun fit, became an increasing effort. 'My competitive participation had been declining for a few years, but then in 2017 I decided to compete in the Scottish Championships, aiming to win the Female V60 category. I did compete, and I did win my category, but it took its toll and I decided to stop competitive running for good after that. Last year my left knee gave up completely and I'm now awaiting a new one.'

When considering her finest achievement in the sport Christine suggested another Scottish Island Peaks Race. 'In 1993 Helen Diamantides and I were part of another all women team taking part in the SIPR. Steph Merry was our Skipper again and our yacht was the super-fast trimaran *Severalles Challenge*, kindly leant to us for the event by the owner. There were about sixty participating boats that year and we rounded the Mull of Kintyre in first overall position! The wind died and we had to row to Lamlash, as a result of which we were passed by the eventual winners, rowing a much lighter boat. Nonetheless, an all-women team were second into the finish at Troon and we were fifth overall on the running stages, out of nearly fifty finishing teams.'

Other high points in her career include: being sponsored as part of a female running pair (with former West Highland Way record holder Betty Hall) to take part in the 1990 Health Australia Tasmanian Three Peaks Race joining a team of Aussie sailors; running in the Scottish Team at a number of international events, including the World Trophy (at Die, Gap, and Bardonecchia), the

European Uphills, and home internationals including Snowdon 1993; winning a Bronze Medal at the 2001 Vets World Trophy in Poland; winning the women's trophy for the Bens of Jura Race in 1989, in 4 hours 16 minutes 15 seconds; and missing the Scottish Team trial for the 1992 International Snowdon Race due to injury, but going anyway and finishing fourth lady overall. Finally, she says: 'I suppose the best point has been surviving, being able to compete in the Scottish Hill Running Championships in my thirties, forties, fifties and sixties but above all, making so many long-term, lovely hill-running friends, with whom I have shared the best of adventures and the best of laughs.'

Christine competed with many females in pairs and team events and particularly remembers those with Helene Diamantides, Lesley Kirkwood and also the late Elspeth Scott. 'Elsie and I did the Karrimor International Mountain Marathon and Lowe Alpine Mountain Marathon together and were involved in the organisation of many events including support for the Scottish Junior teams. I very much miss her. She contributed a huge amount to the organisation of Scottish Hill Running; she was always even-tempered, organised, cheery and down to earth and we shared the same hate of tussocks and high winds!' Christine also laughs as she recalls the 1997 Universal 500 combined sailing and running event. Her partner was Jane Roberston and 'we ran in a complete circle during the night and giggled our way hysterically through the rest of the race!'

Christine concludes that the exercise of going over events has brought back so many memories of races, mainly happy memories! 'Winning is always fun but I think the race I would like to highlight is the 2016 Salomon Ring of Steall Skyline Race. I was feeling old and rickety and needed a wee challenge. I have always loved the real big mountain races – Stuc a Chroin, Bens of Jura, Ben Nevis, Arrochar Alps and so the uncompromising route of the inaugural Ring of Steall race appealed. I paid the rather large entry fee and did some serious training. I had recced the route with a club mate in a leisurely eight and a quarter hours, but thought that with a following wind and a bit of effort, I might be able to knock an hour off that time. My main worries were the steep descent into Glen Nevis and having wobbly joints on the technical and airy An Gearanach Ridge later in the race. Pain was going to be inevitable but hopefully pain of the happy kind!'

It mattered to her, so she avoided socialising on pre-race night and was quite nervous before the start. 'As soon as we started, I was loving it. My race plan was, as in the past for long events, start well back, run within myself until about halfway, do a self-check and adapt my pace accordingly. The route is beautiful, unforgiving and technical; the weather was fair, veils of mist hiding some of the scarier drops, with glimpsed and stunning views of Ben Nevis. I was feeling good along the Devils Ridge, not as nimble as in days of old, but steady enough – and I started to pass folk on the ascent to Sgurr a'Mhaim whilst gobbling jelly baby-coated Ibuprofen in preparation for the steep descent. Contrary to expectation, the descent was relatively pain free; I jigged to the sound of the pipes as I approached the Glen Nevis checkpoint, and welcomed the cheering encouragement from marshals and onlookers. I picked up the pace through the glen and then, knowing that my wee legs have always loved a steep climb, really turned up the effort on the ascent of An Gearanach, picking up a lot of places and feeling very at home in my misty, rock-pillared, sedge-gullied surrounds!'

'The next ridge was wobbly, but once done, I joined a bunch of tired but jovial chaps for the climb to Stob Coire a Chairn, cheering ourselves along with bad jokes. The group dissolved after the final summit of Am Bodach and as I braced myself for the steep, rocky descent, I glanced at my watch. I might just beat the 6-hour mark. How did that happen?! Well, it didn't happen, owing to a bout of calf cramp halfway down; the delay could have been much worse. I was saved by a bag of crushed crisps. I was nonetheless delighted to cross the finishing line in 6 hours 5 minutes and 26 seconds – knackered but buzzing! I finished sixteenth out of seventy women – nothing spectacular but not bad for a rickety fifty-nine-year-old. That night I partied with partner Dave and fellow Westies in my old haunt the Clachaig

Inn and the following day, supported competitors in the Glencoe Skyline Race. All in all, a perfect running weekend!'

Christine Menhennet is now a qualified Mountain Leader which she describes as being a culmination of her life experiences. 'I first did my Mountain Leader training in the late 1970s, but never sat the exam. Then in 2014 I decided to re-do the training and get the qualification. I did the training at Glenmore Lodge with my old pal Lesley Kirkwood, qualified in 2015 (aged fifty-eight), and was over the moon to do so. I had enjoyed the return to real mountaineering, walking not running, looking and absorbing rather than racing and chasing, and being responsible for others – not just myself. Map-reading, years of being in the hills and good fitness helped me greatly in passing the test. After a short spell of shadowing leaders working for Steve Fallon Mountain Guides, he offered me paid work with his client groups and I also led some privately sourced trips. I did some guiding whilst still doing my office job and much more after I retired. I love sharing my passion for the mountains with others and, in particular, supporting the less confident members of any group, quite often the women to achieve their goals. I was just finishing a website aimed at encouraging women of all ages, abilities and background to come to the hills with me, when in November of 2020 my knee finally collapsed underneath me, and I have been grounded ever since! I very much intend to be back in the hills sharing adventures with like-minded souls once I have a new knee!'

Christine Menhennet showed impressive levels of determination, taking pitfalls in her stride, and in many different ways has encouraged others to enjoy the hills, whether running or walking.

The standards for women in fell races were now being raised and widened, as witnessed by the record-breaking spree in 1988, whereby six athletes set twelve new course records between them. Carol Haigh set four, with Ruth Pickvance setting three and Angela Carson two.

There were several highlights in the season. Carol Haigh didn't seem to need recovery between races. When she set the record at Pen-y-Ghent on 4 June it was in her fourth race in six days! Not to be outdone, Angela Carson returned new fastest times at Lords Seat and the Grisedale Grind in a three-day period in August.

In September there was glorious weather for the Three Shires race and a good field in the women's section. Ruth Pickvance put up a new record beating Vanessa Brindle's old record by eight seconds, and the next runner by over six minutes. At the Winter Hill race at the end of November Ruth Pickvance showed she was on a great run of form. Bill Smith reported that, 'Carol Haigh led over virtually the whole course, but perseverance paid off for Ruth Pickvance who was steadily cutting into her lead as they progressed. On the final descent to the finish, Ruth, undaunted as ever, caught Carol to win by nearly half a minute, also reducing the ladies' record by five minutes'.

Yet another new name was to be engraved on the British Championships trophy for 1988. Clare Crofts had a clear win, by 18 points from Angela Carson. There was still some casual sexism in the report of the championships, unnecessarily commenting on the way someone looked.

Clare Crofts had only begun running in 1985, having joined the cross-country club at Sheffield University because they didn't have enough women to make up a team. In a profile in *The Fellrunner* in the year she won the British Championships she explained how it all went:

> I ran in a few cross-country races but became disillusioned because I always finished near the back of the field. I used to think then training meant running 3 or 4 miles every day a week

> before the race and doing nothing the rest of the time. I met Tony Trowbridge and he suggested that I should train with Dark Peak. He encouraged me to do fell races.

This training obviously did the trick, as Clare came second, to Jacky Smith, in the short version of the Edale Skyline race in 1986. By 1987 she was setting course records, at Scafell Pike and Langdale; and in 1988 did so at Chapelgill, Pendle, Duddon Valley and Buckden Pike. Asked about that Langdale record she said, 'I am afraid I can't remember the race in detail. I felt I had nothing to lose in this race as it was the last one that I was going to compete in in the 1987 season. I remember pushing hard up the first climb to pass the other women. From then on I was determined not to lose the lead.'

She finishes by saying she never trained more than fifty miles a week, credits her coach (Tony Trowbridge) for his 'endless supply of advice and support', and gives her feelings about running in the World Trophy in 1987 (where she came sixteenth). 'A mixture of excitement and pride. It was extremely important to me as my father was dying from cancer. I know that hearing about the race gave him an immense amount of pleasure. He died shortly after I returned from Switzerland.'

CHAPTER 11

Further abroad

World Mountain Running Trophy Comes to Keswick then Edinburgh. European Mountain Running Championships Held in Wales. Profiles: Carol Haigh, Sarah Rowell

'Carol spearheaded the domestic challenge, being near the front on the first climb.'

More runners were following Carol Haigh's example by running internationally. Danny Hughes was the driving force behind bringing the World Mountain Running Trophy to Keswick in 1988 – the only time it has been staged in England. Danny later became President of the World Mountain Running Association (WMRA) in 1993. Danny was on the European Commission for Mountain Running and instrumental in promoting the European Championship, which started in 1995. As President of WMRA, he had seen the World Trophy achieve the recognition for which he fought so tirelessly – from 2009 it became the IAAF World Mountain Running Championship. This had a significant impact on the development of mountain running worldwide.

In July 1986 several British runners ran the Lenzerheide/Danis uphill only race again, in the area where the 1987 World Trophy was to be held. Carol Haigh was competing against the women's world champion, Olivia Gruener. Despite leading over the first 4km, Carol could not hold her. They both ran the fastest times ever run on the course.

Malcolm Patterson recalls his first international race in October that year, which was the World Trophy, in

Morbegno-Sondrio-Albosaggia, in Italy. 'There had been a long hard fight (led by women, with often lukewarm support from the men) in international mountain running to achieve greater equality, a fight that's just about been won. At this second World Trophy, we took a team of twelve men and two women. It was also where, if I remember correctly, one of the women was Carol Haigh, and she won the World race, but had no official funding and was sponsored by a private company!' Carol Haigh was indeed only able to attend the event thanks to an anonymous donation, after her situation was highlighted in the local press. In the race she pushed the pace hard and established a significant lead and duly won. The second Brit was Jacky Smith, who managed to finish eleventh, despite also having a bad fall – on the first climb – that later required six stitches.

Carol Haigh

Once again a Facebook link was the starting point for getting in touch with Carol Haigh. She was one of the more elusive contacts, but we established an email connection and she gave the background to her fabulous and varied running career, answering my queries as I presented them.

For most of her fell running career Carol Haigh ran under that name, her maiden name, although she appears in some later results under her married name of Greenwood. She was born in Huddersfield in 1966, and ran cross-country, track and road before she got into running on the fells. She has run at a very high level, having started running aged fourteen with the school team. Her many outstanding performances across the non-fell running disciplines include a second place in the National Cross-country Championships, being a track international as a Junior, and being part of the GB team in the Ekiden Relay.

She explains the background behind her eventually looking at running on the fells. 'I was feeling the pressures of running on the track and wanted to try something new, so I thought I'd give fell running a go and loved it. My dad was also a runner, and he was right behind the change.'

Her first fell race was run unofficially (in Otley), as she was too young to register for the race. Carol adds that she had not done much training specifically for the fells by the time of that first race. 'My training had been focused on track, road and cross-country, and I just thought I'd give a fell race a go and to my surprise I was quite good at it!' She soon joined Holmfirth Harriers.

Her roots mean that she recalls that Liz McColgan was a big inspiration in her early days, even beating her in an indoor 3,000m early in her career. Having said that, she admits that Kenny Stuart's record on the fells is the one she is most impressed with, particularly his Snowdon race record.

Looking back, she feels no sense of having been a pioneer. 'I would say my presence in the races definitely encouraged more young women to have a go at fell races. Although I've noticed there's still only a small number of young women who go to fell races in comparison to cross-country and track races.' Carol has competed for many years, having started in her teens, but says that when she had her second child she didn't have as much time to focus on competing anymore.

Carol Haigh has one claim to fame that very few other women have, in that she achieved international selection at fell, road, cross-country and track. 'I ran for England on the track in Ireland and I got a GB vest to go to the Commonwealth Games on the track, but sadly got a stress fracture right beforehand.'

Carol had run 33-46 for 10km on the track to get in the Commonwealth Games team, but rues the lack of support she got, especially over injuries and funding. 'I thought that I could get to the top on the track and to try to get to the Olympics, but had no help at all with anything, except some free shoes and clothing. There was no physio support or financial support if I had really wanted to go to the Olympics. It got me down. So, I turned to the fells as the pressure was too much. I wish I could have had the help and support athletes get today.'

One unusual international Carol competed at was in being

part of the (winning) Ekiden Relay team in 1984, in Japan. A photo of her in the event seems to suggest it was snowing. 'I was running for Great Britain in the relay and as I was doing the last leg it started snowing, which you can see in the photographs', she confirms.

At a track meet in Belfast in 1984 Carol started suffering with sciatica, but it was intermittent. 'It used to come and go, sometimes lasting for up to six months. This is something I still battle with now.' The issue escalated in 1988 and 1989, and she would often turn up at races and not know until after a warm-up how it would react. Then in 1989 a stress fracture put paid to spring of that year. She came back to top form again from the start of 1992.

Many of Carol's results crop up in this narrative, as she was a very prolific and successful racer. In the 1986 season she set twelve course records, including at the Snowdon race. At the 1986 World Trophy Mountain Race she won, despite a disaster on the descent. She described the event more fully in an interview soon after the event. 'I was quite surprised by the early pace of the Morbegno race over 7,500m, from the town's piazza to the two summits. When we started the first climb I found myself in front and began to push the pace. The first climb felt relatively easy but I had to concentrate hard on the second long climb. My only problem came about a kilometre from the end of the descent from San Marco, when I went over on my ankle on the zig-zags. Fortunately, my lead was sufficient for me to win from Bottarlli of Italy. I was taken to hospital after the race for x-rays on my badly swollen ankle.' She showed her toughness though, as three weeks later she was recovered sufficiently to go back to Morbegno and come first in the Trofeo Vanori fell race.

Then in 1993 Carol had an amazing period, where she won thirty-eight consecutive races, setting twenty-three new record times, including winning Snowdon in 1-12-48, again surviving another issue within the race. 'I think the pressure of running downhill for 5 miles rubbed the skin away on my heel. When I finished my skin had completely gone from my heel!' Being reminded that in 1997 she reportedly won 'at least forty fell and multi-terrain events', she chuckles, and explains that she liked racing. 'Yes, I loved racing, it was great to meet and run alongside other fell runners. Everyone was so friendly!'

She still had time to fit in some serious training though. 'I would do track Mondays, long runs on Tuesdays and Thursdays, easy runs Fridays and races Saturday or Sundays. It would end up being around 60 miles a week. I never did any nav training or orienteering, but my navigation skills are fairly good and the more races I did the better they were.'

Carol Haigh was so dominant at times, yet never won the British Fell Championships. She explains: 'There were so many different races you needed to do to do well, but I was doing other races at the time, like international track and cross-country races, so I couldn't manage them all.'

Although she often trained on a bike and swam, Carol never tried doing triathlons, saying she 'just enjoyed doing each sport individually'.

Even though she had a pretty impressive race range, setting records for Burnsall (16 minutes) and Snowdon (1 hour 12 minutes), for example, Carol never set any records at any Long 'A' races. She says her best long race was when she won the Haworth Hobble, which was 33 miles. She also never tried the Bob Graham Round though, as she thought it was too far for her.

Having set so many records in her career, she concludes that setting the Snowdon record is the one that gives her most pleasure, looking back. 'I am running now and would love to come back but age is not on my side.' Carol Haigh/Greenwood managed to race prolifically for many years, and achieved exceptional results, as exemplified by several records that still stand.

After turning down the chance of hosting the World Trophy in 1986, the FRA worked hard to bring it to England in 1988. There had been considerable enthusiasm expressed by Keswick Town Council for the event to be held there. The plan was for a longer race to take place on the Coledale Horseshoe, with a short course on Latrigg. There were objections from Switzerland, Germany and Austria on the grounds that they did not finish uphill, which were rebuffed. The planned style of race was finally accepted by those countries. It was decided also to include non-championship races to involve all fell runners in the event. The Saturday was to have junior, women's and senior men's races all over the short course on Latrigg. On Sunday the longer course would have the open race, the veteran's World Trophy and the senior men's race for national teams. Responsibility for the short course would be with Keswick AC and the longer course with Cumberland Fell Runners Association (CFRA).

The first races were held on a sunny day on the short courses on Latrigg, described as cross-country in style. In the women's race Fabiola Rueda of Colombia retained her title, with Switzerland again winning the team award (on countback from Italy). The special event supplement in *The Fellrunner* ran an upbeat report, stating, 'it was arguably the strongest field ever assembled for a women's race', and that the Scots were contesting the race for the first time:

> Carol Haigh was just behind Guillot of France on the first climb. She was unable to sustain her pace, however, and by the second climb she was clearly struggling. Angela Carson of Wales, having her best run ever in this event, was first Briton in 6th place. Next [in 7th] was Trish Calder, who led the Scots to 3rd team place, behind the Swiss and Italians. Penny Rother in 11th and Joyce Salvona in 13th completed the team's outstanding performance. Carol's brave run gave her 12th place. Behind her Clare Crofts and Vanessa Brindle fought a desperate battle resolved only by a sprint finish, won by Clare. Their 17th and

18th places gave England a fine 4th place and Jacky Smith, hard on their heels in 21st completed an excellent all-round performance by the English.

A meeting of ICMR (International Committee of Mountain Running) held in tandem with the event was dominated by superior numbers of votes from the 'Alpine' nations, who ensured that uphill finishes would be the norm in future World Trophy events, although this later changed to alternate years of uphill only. From 1989 selection races for the World Trophy were instigated. The selection races for women in 1990 were held at Skipton, with an encouraging thirty females taking part, and Skiddaw.

The World Trophy race in 1989 was held in Die and Chattillon-en-Diois,[15] in France, and saw the debut at these championships of one of the UK's finest female fell and mountain runners. It was Sarah Rowell's re-entry to top-level racing after some issues had stalled her successful marathon career. In this, her first mountain race, she finished a very creditable fourth.

Sarah Rowell

I approached Sarah through Facebook, and we agreed that a (recorded) Zoom call would be the best way for us to chat initially. The recording, and transcript, provided a fascinating insight into this multi-layered athlete. Our follow-up email correspondence was fitted around her travels on World Mountain Running Association business. Several times her responses to queries were what she called 'airport scribbles' – albeit detailed scribbles.

Sarah Rowell was born in Hostert, North Rhine-Westphalia, Germany, in 1962. Her father had been posted there with the army. At school she did cross-county but never trained for it.

15. The World Trophy became the World Championships from 2009 onwards.

Her higher education continued in the UK, with her going to Brighton Poly, now Brighton University, to do a BSc Sports Science degree and then a PhD. At university she says she considered hockey her main sport. 'I also dabbled in climbing, skiing and canoeing. Once I started running seriously, I stopped doing everything else.'

That serious running became a successful marathon career. Sarah Rowell ran 2-39-11 at the age of twenty at the 1983 London Marathon. Later that year she won the gold medal in the women's marathon at the 1983 Universiade (World Student Games) in Edmonton, Canada. At the 1984 London marathon she improved her best to 2-31-28 to qualify for the British team for the 1984 Los Angeles Olympics. In the inaugural women's Olympic marathon, she finished fourteenth. She broke the British record when running her personal best for the marathon with 2-28-06, when finishing second behind Ingrid Kristiansen at the 1985 London Marathon.

Reviewing her road running, Sarah mentions several highlights. 'On the road it has to be London 1985, when my 2-28 was achieving a goal I had set myself, a run which at the time was as good as I could have hoped for. I was also very pleased with two races in 1984 – the Tunbridge 10 (in 53-44) and the Hogs Back (the old race, which was 11.11 miles, in 60-04).'

After the 1985 London marathon Sarah ran the Columbus marathon, and had the start of some leg problems. In 1986 she didn't start the London marathon but was still selected for that year's Commonwealth Games. She had the first of her leg operations in October 1986, to remove scar tissue. In July 1987 there was another operation, this time for compartment syndrome and removal of further scar tissue. This was all to try and sort out cramping issues that she had.

Sarah was coached by top marathon coach, Cliff Temple. 'There was one thing we disagreed over. That was that he thought I was always too thin and that I should eat more. His view was that part of my injury problems was that I wasn't eating enough for my body to heal and for the ops to be successful. While

I would disagree regarding the eating negatively affecting the operations, I would agree I was not eating enough.'

After recovering from the operations, Sarah started training again in 1987/88, but suffered another setback. 'It was under-recovery/over-stress. I was living in Eastbourne, had started doing my PhD, had just had another leg operation, was hoping to get back to running on the roads, and was running 80 to 100 mpw and racing most weekends. It was too much.'

Sarah Rowell confirms that she came off the roads and on to the fells predominantly because her left leg would cramp up when running fast on flat and smooth surfaces, but was fine for off road running. She expands on her change of surfaces. 'I had always been naturally good at running off-road. The fells – or in the first instance a focus on the World Trophy – was a natural move.'

In 1989 Sarah had finished her PhD and had moved up to Leeds to work. 'Increasingly I was moving from roads to off-road, and was finding off-road races to run. I was training with Angie Pain and Véronique Marot, with Brian Scobie. Brian didn't formally coach me, but I joined his group for track sessions and long runs. Unfortunately, Cliff Temple and I sort of drifted apart. Mountain and trail running at that time did not have the profile it has now. Cliff didn't have the motivation to continue coaching me remotely (this being before mobile phones and the internet).'

For her first mountain races she wasn't training as a mountain runner. 'I was getting back into training after under-recovery syndrome and really doing the same training as before, but was now based in Leeds. I fell naturally back into my normal habits, which was to do track training on Tuesday. I started running soft fell races and mountain races off what I would call normal training. No one influenced me to do off-road. I just knew I was good at it. I did Box Hill in 1989 because it was local to me and there. It was my first 'fell race'. Angela Brand-Barker was competing and finished second to me. I remember her coming up to me and asking who I was. I had set a course record.'

Sarah frankly admits that her early forays on to the fells were fairly low key. 'The first time I did the Boulsworth race, Wendy Dodds said to me, "good to see you doing a proper fell race!" My focus to begin with was more on the faster B or C category races.'

Sarah's early inspirations were unsurprisingly marathoners, particularly Grete Waitz, Ingrid Kristiansen and Joan Benoit. 'In terms of the fells/mountains, it was all and anyone, as I was a total newbie, but notably Carol Haigh/Greenwood – as a real competitor.' Sarah does say that she unfortunately wasn't aware at the time of the situation that females who raced on fells faced in the 1970s.

Sarah expands on her attitude to training. 'Running was what I liked doing and is maybe an obsession. I had a period of running full-time. Back then the pre-hab, and re-hab, wasn't being done. Doing a PhD, I used to get up in the morning and run 5 to 6 miles, and then didn't really do anything else until the afternoon. Therefore, running 80 miles a week was easy and 100 miles a week wasn't difficult. I have never had a long commute, so when I was working I could be in the office by 8am. In Leeds my office was right by the track, so I could go straight there after work for sessions. It just fitted in. My friends were runners, so it was easy. Balance is a really interesting thing. I got a first-class honours degree and people say, "how did you manage it?". My answer is simple. I didn't have the social life that most students did. I remember Ingrid [*Kristiansen*] saying "if you come home from a session and you have got a kid who loves you and couldn't care less about how the 400m reps went then it keeps things in perspective". Ideally, you have to have a balance AND be obsessed.'

She tried mixing the British Fell Running Championships and the World Trophy, but found that was too much. 'For me yes, combined with too much training as I did not have the confidence to ease back my training when I knew I was fit – also I always tried to run as hard as possible, not just to win.'

In 1991 she won the Haworth Hobble in a record time with Wendy Dodds, who was a much better known fell runner at that time. 'It was great fun, and yes loads of people were shouting for Wendy!', Sarah chuckles. 'I had a very embarrassing Hobble in 1994. I teamed up with Paul Sheard. Carol Greenwood was running it with Ian Ferguson. It was going to be quite a battle. As we came over Penistone Hill we overtook two Clayton lads to take the overall lead. I turned the wrong way and we ended up in somebody's garden with a load of washing on the line. The Clayton lads followed us into the garden and we ended up with a four-person sprint finish. Paul finished first, then the Clayton lads, then me. Therefore, we finished second team.'

Sarah adds another Haworth Hobble story. 'It involves using the men's shower in 1992 post-race (after finishing fourth overall with Colin Valentine). There were no women's showers. None of the men in there at the time seemed to mind!'

Sarah has said elsewhere that she feels that her 1992 (non-record setting) Three Peaks win was a great performance, as she now explains. 'I would always look at my time relative to the men's winner, and aim for between 108 and 110 per cent of the winning men's time. While I certainly did not achieve that all the time, the percentage gap I had that year over Fergy [*Ian Ferguson*], a great athlete, was a really good one – plus I made the top twenty overall.' For the record, Ferguson took 3-01-11, Sarah (in fifteenth place) took 3-19-11, a percentage difference of 109.

Things didn't always go that well. 'For the 1996 Three Peaks I was way out of it (by percentage values), despite setting the then record, because I was convinced that I could run 3-10 for that race, which of course I never did. When I look at all the splits, I feel I should have been able to do that.'

Sarah had some terrific results in the next few years. Eventually she won the Three Peaks Race four times as well as the Wasdale, Borrowdale and Ben Nevis races. She finished second in the 1992 World Mountain Running Trophy and won both the British and English Fell Running Championships in 1995 and 1996.

In that 1995 season she won the British Championships without losing a race. She quietly says it was a pretty good season.

'I ran really well that year, except at the Worlds in Edinburgh. I feel I had the best chance to win the World Championships, as the Edinburgh course suited me. A great year but for the one race that I really wanted. That I didn't do as well as I could was because I had overcooked the training. I had a really good trial race, but I can remember doing a two-hour training run the day after the trial. I did learn from it, but by that point I wasn't seeing improvements in training. My head was saying do I want to focus on this so much. Then in 1997 I finished second in the trial, a way behind, and just thought, "no – I have given so much emotionally and it hasn't worked", so I sort of drifted off. I did some more cycling, and I wanted to do adventure racing.' She adds that 1992 was a good year too, when she was second in the Snowdon race.

Sarah had to have a back operation in 1998. It was the same issues as already noted and it was causing her to lose her ability to run fast over rough surfaces. The problem seemed to be getting worse. 'My personal belief is that the problems I had were linked. My biking is as good as ever. My running speed is massively lower. My running mechanics are pretty poor. If my back is feeling bad running is an effort and it feels horrible. They injected some dye into my vertebrae and some of the dye leaked, showing a leaky disc. The op was to sort that out.'

She now says she doesn't think *any* of the operations were actually needed. 'The only thing they could find was that I had scar tissue built up in my left leg. For the first op to remove scar tissue, the medic had found a paper showing what Lasse Viren had been through and that he had compartment syndrome. The second op was to deal with compartment syndrome. The trouble was that I had a bit of haematoma and rather than get up and move, which compartment syndrome needed, I had to spend a week in bed. The third op was a repeat on the compartment syndrome.'

Sarah eventually stopped competing at the highest level on the fells and mountains, partly because she always found competition stressful. 'The stress was internal, and for me it was about improving and getting better. When I stopped improving I stopped competing seriously. Internal stress didn't affect my performance, most of the time. Results were more likely to be affected by training too hard. When I won the Seven Sisters Marathon I had done 120 miles that week, so sometimes you can have good performances. When I stopped performing as I felt I should do, then my inability to stop putting that stress on myself just meant I didn't enjoy it anymore.'

Sarah does not feel then (or indeed now) that she was being something of an innovator. 'Not really, other than maybe being someone who took a serious approach to racing and training on to the fells, whether that's innovation or not I am not sure.' It is a moot point – as was not the case in some of the early women running on the fells, who admit to a fairly casual approach.

Asked about trying to make changes happen, in her early years, Sarah replied, 'again, I am afraid to say not as much as I potentially should have been, other than pushing with regard to prize equality. I do not feel I ever had issues being a female.'

She also adds that she was a student and did the World Student Games marathon in Edmonton, Canada, and how that prompted an action she took later. 'One of the things I am proud of is to have pushed to get UK Athletics to treat mountain running teams in the same way as it treated other teams on travel costs and kit (which for the youngsters is important).'

Sarah set a good number of course records on the fells. Commenting on the best and longest lasting, Sarah offers two from races which have not changed their courses too much: Skiddaw (still the record from 1989), and Hutton Roof (a record set in 1994).

She said once 'I do not remember being overtaken by another woman on a descent'. That is a pretty powerful statement, which she explains. 'I was very much better running downhill and on the flat rather than climbing. That's still the case.'

Sarah had a very varied career and tried to summarise it into the highlights, and any regrets from her efforts. 'Regrets, yep, pushing too hard in training and not having the confidence to back off near big races, and also not adapting my training more. The highlights are too many really, some performance focused, some great experiences – such as the Pudsey and Bramley club's successful Pennine Way record, and being team leader for the Worlds in Wales where everyone won a medal.'

Sarah adds a comment on that Pennine Way record. 'When Pudsey and Bramley set the Pennine Way relay club record, one other club put in a complaint to get it disallowed as we had two women in the team!'

Looking specifically at mountain running, with hindsight Sarah reflected that she really only used to do the World Championships. 'I never went and did Tyon or Sierre-Zinal or any of the others [*in my peak years*]. The year that I was thirty-nine I had a minor mid-life crisis and spent a couple of months in France with Graham Patten. We were both in the v40 age group though and we did Tyon and Sierre-Zinal and that was the year it was shortened. We climbed Mont Blanc too in that time. I did the Chamonix half marathon one time on holiday and did UTMB. I started it twice and finished it once. Later I did the Three Refuges race, a relay of three. Someone runs up, someone runs across with a scramble, and someone runs down. I did the scramble leg which suited me. It was a bit strange running in a climbing helmet!'

Sarah says she attempted the Bob Graham Round three times. She got round once but out of time; once she bailed out because of the weather; and once was mainly as a support runner who had hoped to get all the way round.

The first BGR was with Mark Townsend, in June 2010. 'I was supporting him and agreed I would try and go all the way with him. We were going clockwise and were going down the descent to Wasdale and it was obvious we were moving faster than he set out to and I was starting to struggle. I said I am going to stop at Wasdale. By the time I told him I had made that decision in my head. Mark said, "but we have enough pacers, some can stay with you". I said, "I am here to support you". In the end I stopped at Wasdale and then restarted with him again at

Honister and ran in with him. I do think that if I had continued I would probably have got round within the time actually. I had switched my brain off.'

The bad weather one was a Pudsey and Bramley club attempt that failed. The one time she did get round she can remember having Jonny and Helene Whitaker on leg 2. 'Of the five head torches we set off with only one was working due to the rain by the time we got to Dunmail. Goodness knows how those two managed to navigate but they did a bloody good job. Even Helene started complaining about the cold, so it was bad. We were falling back on time. Going up Yewbarrow, Wendy Dodds said that she had got to go down for something. The reason she went down was she honestly thought I was in such a bad state that I was going to have to stop, and she didn't want everyone to leave [*Wasdale*] without me. I had dropped out twice. This time I was going to get round. I knew it was going to be over 24 hours. Scoffer [*Schofield*] was on the last leg and was apparently standing waiting saying, "if she gets here quickly, I can get her round in 2 hours". It was never going to happen. A lot of people had given their time, for which I am grateful, but I just didn't get round in time. We had seriously bad weather on legs 2 and 3, and I got round in 26-15.'

She had varied success in mountain marathons. The best memories were, 'anywhere we managed to have a day or two of clean navigation! I also did the Oxenhope straw race. I am not sure why, other than it was a local fun race. I loved doing it, and yes the fact that Anne Buckley and I 'won' outright one year is a good memory.'

Sarah completed the Three Peaks bike race once, and loved it, saying she would have done it again if it wasn't for having heart issues. 'I decided that, living with Andy [*Peace*], then the Three Peaks Cyclo-cross was something I should do once. In our household that weekend is a sort of religious event. I planned to do it in 2013 but fell off the bike when training for it, and tore the ligaments in my thumb. It didn't hurt but a couple of days later I was with the British team in Italy and I said to the doctor can you just look at this. My thumb had gone floppy. He said you need to see someone, and I had to have an operation. So, I missed that year, but was determined to do it again, which I did in 2014. In the same year, at one of the summer races, just before the start my heart rate suddenly shot up and didn't come down. I remember sitting down with my heart fluttering away, but feeling I can't drop out. Colin Moses said I should speak to his wife, who is a cardiac nurse. "You need to go to hospital", she said. The ambulance arrived and my heart rate was basically at 220bpm. They put some amiodarone into me which brought it down. I spent the next six days in hospital feeling fine. They found that I have got Arrhythmogenic Right Ventricular Cardiomyopathy, which means I have scar tissue on my heart muscle which they believe may be genetic, but brought on by the excessive amount of endurance stuff I have done. I have an annual check-up and I self-monitor it. The main thing I had to do was stop the racing because it only happens if I push my heart rate too high. I can still ride my bike but doing the Three Peaks would just be stupid. Now I have to be slightly careful, especially over the quality of what I do.'

Sarah Rowell has written two off-road running books,[16] one of which was with Wendy Dodds. 'I had written my earlier book for Crowood, and they wanted me to write another, but at the time I was also writing another book – on excellence in high performance sport – with another colleague, so I asked Wendy to help me, and we did it jointly.'

Some athletes have prepared so well that they *expect* to win. Fell icon Billy Bland had that in his armoury and folk would be going to the start line thinking they were running for second. Sarah says she had that expectation – to an extent. 'A lot of my self-belief came from good training. Then what I wasn't able to do was take that self-belief and use it as well as I could have done.' She gives an example from one year. 'I can remember going out doing a loop I used from Leeds, for which I had a best

16. *Off-road Running*, Crowood Press, 2002; and *Trail and Mountain Running*, Crowood Press, 2013,

time ever of 2 hours 8 minutes. I went out one day and ran 2 hours 6 minutes. At that point I should have had the confidence to say, "you know you are in really good shape, you are two to three weeks out from the Three Peaks, you don't need to keep pushing". I did the same with the World Champs in Edinburgh. I would go into races knowing I was in good shape, but it didn't stop me worrying and being nervous before the race. I probably never learned to race. My strength was my endurance. I don't have a sprint finish. Even on the roads, or any surface, I would get out there and I would just push as hard as I thought I could for the duration of the race. It never occurred to me to sit in.'

Regarding preparation and self-confidence, Sarah adds that she ran in an era when unless Carol Greenwood was on the start line 99 per cent of the time she knew she should be able to win. 'Carol, and Menna Angharad for a short while, were the main ones I looked at and thought I could have a good battle with. However, I still always stood on that start line worrying about other runners. If you look at my record then the number of times that I lost to another woman in a race, it is minimal. That is not necessarily a good thing, because I never got very good at losing. When I first started running on the fells, I remember turning up at races and behaving like I'd always behaved. I'd turn up, warm up properly for forty-five minutes, do my strides, stretches, and do the race. I am someone who becomes very introverted and wants nothing to do with anyone else and walks round with a face that says, "piss off and leave me alone". I would do the race, warm down and looking back I can see that people might have thought, "what on earth?". I came in with an attitude and I think women are less able to be good friends with their major opposition, as a generalised statement. I certainly felt that at the time. In general men will tend to be over-confident and women under-confident (in work/life as well). There is a real difference between the subjectivity and the objectivity (think of the Steve Peters *Chimp Model*). If you allow your subjective mind to lead too much, then yes that can really knock your confidence. For example, by the time I did my second Three Peaks my time was fifteen minutes faster than anyone else's. It didn't stop me standing on the start line worrying.'

Sarah nominates four females whose record on the fells/mountains she is most impressed with, looking back. 'They are Pauline Stuart, Carol Haigh/Greenwood, Victoria Wilkinson, and now Hannah Horsburgh – anyone whose performances are in the 8 to 10 per cent bracket of the men's winning time, a level also reached by Jasmin Paris in the longer events.'

Simon Barnes, in writing about the meaning of sport,[17] has a quote on longevity being part of greatness: 'Greatness requires a kind of perpetual thirst'. It seemed that might have a resonance with Sarah, who had to keep coming back from setbacks, and showing her thirst for more. She gives her perspective. 'On the one hand, I can look at my career in international mountain running and see that I ran out of thirst, and maybe it was two or three years before I should have done. Then I can also see that for me having challenges and having goals even if I am not racing is important. I still love the mountain marathons and that is why I do orienteering, because it is challenging. Can I still get better at it? It is also why I climb. They are challenges, to go up things that are going to scare me, but give a real sense of achievement. I do see that, and I have some of it but to really meet that criteria I would have to have had another three or four years of international mountain running.'

Sarah concludes that she is still fit, but slow. 'My running speed has declined much more than my cycling! I still try to do something every day, mixing running, exercises (strength and mobility for the two ACL [*anterior cruciate ligament*] replacements which need looking after), cycling and in the summer a bit of swimming, plus I now do local orienteering just to do something I can get better at. I got round the Saunders [*Mountain Marathon*] OK in 2021!'

Sarah Rowell is probably the best example of a top female marathon runner who turned successfully to fell and mountain

17. *The Meaning of Sport*, Short Books, 2007.

running. She is also refreshingly honest in her self-analysis, being prepared to admit where she may have been able to have done things differently – and maybe to have been even better.

The World Trophy almost floundered in 1993 over a huge row about 'Up and Down' and 'Uphill Only' courses. A compromise was reached to alternate them year on year, and the re-badged World Mountain Running Trophy seemed to have a future again. There is now a proliferation of such championships. Browsing the World Mountain Running Association (WMRA) website shows that there is now a World Championships; European Championships; World Long Distance Mountain Running Challenge; and Commonwealth Mountain Running Championships.

The successful event in Keswick in 1988 set the precedent for UK venues to host major mountain running championships. The Worlds came to Edinburgh in 1995 and the Europeans to Wales in 1996. Just two UK female athletes followed Carol Haigh in winning a major mountain running trophy in the period covered by this book. They were Beverley Redfern (from Scotland), who won the World Trophy in 1990 at Telfes, in Austria, and Angela Mudge (also for Scotland) at Bergen, Germany, in 2000.

CHAPTER 12

More record breaking

1989: A Year of Many Course Records.
Profiles: Angela Carson, Ruth Pickvance

'Obviously records get beaten.'

An interesting comparison is given by figures produced by Andy Walmsley in 1989.[18] He counted the number of course records held *at that time* for all races in that year's FRA calendar. The results are pretty startling. For the women Carol Haigh/Greenwood, who never actually won the British title, had a staggering forty-three; Angela Carson/Brand-Barker seventeen and Vanessa Brindle/Peacock eleven. That record haul for Carol Haigh shows the form she had been in for the last few years. She had not finished yet.

Angela Carson

Angela was put on to me directly by Wendy Dodds, and Angela's thoughts provided another brilliant window into the early days for women. We agreed that a series of questions via email was the way forward, as for her it was useful to, 'not have to rely solely on memory and can check a few scrap books.'

Angela Carson had been performing well for a number of years and had already won the British Championship twice. She was born near Coleshill, Warwickshire, in August 1961, and moved

18. In an article entitled 'The Record Business', in the June 1989 issue of *The Fellrunner* magazine.

to Wales when she was six. Her married name is Brand-Barker, having married in October 1990. She qualified as a physiotherapist in 1985, then worked for the NHS until her retirement in 2016.

At school she enjoyed distances from 400m to 1500m, which were run on a grass track at her school. She reached a very high standard as a young athlete, representing the county of Gwynedd in the Welsh Schools Athletics Events from 1977 to 1979, and being Welsh Schools Champion at 400m hurdles (as an under 19) in 1979.

Before getting involved in fell running Angela was a keen rock climber and mountaineer, and took part in orienteering and cross-country with her respective university clubs. She originally joined the cross-country and orienteering clubs at Manchester University and when she transferred to Sheffield University, joined the same clubs there.

Her introduction to running on the fells came about when she joined other University cross-country club members in running the Snowdon Race in 1981, as she explains. 'It was easy to do from home and I had been aware of this race since its inception. My primary school headmaster's son-in-law was Malcolm Jones – the only person to have run in every race up to the fortieth anniversary of the race.' Angela adds a wry comment about that 1981 Snowdon race. 'It was official. They even had the AAAs blazers there making sure numbers and vests were all shipshape!'

Angela had done no specific training for the fells by the time of that first race. She adds, 'I wasn't aware of the sport of fell running until late 1981. It seemed a natural thing to combine my love of running with my love of mountains. Once I started, I was hooked!'

Another outstanding runner, Rosie Naish, grew up just up the road. Angela says she was in awe of Rosie when she broke the Snowdon Race record in 1982. Showing her own strong competitive spirit, Angela adds, 'once I started competing more regularly, the leading ladies became the ones with "targets" on their backs.'

Looking back, Angela says she cannot recall any problems with race organisers in the early days, before commenting that 'races were a lot less official last century! The prize differentials were interesting at times though: for example, a basket of fruit for 1st man, and a bikini for 1st woman! Or a gallon of whisky 1st man, and a litre 1st lady.'

So, did she feel she was being something of a pioneer? 'I just felt that women were in the minority in this sport. The pioneers who had fought to run over the same courses as the men pre-dated my involvement.'

She was not especially militant, and never got involved in any official canvassing to change things. 'However, I was a bit miffed to learn that The Trunce (a traditional tough cross-country/fell race in Sheffield) was for men only. My friend Kay Whittle and I entered in 1984 (being economical with details on the entry form) and with the help of male friends in DPFR, who surrounded us at the start, we ran in the race, but the marshal who marked your arm at the turnaround point refused to mark us and we didn't cross the finish line but snuck off down a back route a few metres before the funnel.'

Admitting to being a very unorganised trainer, Angela describes her setup. 'In Sheffield, in shared houses with orienteers/runners it was so easy to get out onto the moors and hills to the west of the city. I did the weekly DPFR [*Dark Peak Fell Runners*] training runs. My volume was always low, around thirty-five to forty-five miles a week, but most of that was off road and quite hilly. There was no structure to my running. I never had a coach – I just loved running and followed my nose.'

As far as navigation is concerned, Angela grades herself as normally a solid navigator. 'I learned map reading skills for the Duke of Edinburgh's Award, and have been orienteering on and off since 1980. After hanging up my Welsh vest in 2005, I discovered Mountain Bike Orienteering (MTBO) and have competed internationally a few times.' She cites a W55 Bronze medal in the World Masters MTBO in 2017 as a highlight.

Competing on the fells since 1981, her last official race at the time of writing was Ras Yr Aran, in March 2020, just before Covid-19 disrupted everything. She competed internationally from 1985 to 2005, before just stopping. That is a spectacularly long international mountain running career. 'I decided on a long flight back from New Zealand that I'd had enough of travelling miles just to race for under sixty minutes.'

It can be difficult for someone to specify their finest race or achievement in the sport. Angela says she has a good few race victories with special memories and lists a few. 'Cnicht 1981 – it was my first victory (totally unexpected after I'd found Snowdon really hard). Also, Snowdon 1987, and Ben Nevis 1997. Achievements that stand out for me are: being four times British Champion and International representation over twenty years. I was also proud to perform well in all areas of mountain running – from short fell races to mountain marathons.'

Asked about race records she had set, Angela mentions four local Welsh ones (some not now held), then identifies some more: Bens of Jura in 1988 (she thinks she was the first sub-4 hour woman), nine in 1994 (Muncaster, Blencathra, Coledale, Yr Eifl, Kinniside, Peris Horseshoe, Merrick, Pentlands Skyline, and Wansfell), then four more in 1995 (Craig Goch, Blakeley Skyline, Trefriw, Steel Fell) and Coledale in 1996. That is one impressive set of records, most of which were subsequently beaten. She adds that she 'set the record in the Three Peaks Yacht Race in 1998 with Menna Angharad. This involved taking a multihull into Ravenglass. This record still stands, as the race was changed to monohulls only and included cycling from Whitehaven harbour.'

Which other record setters impress someone setting so many herself? 'Angela Mudge is the greatest all-rounder – achieving UK and international titles/records and also proving her navigation and mountaineering skills by winning mountain marathons.' Angela Brand-Barker also gives a big shout for Carol Haigh's Snowdon record time, for its longevity (having been set back in 1993).

Angela actually holds one outstanding record that is even older than Haigh's Snowdon one, which is in the same area. Angela briefly explains about setting the Welsh 3,000s record, and why she thinks it has not been challenged. 'I have to thank Ken Jones for organising this record attempt. Stel Farrar and I caught the train to the summit of Snowdon on 5 August 1989, and we each had separate pacers for each section of the route. I was lucky with the weather, which was clear and not too hot. It was one of those days when your legs do just what you want them to do.' Angela's time for the 26 miles, taking in fifteen summits, was 5 hours 28 minutes 21 seconds.

Angela adds that 'it will probably be challenged now that Finlay Wild has brought attention to the route.' It will be interesting to see if anyone ever organises an attempt with the strict conditions that are required for the time to be included in the Guinness Book of Records (Finlay Wild has the FKT [*Fastest Known Time*], whilst Colin Donnelly remains record holder in the Guinness Book of Records).

She explains that she met Finlay briefly at the Kendal Mountain Festival and congratulated him on his Guinness entry for the Welsh 3,000s record. 'He gave me a puzzled look and said he had run a FKT and didn't know if this would go in the Guinness record book.'

Angela then outlined the conditions for a Guinness record, and was unsure whether Finlay's time would be eligible for inclusion. 'I guess FKTs are all to do with modern GPS technology, trackers etc which were not available in the late 1980s. In those days, there had to be an approved timekeeper who was at the start and finish, and you had to have two people who would verify that you had visited all of the summits in the correct order. All the info was then sent off to Guinness and they would either approve your record and insert it in the next yearbook or refuse if the information submitted was not felt to be valid.' She says she had Ken Jones to thank for making sure all the documentation was in order for hers.

Angela Carson/Brand-Barker won the British Fell

Championships four times in all (in 1983, 1986, 1993 and 1994). She runs through the decade that these victories encompassed, explaining her main focus for those years. 'The 1983 victory was unexpected and at the time I thought that having achieved that, I would now try something different. It had also meant a lot of expensive travelling and as a student, my resources wouldn't stretch to gallivanting around the UK every year. Doing a Bob Graham Round in June 1984 meant my legs weren't fit for anything else for few months, so no champs challenge that year. In 1985, getting selected for World Trophy was my main aim. In 1986 my fellow Eryri runners were travelling to the British Championships races so I went along to assess my form and ended up with the victory. During 1987 I suffered with illness, which was possibly Lyme disease. In 1988 I moved to the Lakes from Wales, via Australia for six weeks, so missed too many races. For 1989 I concentrated on the Welsh 3,000s record, and my son was born in 1991. For 1992 my main target was selection for Wales in the World Trophy. Finally, for 1993 and 1994 Keswick Ladies targeted the English and British Champs so I was lucky to compete with great teammates there.'

Angela reveals that the Bob Graham Round was certainly not planned. 'I was training with a DPFR group on Wednesday nights as a way of switching off from exam revision. I was asked if I fancied a trip to the Lakes one weekend. Seeing it as a great way to unwind after exams, I replied "yes". I was then told that I could "have a go" at the BGR if I wanted. I asked what I needed to do and was told to pack various sets of running kit and provide food for the communal store (rice pudding, soup tins etc). Thus, I became a part of the DPFR Bob Graham machine.'

Looking back on 1987, Angela recalls that she suffered with serious fatigue from late summer onwards. She had two weeks off sick and was unable to run for six weeks. There was then a gradual return to fitness from early 1988. 'I had no blood tests done and I wasn't aware of Lyme disease in those days. I had had to remove dozens of ticks in the spring and summer having spent a few weeks in Scotland and had red rashes that I just put down to mild skin infection as the rash went after a week or so. Having read up about Lyme's now, this was the most likely diagnosis, but obviously I can never prove it.'

Angela was competing at the beginning of international running competition. 'There was an international fell race in Zogno, Italy on 30 September 1984. This was a men-only event! Danny Hughes then organised an international mountain challenge in May 1985. There were three races – Buttermere Sailbeck, Grasmere and Rydal and there were women from UK racing in these races. Then Pauline Howarth/Stuart and I competed for England and Wales respectively in the first World Trophy in 1985.'

Angela then came sixth in the World Trophy when it was held at Keswick in 1988, although it didn't go that well. 'I remember being fourth near Latrigg summit and thinking that I was bound to get overtaken on the flatter section by the speed merchants (my strengths were the steep sections). The bridge over the A66 at the end felt like another mountain! I had blood in my socks from blisters at the end. Once I stopped running, I could barely walk back to my car.'

Latterly Angela has taken up mountain bike orienteering (MTBO). She says she had a love–hate relationship with traditional orienteering for many years. 'I discovered MTBO in 2006. It seemed like a fun challenge – navigation without the brambles! It was also a sport which the whole family participated in and enjoyed.'

Angela had a very proud moment prior to the 2012 London Olympics. 'On 21 June 2012 I carried the Olympic flame through the southern edge of Maryport which is where I had worked since 1994. The rain stopped for the torch journey and it was wonderful to see nothing but smiling people – many of whom I knew. What made it even more special, was that I passed the flame onto Joss Naylor, a true fell legend.'

Angela Carson/Brand-Barker performed exceptionally well over an extended period, and was a female competitor very early on, including the first official Ben Nevis race in 1981, although she does acknowledge that those running in the 1970s may have been more pioneering.

In the 1989 season Sarah Rowell was running really well and was setting course records regularly. In April, May and June respectively she set new marks at the Hutton Roof Crags, Pen-y-Ghent and Skiddaw races. The latter, with a time of 1-13-29, has not been beaten. Prior to those, Vanessa Brindle had beaten her own Three Peaks record in early April, and then in June Ruth Pickvance set a new record for the Coledale Horseshoe.

In April Carol Haigh had set a new record for the popular Chew Valley Skyline race (2-02-31) that had not been beaten when it was last held as a straight race (the Chew Valley Skyline stopped in 2010, and became an orienteering event, the New Chew). At the end of the season Ruth Pickvance was crowned Champion, having had a fine season.

Ruth Pickvance

Ruth was the second interviewee that I spoke to via a Zoom call. Of all the methods used in the research a Zoom call was definitely the closest it was possible to be to a face-to-face interview. It is somehow easier to feel you are properly getting to know someone if you can see them. Ruth patiently answered my questions as she ran through her career and present life.

Born in Blackpool, Lancashire, in 1961, Ruth Pickvance's parents both worked in education. Ruth spent the latter part of her childhood in Halifax, West Yorkshire. After leaving school, she did a degree in English Literature and then worked for a year in the Lake District, at Brathay Hall. 'This was a wonderful year and one in which I spent a lot of time exploring the Lake District – climbing, walking and camping out,' she recalls.

She shied away from athletics at school, clearly remembering staying off school once when it was the annual cross-country race. 'I did, however, play tennis quite well and played for the school team. I've always walked – we had a dog and I'd often just set off on my own in my teenage years with the dog and walk for miles.'

From a young age she had family holidays in the Lake District, sharing with another family. They'd all stay in a tiny cottage in Little Langdale and as kids they'd just roam free. 'We walked up and down the fells, often in the rain in August, in wellies. I couldn't have any boots until my feet stopped growing, my mum said. It was truly wonderful. It set in place a love of the Lake District and quite possibly is the roots of my fell running passion.'

Ruth always cycled, swam and walked. 'I had no car until my mid-twenties and used to travel by train with my bicycle in the heady days when there were goods vans on trains. Looking back, I had a definite need to be outside. I'd just go off for a long walk or for a whole day on my bike sometimes – I've always enjoyed days out on my own. I do enjoy days with other people, but I also notice that unlike some people, I really enjoy time outdoors alone. It's when I sift and filter what's been going on, it's when I have my most creative ideas.'

She reckons she found her own way into fell running. 'A couple of my past boyfriends were interested in sport, but it was very much something that came from within me.'

Ruth thinks her first race was the Wansfell Race in late December 1985. 'I'd been up in the Lakes the year before and had seen the race on a snowy day under blue skies never having seen a fell race before. My sister and I just happened upon it while out walking. It was like a blow to the heart for me. I was utterly captivated, despite the fact that I didn't run at all and that I knew nothing about running. I vowed that I'd come back the following year to do the race and so started running. At the time I was working in my first teaching job in the Midlands, and started to run round the block at lunchtime, much to the amazement of most of my colleagues. Women just didn't really run back then.'

Looking back on that race, Ruth says she doesn't think she had any expectations, and therefore she was just pleased that she had actually done it. 'I knew so little, and I was so ill-prepared, and so badly dressed. At the time it was a case of ignorance is bliss. I thought "that is amazing, I did it". It took a couple of years for the obsession to kick in.'

Things were so different then that Ruth had one job where she used to drive around the corner and change in the car to run at lunchtime, 'Out of sight of judgemental eyes!' she adds, before trying to explain her feel for the sport. 'I did the Wansfell race in my blue V-necked wool jumper, Adidas trainers and I think finished almost last. I remember wondering how people had finished so fast. However, despite the pain that I most certainly remember after that run, I'd found something. I think the values of self-sufficiency, non-commercialisation and simplicity that lie at the heart of fell running sat well with me and my character. It was a passion ignited.'

In the decade from 1985 onwards Ruth Pickvance won the British Championship (in 1989), competed in many classic UK fell races and also some early European races. She was a member of firstly Clayton-le-Moors Harriers and then Kendal AC.

'In the late 1980s I was desperate to get a job back up north and began a weekend commute to do more races, before I finally landed in Blackburn to work at a boys' grammar school. There were so few women teachers that we were called *Sir* – I'm still trying to figure that one!'

In those early days Ruth looked up to Vanessa Brindle, Carol Haigh and Pauline Stuart. 'Helene Diamantides was already racing very well and was the female runner for whom I have a lot to thank. She dragged me round my first Rock and Run Mountain Marathon. What a frustrating experience that must have been for her – they'd even packed up the finish tent when we finally finished. It was the year that 50 per cent of the field retired due to appalling weather, so it was certainly in at the deep end for me. I recall standing in snow-filled puddles to try to take the pain in my feet away. We went on to be good friends and good partners for Mountain Marathons, as well as racing rivals. Helene had more endurance than me (she had more endurance than almost anyone) and was better on rough ground whilst I had more natural speed. I'm still in awe of much that Helene has done – her return to the Dragon's Back race as a solo competitor and her second position was incredible. She has a tenacity and a resilience that is rare.'

Ruth adds that as early female fell runners they were surrounded by men because females were few and far between. 'I raced with men around me, I raced against men.'

Ruth completed the Bob Graham Round on 7 May 1988. She was supported by Martin Stone, Helene Diamantides, Mark McDermott, Selwyn Wright, Elaine Wright, Mike Rose, John Brockbank – amongst others. She says it just felt like a wonderful day and night out in the hills with friends.

As she got fitter Ruth simply loved racing, but in the very early days had no expectations about winning anything. 'I loved the camaraderie of fell running, loved getting to different mountain areas that I'd otherwise never have been to, loved the de-stress from working life and loved the sense of freedom. I'd read *The Fellrunner* from cover to cover, and I wanted to know everything about this sport. I've never been mathematical, and times and stats evaded me for a long time. I didn't even have a sports watch until I started training seriously for marathons and this was like a whole new world to me, to which I came late.'

One of the very early European races Ruth did was the Davos Swiss Alpine Marathon in 1989. It was 42 miles and went up to a height of 8,310 feet. 'It's one of my most memorable races. I'd gone out to Switzerland the week before on my own, with my little tent to acclimatise and to train. I remember how I camped next to a lovely Dutch couple with a huge tent who looked after me and fed me all week. They told the campsite that we were together, so I didn't have to pay any fees as my tent was so small. I look back now and marvel at my own independence being fuelled by fell running!'

Ruth was really inexperienced, having never run that kind of distance or at that altitude and yet she almost won the women's race. 'If I'd known more, I'd never have entered!' she chuckles. The race finishes round the running track in Davos where hundreds of people had gathered, and it was this flat run-in to the finish that proved her undoing as her legs just buckled with less than a mile to go. 'I literally staggered and almost crawled to the finish line. I'd been eight minutes ahead of Lesley Watson after the descent and she passed me on the run-in to the finish. I finished second, and I think it was the only race that I've ever given more than one hundred per cent without realising it due to inexperience. I couldn't walk properly for a week afterwards.'

The Times journalist Michael Coleman was covering the race and helping find marathon runners for the GB team. 'He asked me if I'd like to be coached, and if I'd like to become a marathon runner. He gave me a free place to run the Marrakesh Marathon in the January to see what I could do off no training. I recall travelling out there on a completely smoke-filled plane as everyone was smoking. I finished just inside 3 hours in the most chaotic of races, but I didn't enjoy it. My heart was in the mountains – I've always run quite a lot with my heart – where I raced was always important to me. I told Michael I just wanted to run on the fells, and I'll always remember him saying, "Honestly Ruth, you want to waste all your potential on winning pairs of socks in races rather than going to the Olympics?". That still makes me smile. Such was my love of the mountains, and the mountains were where I wanted to be. In retrospect, having come to marathon running late in my career I'm glad I made this choice. There's real value in road running, as it teaches you focus and drive in a way that fell running doesn't. HOWEVER, it also trashes your body in a way that fell running doesn't. It is relentless, and repetitive. If I'd gone into marathon running in my late twenties

I don't think I'd have had the long and uninjured fell and mountain running life that I've had.'

Ruth loved racing in Europe. It suited her and played to her strengths as a runner: long uphills with downhills mainly on tracks. 'I've never been particularly good on very rough downhill terrain (like at the Bens of Jura race). The other European race that I did and won twice in this period was in France at La Plagne. It's 55km with 6,000m of dislivello [*difference in height*]. It was popular with us Brits in the early 1990s. Martin Stone, Mike Walford, Helene Diamantides, and several others did the race in 1993. That year I finished twenty-third overall and first woman, beating Helene into second place.'

In 1994 Ruth went to live and work in Singapore. It couldn't have been more of a polar opposite to life in Cumbria. She was ready for a change and an adventure, and this certainly was it. 'I think I'd read somewhere that Singapore was a garden city and thought that sounded fine. I had no idea that I was committing myself to an island city of 5 million people, in humidity and heat like I'd never experienced.'

On the way out to work in Singapore Ruth stopped off in Sabah, Malaysia, to do the Mount Kinabalu race. 'I'd never done anything quite like it, starting at 6,000 feet and going up to 13,455 feet and then down again, and it's the down that is the hard bit. 1994 was the year that the British army expedition became trapped and lost in Lowe's Gully which had made headline news in the UK and so there was significant media interest in this British *blonde girl* (the papers love a blonde girl don't they!) getting to the summit as first woman. I was passed on the way down by a local woman who worked on the mountain as a guide, Hasney Salagan. The winnings from the race were worth more to her than a year's salary. If memory serves me well, I think she was airlifted to hospital at the end, as she collapsed.'

Singapore saw Ruth not racing too seriously while there. 'I became good friends with Yvonne Danson (a GB marathon runner) who was based in Singapore. A lovely international group of us ran early on Saturday mornings, but the heat and humidity was so difficult to train in and there was much else to do, like cycling, exploration and travel. I also had quite a demanding job during these five years.'

Looking back, Ruth admits that she didn't race as often during this time, but thinks it's probably part of her longevity as a runner that she had the capacity to step out of it while in Singapore. 'It did me good. Life can become very narrow as a runner if you don't watch it! It's that passion and obsession thing again.'

In 1999 she moved to Wales and got a job in an unusual International School, UWC Atlantic College. The College was out on the Welsh Coast in an old castle. 'Staff lived on site, and we worked a yearly timetable with long terms and then ten weeks off in June and July. The school encouraged staff to follow their passions, particularly in the outdoors, and as we had some evening commitments, we could usually find time during the afternoon to train. I was marathon and road running during the winter with the odd fell and trail race while I worked there. Then Skyrunning in Italy during the long summer break as well as running many of the European Grand Prix races and for England and GB. I had learned the importance of speed work and tempo runs. These were what I consider my serious years! It was during this time that I got a proper sports watch and got dragged, metaphorically kicking and screaming, to do speed work by the two running colleagues that I worked with. For the first time in my life I followed a training schedule written for me by my French colleague Nic Janvier, who was himself a 2-23 marathon runner. It paid dividends and had a super-positive effect on my mountain running and I clocked some top times for road running as well.'

Ruth was in the middle of doing up an old semi-derelict house in the Italian Apennines. It was a busy life as she was Head of Faculty at the College, but they were very supportive of giving her time off to race. 'I spoke Italian and got involved with the emerging Skyrunning scene in Europe. I thought that these races were astonishing – beautiful and professionally staged – like a hyper version of UK fell running. I was certainly one of the first female Brits on this scene.'

Along with Matt Ward and Tim Lloyd, she tried to stage the first Skyrace in the UK. Ruth knew the organisers of Skyraces in Italy, which were already well established. 'They were keen for a Skyrace to take place in the UK. We were saying, "well we haven't got the same kind of mountains". We thought that we could make it happen. We didn't have any specific route or venue. It must have been about 2008. There was no interest at all in the UK. We went to the FRA and approached some of the longer races, but there was no interest. It was just too early for the UK. We were ahead of our time really. It's nice to see that this has finally happened.'

At one stage Ruth ran four marathons in ten months. 'I think the *love racing* thing was still with me. I never clocked a high mileage in training. I got ill if I did. I think my background in long-distance fell running meant that I had excellent endurance. Getting some speed was much more of a challenge. The 1980s hangover was still with us, believing high mileage was a good thing: train, train more and then train even more. I just couldn't do this and have never run more than seventy miles a week and it was usually more like fifty miles.'

Those four marathons (London, New York, Reggio Emilia in Italy, and Genoa in Italy) were done in three different countries, over different courses, at different times of the year and yet Ruth clocked 2-45 for each one. 'I should have got a 2-40 but there's always something with the marathon, usually a headwind in the last 5km! Possibly the most memorable was New York, which was in the November after the 9/11 bombings in the September, and they weren't sure at first that they'd hold the event. I think every person in New York came out to watch as it was somehow testimony to the spirit of the city. I'd intended to just run for fun. It was on the back of a long Skyrunning summer, and I hadn't been road training at all. However, when they asked for my best time at registration, they hooked me out of the mass race and put me in the elite start. I was right on the front line on the Verrazano Bridge and watched the release of doves as a symbol of peace. A beautiful moment. New York, unlike London at that time was run as a mixed race (in the April I'd had the lonely experience of running 10 miles on my own in the London marathon as they set a moderately sized women's field off which soon became dissipated) and I had company and ran strong and well. I finished behind Joan Benoit (she'd won the first ever Olympic marathon for women, in 1984) and being in the same age category we shared the podium together.'

Skyrunning was what Ruth most loved during this period, though. 'The Europeans certainly know how to put on a good race, and the Italians know how to eat after a good race. I made some lovely friends, and the racing took place over courses that suited me. I *can* navigate to get myself about in the mountains, but I struggle to navigate at speed on the run. I never competed much in the Mountain Trial because of this. I always did the KIMM and other mountain marathons with much better navigators (including Helene Diamantides). British fell running is unique, and I love that uniqueness, but I have to be honest here and say that I loved the fact that European Skyraces were on marked routes!'

Early on in her running career Ruth used to train at lunchtimes in the winter. 'I'm hopeless in the evening and am very much a morning person. I could never do track sessions at night. Early on, I think my racing was like training.'

Ruth says she was very lucky to have never been injured in over thirty years of running. 'Of course, I've had major aches and pains like everyone. I think it's due to a number of things, including not running until I was in my mid-twenties. I've always swum, walked and cycled for pleasure and so this gave me some active downtime. I didn't start road and marathons until late on. I think I came at things from an enjoyment angle for many years. It was only when I started seriously on the roads that I had periods of disillusionment and more physical pain. It's a knife-edge getting it all balanced.'

Running seems to have become generally much more serious

and Ruth says she is constantly amazed by the extent to which everyone relies on technology. 'It's useful and can be fun, but it can also start to dominate, and everyone seems to be forgetting to literally and metaphorically look at the view.'

Ruth also reckons that another thing that has changed running (and life) for both better and worse is social media. 'When I look back, I raced lots. It was something that I did almost every weekend, and people beyond my running life knew little about. Basically, you'd get out, have major adventures at the weekend and then go back to work on Monday aching all over and saying nothing because most people wouldn't understand and often just thought you were mad! Social media certainly has its uses and it's fun and I use it. I feel that there was a kind of humility to running before that now seems to have been lost amidst the social media shouting about it. It's made superstars out of those who are the top end and perhaps has created a false world of aspiration. It's a bigger topic than for here but I'm grateful to have been part of the simple grassroots that fell running came with.'

These days Ruth says she gets out for a jog. 'It really is a shuffle. I walk a lot. I cycle and mountain bike. I swim. I do yoga. I still absolutely love being in the mountains and I don't race any more. The only problem I've ever had is a bone spur on my heel which affects the Achilles tendon and developed badly about ten years ago and these days it is much aggravated by running. I miss racing, but I also recognise that it's no longer for me. I think you have to be intelligent about self-preservation as you get older.'

Ruth Pickvance set quite a lot of records in her prime but says now that she can't recall them at all. 'I think the only one left now is for the Stretton Skyline. Martin Stone told me the other week that our record for the Old Counties Tops mixed team only went a couple of years ago. I did this event on different occasions with Colin Valentine, Martin Stone and Alan Gillard.' She does still hold the record from Stretton, from 2005. In 1988 Ruth set records at the Buttermere Horseshoe race, the Three

Shires, Winter Hill, and the Coledale Horseshoe, all of which have been broken subsequently.

She then looks back at those female runners that left a lasting impression on her. 'I'm super-impressed by Helene Diamantides – her resilience, focus and self-sufficiency and endurance. Carol Haigh was always in a speed category that I could never get anywhere near. I was really impressed by Sally Newman, who just pipped me for first place in the World Masters. Lots of the women and it's great to see women's running developing in the way that it is doing.'

Ruth says she felt like she was doing something that she genuinely loved and that she was doing it for herself. 'There's no doubt that some people did think I was odd and it didn't fit with conventional expectations. It was also hard to find like-minded women to share the mountains with back then.'

One time she won the Wasdale Fell Race, Ruth was presented with her prize of a set of heated hair curlers by Danny Hughes. She shares her thoughts about those situations, and how she might react differently today. 'All the men were given North Face jackets and I had these heated hair curlers bought from Argos. I reminded Danny of this when I met him at the Susa International race many years later and we did (kind of) laugh about it. It's interesting for me to reflect back on this. At the time I said nothing out loud to Danny – I'd have mumbled to myself, said something to my friends and I think we all laughed a bit – but I didn't openly challenge it. Perhaps it would have seemed strident, and it might have looked like I was being mercenary. Fell running wasn't about the prizes, was it? Yes – I'd certainly say something today. It makes me think now about the cycle of perpetuating sexism and that if women are treated in a certain way, it leads to an expectation that they'll be treated in that way. In no way is this a personal attack on Danny. He was famously like this at times and yet very good company, we became friends. He was very much a product of his era and viewed things through the lens he inherited from that era. If in some way us early women fell runners were a presence to initiate a different way of looking through that lens, to cause question marks to be raised in assumptions that were being made, then that's all good.'

Ruth mentions that she didn't feel like a pioneer at the time, but that perhaps by, 'doing what I did in a minority, putting in some great performances I helped the ground-shift in women's fell running, helped attitudes to be questioned, and helped to show other women this is what they could do – something which I've become much more involved with recently.'

She then comments on other anomalies. 'It now seems bizarre that women should have been denoted as Vet category runners at the age of thirty-five. It was bizarre that women couldn't compete in a British Champs until much later than men, that they couldn't do the Ennerdale long course . . . the list goes on . . . bizarre that there was ONLY a Mountain Trial short course for women, that there were no perpetual trophies back in the day for all the classic races for women, and that the women's prize giving always took place last of all.'

Ruth reflects on her attitude to racing, and how that meant that she only won the British Championships once, in 1989, despite some brilliant racing results. 'I absolutely LOVED racing – far more than training. In my early years I was hopeless at resting or training properly. I just wanted to race. I had a complete lack of seriousness back then about the whole thing. In a way I found doing the British Champs a bit constraining. I wanted to do the races I liked but doing the Champs would force a pattern on that year and the outline of the year would take on a lack of spontaneity. I recall going all the way up to Scotland to run the Dollar Hill race, which was a Champs race, but running Goat Fell on Arran the day before and hoping the ferry would get me back to the mainland in time. I look back at myself now and shake my head in disbelief! There was a lot of travel involved, much of which I had to do on my own. I remember travelling to the final British Champs race in 1989 at Y Garn in North Wales on my own – pre-sat nav and old road atlas open on my lap. I arrived at what I thought was the venue only to be told by a local that it was the wrong Y Garn from the one I wanted! I literally arrived at the race venue with seconds to spare. Everyone was on the start line, so I think I simply ran out of the car and raced. Norman Matthews was there on the start line and told me that if I won that race then I'd won the Championship – not exactly the best preparation in that situation! I think, simply, looking back that there was much I wanted to do on the racing scene and planning out a year I saw how much the British Champs had to become a focus for the year if you wanted to do it.'

She reviews her own performance levels at different types of events. 'Until I learned to focus on road running and train properly, I think I was a real natural on the long races. Once I started running marathons more seriously and upping the speedwork I got much sharper. I was pretty good at medium [*fell races*] and good on the longs. Running on real rough stuff is not my strength which is why I have done really well on the continent, because they have races on paths and don't go down screes.'

Ruth rounds off her career review by considering her finest race or achievement. 'This is hard. It's a bit like being asked what's your favourite book. Different things for different times, different things for different purposes.'

'One race I'd put at the top of the list of favourites is the Skyrace Valmalenco-Valposchiavo. It's a 30km mountain race that starts in Italy and finishes in Switzerland and follows an ancient smuggler's route through the mountains. It was always hotly contested on the female front, with an international field. I never won it but always finished in the top three. I also loved the Tre Cime di Lavaredo in Italy, an uphill only race that finishes by three iconic rock towers in the Dolomites at 2,450m; and I love the Monte Rosa Skyrace for sheer landscape inspiration.'

'I always really enjoyed running at the Man v Horse (I had two wins).' She ran 2-40 for the Man v Horse in 2000, and just missed the record, and went back in 2001 and ran 2-38 which was a new record. She notes wryly that, 'from looking at the Wiki entry for the race ALL the male winners are listed and none of the female. Hey ho, *plus ça change* and all that!'

She says she also loves the Black Mountains Fell Race and the Llanbedr to Blaenavon for the reminder of all that good, classic fell races should be. Also, the classic race rounds such as Ennerdale. 'I'll never forget doing this early on and running with Joss Naylor – at one point he dibbed off into the mist and I followed him. That was it, I had to stick with Joss or be lost forever. "Come on lass" he said, "Stick with me." That gained me some places for sure.'

'There was a huge sense of achievement running a marathon to plan at London and finishing in 2-45. I was hugely pleased to run New York Marathon in 2-45 when I'd only gone to fun run it. I got a great sense of achievement breaking 35 minutes for 10km at Boughton on the Water (34-50 on a hilly course).'

Ruth digresses slightly, by saying, 'I just have to add – I think parkrun is THE BEST thing to have come out of running. It's inclusive, free, connects people, is unthreatening, community orientated and all the rest. Makes my heart sing.'

Ruth comments on race organising, which she is now involved with as she currently is Race Organiser for three races. 'This started when I was working at Atlantic College and we organised a 10km road race, which became quite famous. It was before there were masses of races. We hosted the Welsh 10km Champs one year. That gave me a real insight into what race organising is all about. I think the continentals organise races brilliantly. They somehow manage to get everyone out, have a great atmosphere and have food afterwards. It is like going to a party. So, I always work hard at doing it well and if you're a runner, you know what doing it well means. The cost of putting on races has really risen, and there is an expectation of immediate results. I believe strongly that we still need to push to keep fell running as "grassroots" as possible.'

She finishes discussing race organising by adding, 'there's a LOT to think about. It's a hard thing striking a balance between enabling people to be self-sufficient (one of the tenets of fell running) with good, responsible organisation in the modern day. I don't know what's harder – racing or organising to be honest!'

Coming right up to date, Ruth explained what she has been doing recently, which she sees as bringing together several strands from her life. 'The way that my business, Element Active, evolved is that I find I'm now running courses and events mainly for women, giving women confidence in the outdoors and an appreciation of our surroundings. I'm becoming aware that women are great perfectionists and won't often have a go until they feel completely ready. Under-confidence can feed under-confidence. We can be our own worst enemies. There's something about the supportive and collaborative nature of a women's group that feeds confidence.'

She is also involved in what she describes as, 'raising awareness of nature and a much-needed re-think about landscapes and diversification.' She reckons that a lot of landscape has been changed by farming, particularly by over-grazing by sheep. 'I have always been keen on nature. I have got 10 acres at the moment and we manage it for diversity. We have got the sheep off and are creating meadowlands. We are putting in hedgerows and planting new trees into the woodland and we have got these old oaks but there has been no regeneration as the sheep ate all the young trees. In a weird way I think I have taken this idea through from fell running. I get out now and don't run that much but I love a good walk uphill and a good look. I just love being outside.'

She concludes by commenting that she has had a really long, sustained, consistent and interesting running career. 'I think a lot of people in UK fell running think I dropped off the scene because I wasn't racing much on the UK fells after the mid-nineties. I didn't. I was Skyrunning in Europe. It's been fascinating to look back over a lifetime of running – most importantly, I always feel that if you lose the poetry in it all you've lost the sense and point. It's a bit like life really. Running and life ... don't lose the poetry ... there are lots of parallels.'

CHAPTER 13

Home and away

The 1990s: More Races Abroad. Race Start Issues.
First Dragon's Back Race Across Wales.
Profiles: Tricia Calder, Jackie Hargreaves,
Alison Wright, Elaine Wright

'An increasing number of women have consistently competed to a very high level in fell races throughout Great Britain.'

Thus wrote Judith Johnson in a letter in the June 1990 issue of *The Fellrunner*. She added that they had also had success at mountain races abroad. She argued that, 'it would therefore be timely if the FRA and fell race organisers recognised "the coming of age" of women and presented similar awards on a par with the men.' Among the suggestions made were: a female British Vets championships award, and a British women's team championship. Johnson finished by criticising the FRA further: 'let's have all women's records published for *all* the races, as well as the men's!'

Meanwhile, Tricia Calder had become a major force on the fell scene by 1990. At the Edale Skyline race in March that year she smashed Carol Haigh's previous record by six minutes. Tricia went on to be British Champion for 1990 and repeated the feat in 1991.

Tricia Calder had a real purple patch in June of 1990, setting new records at the Glen Rosa Horseshoe, Eildon 2 Hills and Cairngorm races. Later in the summer others were getting in on the act, with Sarah Rowell winning at Turnslack, and Cheryl Cook at Latrigg, both in new course records.

Tricia Calder

Tricia's contact information was passed to me by a mutual friend, and we agreed on emailing questions and responses. Tricia claimed to be 'not be very interesting', but like all the others I spoke to has her own story and is part of the bigger picture of the developing sport.

Tricia Calder (nee Aitken) was born in Berwick upon Tweed, and was brought up in Duns, Berwickshire. She did the usual athletics at school, being more of a 400/800m and cross-country runner than a sprinter. It was all very low key, with no training and just PE once a week. She did run in the Scottish schools' cross-country championships. She says that later she, 'moved to road running when marathon mania had kicked off. Even when moving to the fells my training was more on roads, although I used the small hills around where I lived.'

Tricia joined Edinburgh Athletic Club during her road running spell, then joined Hunters Bog Trotters for a short spell, but mostly was unattached. She had two children and started running the fells when she was around thirty years old. She says it was difficult fitting running in with a family. 'I still think I was a bit selfish, being away at weekends and racing a lot, but I usually trained later in the evening or when the kids were at school.'

Alistair Lorimar persuaded Tricia to try for the World Trophy when it came to Keswick in 1988, as it was the first time Scotland had put in a women's team. 'It was my proudest moment getting that first vest at Keswick. We were all up for the whole weekend and met other teams from all over the world. I remember the winner of the women's race [*Fabiola Rueda Oppliger, from Colombia*]. I came off the hill feeling great in my Scottish vest. It was a fabulous atmosphere.' She came seventh that day and improved to sixth at the next World Trophy event in Die and Chattillon-en-Diois (France). Her memories of particular race dates are a bit uncertain, but says, 'probably my best run was at

Ennerdale. I can't remember when it was, but I remember going OK that day. I did get to admire the talented runners I competed with.'

Tricia mostly trained on her own, saying she, 'hadn't a clue really, so just went out and ran and raced – so not the best science behind it. As to navigation, I can't get myself round a lamppost, but seemed to manage when I did mountain marathons with my brother, but he did the nav mostly.'

She says she had no problems with race organisers. 'It was a great time as I was accepted as a fellow runner. We all bunched together, and nobody cared whether you were a man or a woman. They were happy times, as from my point of view it was completely inclusive.'

Tricia was British Champion in both 1990 and 1991. 'I wouldn't have done the races to win twice without Peter Marshall, who encouraged me to go for them and drove me round the country both years. It was a grand experience as I met a lot of other runners and got to do races in Wales and England.'

She recalls that spell of races in June 1990, particular the new record at the Glen Rosa Horseshoe. 'There were loads of midges at Glen Rosa as it was a really hot day. Amazing scenery although you don't get to see it when racing. I now live near the Eildon Hills and always remembers the first part of that race from the rugby club, going up the steps. A hard old race.'

Other highlight races for Tricia were quite varied. 'A road race in Portugal. I made the Scottish hill running team a few times. Oh, I forgot, I also did the Snowdon home international.'

Tricia Calder (now Bell) ran on the hills for around a decade. 'I had a spell of windsurfing. No running races now, but I started cycling when I was around fifty-seven years old. I started doing triathlon in 2011 and am still doing that sport and love training in the hills around where I live now.'

Tricia Calder's story illustrates how the sport had become inclusive by the 1990s, and that women didn't normally have any equality problems by then.

Running in the Coledale Horseshoe race in June 1990 in her first 'real' fell race was an athlete who went on to have a long career, and make a big impact on the mountain racing scene. Jackie Hargreaves recalls how that race baptism went. 'I was first to the top, but the wind was so strong it kept blowing me over towards a little ledge with a steep drop. I remember being scared to death when a really skinny man grabs hold of me and whisked me out of the wind saying, "come on Jackie lass". I will always be grateful to him otherwise I think I'd still be stuck up there.' The V50 winner of that race was Ken Hargreaves, who would soon be her father-in-law.

Jackie Hargreaves

Jackie's was a contact that Norma Hughes gave me, as a fellow CFRA member. She agreed to precis her running career, which she planned to do by 'looking through all my running diaries, and gathering some information on the races that I did and any course records I managed.'

Jackie Hargreaves (née Reid) was born on 20 July 1965. She loved sport at school and was a good all-rounder, making the school teams for netball, cross-country and athletics. 'It was running that I excelled at, though', she adds. 'I won all the school's cross-country and long-distance track races and competed in the Cumbria inter-schools cross-country champs and finished second twice and won in 1979.' She represented Cumbria at the English Schools cross-country championships, finishing around seventieth, which she was pleased with as she felt she had run well and was proud to be running for Cumbria. 'I always felt a sense of pride and achievement whenever I ran for Cumbria then, and later England and Great Britain. I still to this day have a massive sense of achievement.'

Jackie was born in Carlisle and moved to Cockermouth with her four brothers and a sister and lived in a caravan for six years. 'We had no spare money, it was pretty tough, but we all got along. To make some money I got a job on a milk round, and they called me the fastest milk girl in the west. I ran everywhere carrying eight pints of milk at a time. I would do two hours on the milk round every day before school and I think this made me strong and gave me a good endurance background. I also got the house with the geese [on my round] and this usually turned into a sprint session running away from them!'

She admits to being bullied at school because she didn't have any friends from junior school, having moved from Carlisle, and also living in a caravan, so got called a gypsy. A difficult start in life which she has risen above, using running as a positive motivator. 'I hated school but loved sports day, as that was when I stood out and I could show them all how talented I was. I won the races I was put into, and also broke the school's 1500m record. I also won the discus and high jump, no one got close to me', she adds proudly.

Having decided she loved running so much she joined CASA (Cockermouth Amateur Sports Association). 'The coaches were absolutely fantastic and gave me so much encouragement, confidence and self-belief. My first coach was Carol Thompson, and she worked us really hard. We used to do a lot of handicap races, so I was always pushing myself to try and win.'

Jackie did a lot of racing from the age of twelve to fifteen, with her first race being a 1500m on the track. 'I remember my Mam saying, "bring me back the rose bowl". I was so nervous, but then the gun sounded and I was off. One girl was in front of me for the first and second laps then I got alongside her. We kept swapping places until the last lap, and I just went for it and won. I was ecstatic and my mum was so chuffed with the rose bowl [that I won]. I loved the race meetings. We were a small club, so my coaches used to put me in everything from the 400m, 1500m, 3000m, shot putt and discus. I remember having to throw my discus then sprint to the start of the 3,000m which I just made. It was good for getting the adrenaline going! My best times for 1500m were 4.46 and for 3,000m 9.46. When I left school I still competed for CASA on the track and for cross-country at county standard. CASA was a great club with a great atmosphere. Sadly, it has finished now, but I have great memories of it and the people who ran and supported it.'

After leaving school Jackie mainly ran for fun and did a few local races. 'I did the Cumbrian run and ran round talking to a lad who knew my brother. I didn't realise it, but I finished in second place. If I'd known I was doing so well I am sure I could have won it. I was mainly going out to discos at that time.'

Around this time Jackie Hargreaves ran her own paper shop at Moorclose, Workington. 'I still had to run to catch people who tried to pinch from the shop. I caught a few, including one lad who was on a bike!'

Jackie met her husband Rob, when she was twenty-five, at a circuit training class in 1990. He asked her if she wanted to go for a run with him. They chose Blake Fell which was only fifteen minutes from her house and one Rob trained on all the time. 'I only got a little way up before I was in oxygen debt and said to him, "this is too much like hard work!" We laughed and ran back down, which I enjoyed. I also enjoyed the views and the terrain. I like a challenge, so we tried again and then I got the bug. Rob encouraged me to do my first fell race. At the time in West Cumbria there was a race called Two Lakes, an anticlockwise run around Crummock Water and Buttermere. It started from Buttermere village, immediately going over Rannerdale. It was a really good race for first timers. I managed to win the race [first lady] and got the course record. I remember the adrenaline I got out of pushing myself and the great feeling of passing people. I knew then that I was going to love fell running, especially attending the prize giving where everyone was friendly and genuinely happy for me. I also ended up in the local paper!' Rob was already a member of Cumberland Fell Runners Association, so Jackie joined up too.

Jackie recalls that she has had loads of people who have inspired and helped her achieve what she did in running, the main ones being her coaches. In the early days it was Carol Thompson and Kenny Lowther at CASA, then Tony Daley, and Gary Byers. 'I used to go to Gary's for a training session, and I remember feeling very nervous, as I knew these sessions were always eyeballs out. I also used to run with some really good fell runners such as Willy Bell, Brian Thompson and Gary himself. We would do tempo runs on hilly back roads doing forty-five seconds on, fifteen seconds off, which was like a race. We also did hard hill rep sessions, some short and fast, some long climbs as hard as we could sustain. I always had someone in front to try and catch and someone behind who I didn't want to be caught by.'

Jackie and Rob had their first son, Alex, in 1995. 'He was my new inspiration and I somehow felt stronger afterwards. I remember I would breast feed him before training. Later when racing at the County cross-country championship in Carlisle, which I managed to win, Dave Farrell (the organiser) announced over the PA that the ladies' champion was in the stands breast-feeding her new baby. Talk about being embarrassed! I had really supportive friends and family to look after him and I also had a running buggy and used to enjoy passing other runners as I trained with Alex in it.'

Jackie's first international race was at Snowdon in 1997. She remembers the feeling of excitement and pride to be running for her country. 'It was such an honour. I was so excited that I remember running well to finish fourth and running down the finishing straight shouting "England, England" and punching the air! Pete Bland pulled me over after the finish and said he didn't ever want to see me finishing a race that well again, as I could have won it.' Jackie ran in the England team again at Snowdon four times between 1998 and 2004.

Later, in autumn 1997, she made the England team for the World Mountain Running Trophy in the Czech Republic. 'I was again ecstatic to be going to a global event and proudly carried the flag at the opening ceremony. I was beaming with pride. I was a vegetarian at the time and recall it was beef stew and soggy mash swimming in butter for our evening meal the night before the race. It turned my stomach, and I couldn't eat it. The Italians were eating fresh pasta cooked by their own chef! I went back to my room and ate a load of nuts, but it wasn't enough, and I didn't race well finishing a disappointing twenty-fourth. I just had no energy.'

Jackie continued running well into 1999, gaining selection for the England team in mountain running several times, and gained bronze medals in the W35 category in the World Masters mountain running championships in Innsbruck in 2002, and in the W40 category in 2005 when it was held in Keswick. [At the World Masters, athletes were running for themselves, not their country.]

They had their second son in 2001, and again this gave Jackie strength, inspiration, and a boost to her running. She remembers that having a baby just gave her more energy. 'I made the World Masters in 2002 in Berglauf, Innsbruck, in Austria. I had been training and racing well and knew I was in good shape going into the race. I set off feeling good and remember working my way through the field to third position after overtaking an American girl, and then the race was on for the bronze medal. I put my head down and worked hard to drop her, but she stuck to me like glue. I could hear her breathing and knew she was working hard to stay with me. I saw the 800m to go sign and picked it up again saying to myself, "you are not going to lose this medal, now come on dig in". With about 40m to go we were both flat out, but there was no way I was letting her get past me. I was absolutely knackered, but so chuffed at the same time.'

She then met noted coach Norman Mathews (in 2003) and says he was her biggest inspiration. 'I had a trial with him to see if I was even good enough for him to take me on. He really put me through my paces, and I was chuffed when he agreed to coach me. He changed the way I trained completely with a lot more emphasis on heart rate.' She then adds some notes she made at the time from this 'trial session' she did with him:

> Pulse 41bpm. 1m warm up. A few strides on toes, then 10 x 200m flat out, all at 33 to 34 secs. HR up to 180 and down to 120 after 2 mins. Felt good. Felt like I had run my heart out. Very surprised how hard this session was, but very happy because I didn't think I could run that fast. Back to Norman's for strength and flex assessment to see my strengths and weaknesses. 40 mins circuits, very hard. Enjoyed it. 6 miles (easy run). Felt good.[19]

Norman Matthews taught her how to train hard but smart. He would email or ring her every week to tweak things and see how she was. 'He was very supportive, but would also tell me off if I did too much or pushed my heart rate up too high, which I often did when I felt good, as I would want to beat my times. This had backfired on me a few times before Norman started to train me.'

One time being at the Knockdhu International in 1999. 'I had raced the Round Lattrig race in Keswick on the Wednesday before Knockdhu. I broke the course record finishing sixth overall, but then raced tired at Knockdhu, finishing a close second. Had Norman been training me he would have told me to forget Lattrig and save myself for Knockdhu. The two slices of soda bread for breakfast probably didn't help either!' Subsequently Jackie adds further details of her poor preparation for that race. 'I really messed up. I went to a wedding on the Saturday (1 May), then did a 1500m and a 3000m track race at Blackpool for Border Harriers in the Northern league (winning both) on the Sunday, followed by Penrith Beacon race on the Monday (3 May), winning and getting the course record of 28-15. No wonder I was still tired the Saturday after (8 May)

19. That is a pretty tough and testing session and the numbers show how fit Jackie was at that time.

for Knockdhu! My diary says I had a tight chest all week prior to the event.'

Despite Norman's tellings-off, Jackie always felt she could talk to him when things weren't going well, and training was feeling really hard. 'He would encourage me to stick with it, told me I would get stronger. It would eventually feel natural, but it was still very hard. He was really supportive and that gave me the confidence to follow everything he set out, including sending him a weekly report. This was really useful for discipline. Knowing someone is going to read what you have done and give you positive feedback, or a telling-off, helped to focus my training. It must have been a massive undertaking for him as he had quite a few runners that he coached at the same time as me.'

Discussing the proudest moment of her running career, Jackie comes back with running for the GB team in Korbielow Poland in July 2004, at the 3rd European championships. 'I had just made the team as the fourth counter and finished third counter in the race. I finished in twenty-first place overall and helped GB take the bronze team medals. I had written in my diary that we were fourth team going into the last lap and I was in twenty-seventh place. I wrote that I killed myself up the last climb and then overtook loads on the rough descent and helped get the team the bronze. What a feeling – I was over the moon.'

This recollection was quickly followed by her recounting what was probably the worst moment in her running career. 'I went to the World Masters in Sauze d'Oulx, Italy, in August 2004. I was in the best shape of my life and had loads of confidence after helping GB to that team bronze in Poland. I had won the County cross-country and other races, and in training sessions I had never run as well before. Disaster struck the night before when I caught my toe on the edge of the bed. It went right back on itself, was excruciating and I was rolling around the bed in agony and knew I had done something bad. I woke up the next day and tried to put my shoes on, but the pain was too much, and I knew I wouldn't be able to run. I was gutted to hear that the girl I had beaten in Poland had won the silver medal.' Not afraid to acknowledge disappointments, Jackie notes another one. 'I had been selected to run in Malaysia in Sept 1999. Unfortunately, I came down with a bug and the doctor diagnosed pericarditis, so I had to pull out. It was a worrying time, but thankfully everything cleared up.'

Jackie Hargreaves always did well in the Cumbria Cross-country county championships, winning six times between 1993 and 2004. 'In later years I entered as a Senior even though I counted as a Vet because of a strange rule they had. I was first over the line in 2001, only to be told I was first Vet, not the county champ. How could that be? I didn't settle for that and argued the point (it is crazy that I had to). I wasn't leaving until I got my medal, and afterwards I didn't take any chances and entered as a Senior and won another two championships. I was also the Mid-Lancashire Cross-country champ in 1996 and 1997. I also ran for the North of England a few times on the road, the first time being the Canterbury half-marathon in 1998. I finished in seventh after a bad run, but still had a not bad time of 1-21.' She also came thirty-third female in the London Marathon in 2000, in a time of 2-50.

Continuing the theme of unfair prize situations, Jackie cites the Rutland county show race. 'I finished the race in fifth place overall. We went along to the prize giving and watched as all the prizes were dished out. It was a generous prize list going down to tenth, and I stood there thinking they would call my name out, but then it was over! I went to ask about my prize to be told there isn't a prize for women. I pointed out I had actually finished fifth overall saying quite loudly, "how is it that a woman isn't worthy of a prize?". Eventually I was given twenty pounds, but the first man had collected one hundred pounds.'

On a roll now, Jackie says this was happening in a lot of races, including a British Championship in Wales with a massive field. 'I won a small Easter egg and the men got big ones! I remember thinking the greedy gits. I missed the prize presentation and CFR's Brian Thompson (an international fell runner himself) gave me my prize later. I thought he was winding me up and I laughed and said, "OK where's the real prize?" Hopefully, things have moved on now.'

Jackie Hargreaves achieved a performance level that was good enough to attract sponsors. She mentions that she was sponsored by New Balance and Allsports International for a few years.

Jackie mentions some of the people who inspired her in fell running, including Carol Greenwood, Ruth Pickvance, Helen Diamantides and Andrea Priestley. 'Carol was a machine. She would race two or three times a week and win all the races. Andrea and I would have some good battles. At the Three Shires race we kept overtaking each other, and she just beat me but in a really tough race. Helen Diamantides was also very inspirational. She wrote a piece in *The Fellrunner* and she mentioned I had changed fell running by turning up looking glam wearing bright red lipstick. It seemed to be a big deal back then and my club presented me with the lipstick trophy at the presentation night.'

Off the fells, Helen Pattison [later Helen Clitheroe] was a really big inspiration, as she and Jackie used to have some good battles at cross-country races. 'She went on to become a household name and one of GB's best track runners from 1500m to 10,000m, and also won the European indoor 3000m. I used to say to myself, "if Helen can do it so can I". A great inspiration', she recalls.

Jackie adds that Joss Naylor was also a big inspiration to her. 'He was our club president, and at the famous club presentation nights he would give talks and I would listen to his every word. He always talked so well and inspired us all. I helped him on one of his challenges, I think it was his 'sixty at sixty'. He is humble and was always very kind to me. His records speak for themselves. Kenny Stuart's records always amazed me, standing for so long, too.'

Concluding by talking about how she used to get asked to speak at presentations and at schools, Jackie says she used to really enjoy this as she could see that she inspired the kids to reach their goals. 'I used to run voluntary running sessions near where I live. They started to get a bit too popular, but all the kids really enjoyed it no matter what level they were at because I made it hard but fun. I remember being really proud watching them improve in races. One girl (a woman now), Charlotte Wilson, went from one hundreth place in the Cumbria Schools Cross-country to second the year after. She still runs now and says it was down to my influence. One lad actually wrote about me at school saying I was his sporting hero because I had helped him get faster.'

A fine thought to finish on from Jackie Hargreaves, who was a great competitor, and is one of several noted in the book who had a productive relationship with one of the top coaches who worked with fell runners in the era.

At the 1990 Wasdale race Helene Diamantides had a brilliant run, beating Angela Brand-Barker's previous record by eight minutes, and came in thirteenth overall on a very tough course. Helene's friend Alison Wright also completed a fast Bob Graham Round in 19-18 in that year, just seventeen minutes off Helene's record. This was just one of several endurance challenges that Alison Wright should be remembered for.

Alison Wright

Alison Wright is a friend of Helene Diamantides, and also has a unique niche spot in the sport. She patiently explained her background and experiences to me in a couple of email exchanges.

Born in North Harrow, on 2 September 1965, Alison Wright says she positively avoided running during most of her childhood, which was spent in South Wales. She became interested in running when she moved to Bakewell (Derbyshire) aged sixteen, but at that time the teachers didn't pick her for teams because she was the new girl they didn't know. She can laugh about it now, adding that, 'I was once accused of skiving off cross-country by a PE teacher, because I was back showered and changed long before anyone else returned.'

In her late teens Alison took up fell running, as she explains. 'I started competing in local hikes, like the Four Inns Walk (40 miles) and the Masters Hike (50 miles) through the Venture Scouts when I moved to Bakewell. You had to wear boots in those days and compete in a team. I had a few years winning trophies in these two events, while I was still at school.'

The summer before Alison went to university, in 1984, she got a job leading outdoor activities at Thornbridge Hall, a few miles from Bakewell. Colin Henson was in charge of the centre. 'He'd been part of the Venture Scouts scene in Doncaster, coaching and encouraging teenagers like Elaine Stephenson [*now Wright*]. He was also a marathon runner. I ran most nights with Colin over the summer and entered the Bolton Marathon with him. We had six weeks to train, but it was far too tempting to run in the hills instead of on the roads. So, when we rolled up to run the Bolton marathon on a very hot day, running on the roads came as a bit of a shock. It was my nineteenth birthday and I ended up on a stretcher completely dehydrated after taking 4-30 to get round.'

Despite this, a few weeks later Alison went up with Colin Henson and another friend to do the Three Shires fell race, which was organised by Elaine and Ian Stephenson. She had been running in the hills in the White Peak over that summer. 'I loved it! By the time I started university I was obsessed by the sport. I did some orienteering at university. I also did rock climbing a little in my teens, but started climbing more and mountaineering in my twenties.'

Alison soon joined Dark Peak Fell Runners, shortly after the Three Shires race. When she started she looked up to Pauline

Haworth, and later when she started doing Karrimors, Ros Coats. Although she feels she was never a pioneer, Alison did start a fell running club at Durham University.

Looking back now, Alison Wright reckons that her peak was probably between 1990 and 1991 before she went to Oman in 1992. 'I was in Macclesfield Harriers by then and trained with Mike Greenwood, Dan Parker, Karen Parker, occasionally Anne Stentiford (although I don't think she was around much), and sometimes Mark Hartell when he wanted a slower run (instead of chasing after my husband Mark McDermott). I was married to Mark McDermott for a while in the nineties but didn't use his name.'

She spent most weekends running in the hills somewhere, encompassing long days out, often racing or supporting Bob Graham Rounds. 'During the week it was a 10-mile hilly road run in winter on a Monday night (best time 67 minutes), or a shorter run across the fields in summer and a club run with MDOC [*Manchester and District Orienteering Club*] on a Wednesday night. I wasn't orienteering at this time – but the club runs at MDOC were worth joining the club for. I would sometimes fit in a few other runs, but often I was tired from racing at weekends. My navigation was not brilliant, but I find I'm better than the current generation who rely on GPS. I did a fair amount of orienteering at university but wasn't very good at it. It also spoils a good run!'

Alison considers her best races on the fells to have been winning at both Ennerdale and Duddon, one week apart in 1991. On the wider scene she adds winning the Three Peaks Yacht Race with Helene Diamantides, but is not sure which year, and also, 'doing the BGR in 19 hours 18 minutes in 1990 chasing and missing Helene's record! [*by seven minutes*] Also I had a Karrimor Ladies' pairs win with Helene in 1992 (and possibly one other time) and in the Mixed pairs with Dan Parker (the year before).'

Alison thinks her finest achievement in the sport was something completely different. 'I think I'd still say it was the Everest

Base Camp to Kathmandu record, in 1987. It was crazy especially trekking from Kathmandu to Shigatse in Tibet before the record run. It was an incredible adventure at that age [*she was just twenty-two years old*]. It took about a year to plan, and it was very hard to get any maps. I met up with Richard Crane, who had the record at the time. I am pretty sure I did most of the planning. I think a lot of people underestimated the record we set (which is why it stood for so long) and the amount of effort we put into nailing the route. Helene and I were training for three months in Tibet and Nepal before the run.'

Alison thinks that the Everest Base Camp to Kathmandu run had a massive impact on the British press. 'I think it was just seeing two young women doing something so adventurous. This was before it was de rigueur for students to take gap years. We were covered by every national newspaper with a full-page article on the back page of *The Times*. We even made the BBC evening news. Of course, these days that sort of coverage would have led to a massive social media following, but apart from a local news reporter and photographer showing up when I started my first job a few months later in Reading, life quickly went back to normal for both of us.'

When it comes to other people's achievements on the fells that impressed her, Alison gives some interesting nominations, 'Mike Hartley's Pennine Way record – because it took so long to be broken, and Mark McDermott's 24-hour Lakes record – because I saw the effort it took and there was the mental challenge of breaking Joss Naylor's "unbreakable record". More recently, Jasmin Paris for taking such a huge slice of time off the women's Bob Graham Round record. I always knew the record should be sub-17 hours, but it took until Jasmin came along before someone had the confidence to do it. Her 15-25 time rocked the fell running world, maybe even more than the faster time a few years later by Beth Pascall.'

Even before the Everest record Alison had another amazing achievement. She was the youngest BGR completer, at nineteen, in 1985. She explains how that came about. 'Colin Henson was obsessed with completing the BGR and got my interest. I had helped out on the Dark Peak caravan a few weeks before. My boyfriend at the time, Mathew Owen, also went along to help out, and was talked into going round (successfully). He was just eighteen. I probably would have been happy enough to join the Dark Peak attempt, but Colin was worried about them setting off too fast. So, I delayed my attempt at the round, to do it with Colin a few weeks later. I ended up joining an attempt with some friends from Nottingham, Roger Moates and I think the other guy was David Ramsden. Colin dropped out just after Wasdale (he completed the round a few years later).' Alison finished in 23-19.

Alison Wright is still competing. 'I've had years when I've done mountaineering or climbing. I also lived in Oman for five years, and had time off for injury or was distracted by work and family. At the moment, I'm trying to get fit again after a few years recovering from an ankle injury.' She concludes that her current fitness state is, 'slow but improving! I have been running a lot of races lately. I have dodgy knees and a dodgy ankle but am still getting out!'

Alison Wright is someone who may be under many people's radar, but stands out for doing the BGR so young, and also for showing the way by considering, planning and executing a challenge like the Everest Base Camp record. She was very much showing the way for others, directly or indirectly.

The team for the World Trophy, in Telfes in 1990, was announced as: Cheryl Cook, Kath Hill, Yvonne McGregor and Sarah Rowell. It was also announced that there would be both a women's team and Vets title to be run for in the 1991 British

Champs, to be scored as best four races from the six nominated ones.

The 1991 season witnessed a plethora of new course records, from a wide range of athletes, with the following all setting at least one: Helene Diamantides, Yvette Hague, Wendy Dodds, Sarah Rowell, Cheryl Cook, Janet Kenyon, Kath Hill, Jill Teague, Tricia Calder, Anne Buckley and Maureen Laney, and inevitably Carol Greenwood. One particularly stunning record was that set by Sarah Rowell at the Three Peaks race. She knocked sixteen minutes off the previous record, and finished in a magnificent twenty-second place.

Roger Boswell's race report for the Half Nevis race that July included a wry comment on the female winner that day. 'Ros Evans (Coats) paused in the home straight to collect her eldest offspring and carry him over the finish line – he was disqualified on account he did not run the first part of the race, and furthermore he accepted external assistance over the last bit.'

In the British Championships for the year Tricia Calder was first (with 48 points), from Clare Crofts (35), and Helene Diamantides (29). Calder also won the British Vets title. In the inaugural women's team championships Ambleside won from Dark Peak Fell Runners and Clayton-le-Moors. No one team dominated the team championships in the coming years though. The following five clubs won the remainder of the titles that decade: Keswick (1992 and 1993), Fellandale (1994), Pudsey and Bramley (1995 and 1996), Carnethy (1997, 1998, 1999) and Bingley (2000).

Helene Diamantides was part of that winning Ambleside team, along with Elaine Wright, Nicky Lavery and Julia Laverack. In a retrospective, published in *The Fellrunner* in February 2004, Helene makes some interesting observations: 'The problem at the time was how to encourage more women into the sport. We were in a vicious circle. There were not enough women entered in races to justify the organisers funding prizes to third place. Certainly, the introduction of the championships and increased depth of the prizes has contributed to participation.

Most women are paralysed by their own fear that their failure would be revealed, and team events have had a significant role in introducing women to the sport from mountaineering and road running backgrounds.'

Elaine Wright

Elaine Wright is an active race organiser, with husband Selwyn, and answered my questions by email in between those organising duties, which were just coming back into play after lockdown. Playing down her own running, she added, 'I'm not sure if any of this is useful to you, but it has brought back some great memories.'

Running in that winning Ambleside team was Elaine Wright (née Stephenson), who was born in Doncaster in 1963. In her mid-teens she joined the local Venture Scouts unit, the 68th (Doncaster) Scouts. They often competed in scouting distance events in teams of four, such as the Masters Hike (from Huddersfield), and the Four Inns (Derbyshire). 'We were increasingly competitive as the years went on and succeeded in winning sometimes. I can name many fell runners today who came into the sport through the scouting movement. Colin Henson, our Scout Leader, shared with us his enthusiasm and love of the outdoors and was a keen competitor himself.'

By the late 1970s the teams were competing in many LDWA events, along with events like the Fellsman. Elaine adds as an aside that 'looking back at historical results I notice Selwyn and I both competed in the Fellsman in 1979 and 1980, though I didn't actually meet [*my future husband*] Selwyn until my brother's Bob Graham Round in 1982.'

By the mid-1980s the 'running venture scouts' had all gone their own way, although a few of them ended up living in the Lakes. 'Colin meanwhile moved to Derbyshire where he became a valued member of DPFR and a very competitive veteran on the fells. At this stage I believe Colin was also a mentor to Alison Wright.'

Ambleside AC was established 1983, just before Elaine moved to the Lakes – in that winter. 'I held the post of Club President for three years in late 1980s, not a very onerous position but I managed to keep the guys in order during our short AGMs!'

In June 1984 Elaine completed her own Bob Graham Round, a couple of weeks after she had run in the Jura Fell Race. Elaine (Stephenson as she still was at the time) was the eighth female completer, with Bridget Hogge and Angela Brand Barker (Carson) also completing their rounds on the same day, running together. Fred Rogerson (the BGR administrator/guru) was 'going bananas', according to Elaine, as he was just so excited to see three women going round on the same day. Elaine also adds that she was the youngest female completer (at twenty-one years old) for a couple of years, until Alison Wright went round in 1986 at nineteen years old.

From the mid-1980s, Elaine's life was full of training and racing (with Ambleside AC), together with mountain marathons and the occasional trip to the Alps, for Sierre-Zinal or the Swiss Mountain Marathon. 'I just enjoyed competing in the Lakes with familiar faces each week. I won the odd minor west Cumbrian event – Blake Fell, for example, only to be timed out the following week at Ennerdale on the first checkpoint! I believe the race organiser did subsequently increase the cut off times and I did finish the race another year.'

By the late 1980s Helene Diamantides had moved to the Lakes and was running for Ambleside AC. 'Along with Keith Anderson they brought more focus to the club', says Elaine. 'The men were keen to compete in the British Championships and were successful in 1990 (and 1991 and 1992). The women wanted the chance to do the same. We had won the mixed relays in the Hodgson in 1989, which probably spurred us on. So, our small group of female Ambleside runners lobbied the FRA committee and put forward a motion for a Women's team championship at the FRA AGM in 1990. It was passed and the following year, in 1991, we competed in, and won, the first Women's Team Championship.'

That year Elaine had some of her strongest races: at Stuc A'Croin (finishing in 2-45); Borrowdale (3-54 for eighth place in a really strong field) and Thieveley Pike. 1992 was also a good year for training and racing: with Duddon (3-59); the Ben (2-10); Langdale (2-52); and the Hodgson Relay (Angle Tarn leg) first mixed team. She points out that Ali Crabbe, Nicky Lavery, Helene Diamantides, Julia Laverack, Mari Todd, Carol McNeill, and Sue Hodgson were the club's most active members, and that they were only a small team and mostly just had three runners at each championship race.

Then Elaine and Selwyn started a family, with Jack being born in 1993. 'I got back to fitness and to racing in the Lakes. Further afield our favourite trip was to Jura (we have been nearly every year since 1984). I've run it eleven times, though to my regret never beating 5 hours. It is now Jack's favourite too, along with the Three Shires Race.' Daughter Katie was born in 1996, and is also a fell runner and climber, having been a member of Ambleside women's relay team in the Hodgson for a couple of years. She is now in Sheffield and a member of Totley AC.

Elaine Wright has helped on many races on checkpoints over the years. 'Selwyn and I organise The Three Shires Race. My brother Ian came up with the route, and the first race was held in 1983.'

Having just read the updated version of *42 Peaks* (the Bob Graham Round booklet), Elaine says it brings back many memories: 'Helene Whitaker's Bob Graham Round, Paddy and Ramsay Rounds; and Anne Johnson's 24-hour Fell Record – all epic achievements. All the more so because these record-breaking challenges went quiet for many years, even though the number of females doing rounds increased steadily.'

Elaine explains that for the last twenty years or so she has used running and biking to keep some fitness, 'more so since selling the hotel in Little Langdale in 2018 and finding the joy of free time.'

She concludes that she feels very lucky to have been around from the early 1980s. 'I have been happy to have been running and competing on the fells in the Lakes amongst great friends at a time when the sport was growing in popularity, and an increasing number of females were running and some completing extraordinary challenges. At no time, then or now, did/do I feel I was in any way a pioneer.' A modest summary of a full life, with much time and effort given to the sport. Elaine Wright has done much for fell running over the years, helping immensely in encouraging women into the sport and increasing competition levels.

There were some amazing performances in the 1992 season, only some of which can be included here. Carol Greenwood had got over her injury and was on the record trail again, and Sarah Rowell was having a splendid season and set several new records. In April Sarah had a storming run at the Three Peaks race, finishing an impressive fifteenth overall in 3-19-11. Not a record, but it is the Three Peaks result that she considers her best performance for the event. At the end of the fell running season Clare Crofts was British Champion again, well clear of Angela Brand-Barker and Janet Kenyon.

That year also saw one of the most amazing performances by a woman, when Helene Diamantides and Martin Stone won the Dragon's Back race, a five-day event covering 220 miles from North Wales to South Wales, over many of the country's highest peaks. This is covered more fully in Helen's profile in this book, but it will suffice to mention here just one thing from Helene's humorous report in *The Fellrunner*, in her 'Guidelines to success in the race'. 'Don't win the first day. Especially if you are female as this enrages the opposition and spurs them on. It also upsets the paras who set up the showers (I thought they were SUPPOSED to be mixed).'

Reviewing the early days for fell running females, in two articles in *Up and Down* magazine that were published in 1992, Eileen Woodhead commented on women still not being fully integrated in the sport, citing the fact that there was no women's team championship until 1991. She added that, 'as well as women simply being not allowed at many races, would-be entrants had to contend with problems no man would put up with.' Looking at the scene in the mid-eighties, she noted that, 'despite the calibre of the individual competitors, women as a class were still very much seen as second class citizens. The debate on whether to give them a separate race, set them off before/after the men was still going on. To the women themselves it almost seemed as if they were considered a nuisance that might hopefully go away.' Striking a more positive note, Eileen added, 'but increasing numbers and determination throughout the eighties slowly but inexorably put women's fell racing on a proper footing, and showed a foretaste of the future. What the pioneers didn't realise was they were opening the floodgates.' Wise words indeed.

There was still an issue about race starts. There was an informal discussion at the 1993 AGM on 'separate starts for ladies at championship events'. There seemed to be disagreement among women runners on the matter, and some considerable bad feeling developing. Geraldine Walkington wrote a letter, headed '*Second class?*', which was published in *The Fellrunner* in February 1994. She suggested it would be a retrograde step, adding, that 'the cross section of women I have spoken to, do NOT want segregated start times and I feel very strongly that this has been foisted on the women's running sorority by a small number of women who might prefer to run in a smaller field. Not so long ago, women sought, and fought for, the right to run with the men, and the laws changed to accommodate this.'

Immediately below it there was a letter in support of the change from the recently crowned British fell champion, Angela Brand-Barker. On the next page (there were plenty of letters to the editor around this time, before social media was there for you to put your viewpoint out there) was a letter from Linda Lord asking for better treatment for lady vets in races, concluding that an improvement in this area might, 'also serve to encourage back into racing those women who have had a break to raise a family, and indeed, the women pioneers of early fell racing days who have permanently hung up their studs.'

The split starts issue rumbled on, and was discussed, but unresolved, at the FRA committee in 1994. Meanwhile, on the racing front, Angela Brand-Barker had become the 1993 British Champion and managed to retain her title in 1994.

Despite not doing enough championship races to finish better than tenth, Carol Haigh (now Greenwood) had an amazing season, amassing new course records, seemingly at will – twenty-three at one count. One of these was at Snowdon on 24 July, where she set about her own record, set back in 1986 – a record that some, including race organiser Ken Jones, reckoned would never be broken. *The Fellrunner* reported the 1993 race in detail, with comments from Carol:

> The race was held as an International again. "I was lucky enough to be asked by Manager Pete Bland to run for the English team. That was great because I knew that there would be fierce competition among the teams." As the race progressed though, Carol quickly found that the competition she was up against was not of the other *female* teams. Out of the 450 competitors, Carol turned at the summit in 39th place, 4 minutes ahead of the next lady. A glance at her watch told Carol that she was 10 seconds inside her record ascent time of 47-52.
>
> As Carol raced down the mountain she remembers, "I just kept concentrating on keeping from falling or twisting my ankle or anything silly, but I could feel the soles of my feet getting hotter and felt my heels beginning to blister. As I hit the steep road section at the bottom, my left heel seemed to pop! By now I'd caught Gavin (Bland) and he gave me lots of encouragement, though he'd fallen quite badly and the blood from his injuries was spattering onto my lovely white England vest."

> Carol had shattered her previous record by 2 minutes, finishing in 36th position overall. The 'pop' she had felt was as the whole of the skin on her left heel came away, leaving a neat raw area 2 inches long and extremely sore.

Despite the pain she made up two places on the run past the Royal Victoria Hotel to the finish. Her summit time – of 47-07 according to the Snowdon race website, not as incorrectly noted in the race report – has never been beaten in subsequent races, although Emmie Collinge managed 46-55 in the uphill-only Super Cup in 2015. Carol's Snowdon race record time of 1-12-48 has never been beaten.

CHAPTER 14

More challenges

More Big Rounds: Paddy Buckley, Charlie Ramsay, and a Bob Graham. Let's Do All Three.
Profile: Helene Diamantides

'She finished with a fast run down from the last peak', was the conclusion of another major challenge round.

Fifty years after Bob Graham did his round, a Welsh equivalent was devised by Paddy Buckley, with the help of Chris Brasher. The Paddy Buckley Round is a circuit of just over sixty-one miles with 28,000 feet of ascent, taking in forty-seven summits in North Wales. Wendy Dodds was the first to complete it in May 1982. Wendy had set out with Bob Roberts and Paddy Buckley himself. However, Roberts had to retire with stomach trouble and Buckley with cramp. A report of the effort in *Compass Sport* magazine notes how it panned out, after the other two runners had dropped out. 'Wendy, now solo, continued to Moel Eilio from where a slight navigational error took her too low into Llanberis instead of to the youth hostel where her support team waited. This resulted in a climb back up the hill and a falling behind on the time schedule.' Wendy came down that last hill to finish at Capel Curig in 25 hours 38 minutes.

The third of the big national rounds is the Charlie Ramsay Round, in Scotland. It takes in twenty-four Munros (mountains over 3,000 feet) on the ridges of the Grey Corries and the Mamores. The round is essentially an extension of Tranter's Round, which was 36 miles with 20,600 feet of ascent, completed by Philip Tranter in June 1964. Charlie Ramsay decided to make it more of a challenge and added five more Munros to make it twenty-four Munros to complete inside 24 hours. This version was established in 1978 by Ramsay, a member of Lochaber Athletic Club. The route is 56 miles and has 28,500 feet of climbing, which he completed in 23 hours and 58 minutes.

In July 1989 Helene Diamantides became the first female and the fourth person to complete the Ramsay Round setting a new fastest time of 20 hours and 24 minutes with Mark Rigby. The Ramsay has proved much less popular than the Bob Graham over the years, with the second female completion in July 2000, when Jane Meeks finished with just one minute to spare. Hers was only the twenty-sixth Ramsay Round completion.

That same year (1989), Helene Diamantides was the first female to do the Paddy Buckley Round in less than 24 hours, following completions by Sue Walsh and Wendy Dodds, both over 24 hours. Remarkably, Helene's Paddy Buckley Round was part of a triple of all three Big Rounds (Charlie Ramsay, Paddy Buckley and Bob Graham) that she completed that year all within three months.

Helene Diamantides

I had spoken to Helene a few times before in my other book research, and re-connected with her to cover her activities in the earlier days. She also very kindly introduced me to two other runners that I subsequently interviewed. Through a series of emails she patiently provided the extra information I was wanting about her running.

Helene Diamantides was born in 1964 in North Yorkshire, but she spent most of her childhood outside England. She lived in Ghana and later Greece, spending much of her youth there. Helene once described Greece as, 'an environment where women weren't allowed to do anything that involved sweating, let alone stand on the same start line as men and embark on an endurance test in which being aggressive and competitive were essential to success.' As a teenager she was Greek Pentathlon Champion, also excelling at 400m hurdles and cross-country.

Helene took part in many different sports and was good at a multitude of things. 'It tended to be individual sports though. At the time we did pentathlon not heptathlon, which I tried to continue with when I was at Durham University. I used to get the train and bus to Gateshead for a while, but the travelling put me off and actually I wasn't that good at it.'

There are often contrasting backgrounds in the athletic prowess of athletes, and Helene's gene pool is no different, as she explains. 'My mum could have been a very good runner. My mother's side are incredibly long lived and have always done manual jobs like boatbuilding. My father's side were as inactive as it was possible to be.'

She lived in Greece, home of the marathon, and ran one at the age of sixteen, raising money for the school trampoline. 'The school used to have a marathon over the original course, and kids and staff used to do it. I wanted to do it when I was fifteen years old, but my parents quite rightly said no. They said if I trained, I would be allowed to do it the following year. I trained and ran with my PE teacher and found it a miserable experience. I can still remember how awful it felt.'

Fell running came onto Helene's radar when she went to New College Durham to train as a teacher and joined the University fell running club at Alison Wright's instigation. 'I was eighteen and we trained together for the Sheffield marathon [which Helene won with a time of 3.30] along with other things including fell running. The orienteering club was very strong, but I wasn't that good at it so I joined the mountaineering club, as they went to nice places. I made good friends there.'

Helene's introduction to fell racing was through some of the standard fell races, although she was uncertain of dates when asked recently. 'Kentmere was my first race in 1984 I think. Alison [Wright] and I went orienteering in the morning and she wanted to do the race, so persuaded me to do it as well which I enjoyed. I think I did Buttermere Sailbeck next and Alison then persuaded me to do the Three Peaks. You have to have experience to enter this race which Alison had and I certainly didn't.'

Helene claims to have had no interest in the fell championships, and just enjoyed the running. 'I wasn't really at that standard. I joined Dark Peak Fell Runners, and was thrilled to be third counter for the club once when we won a prize. It was just fabulous and unexpected.'

Her partnership with Alison Wright took them to a win in the 'A' Class of the Karrimor International Mountain Marathon in Galloway in 1986, in what were atrocious conditions. She recalls it well. 'Nearly everybody else dropped out. It was one of the Galloway years! We got washed down the river under Merrick. Not good memories. We pitched our tent over a ditch, taking turns sleeping in the ditch. It was an awful night. Because we had come from mountaineering we had good kit, such as thick Gore-Tex jackets. I relied on Alison to navigate. I can now navigate but look up to someone like Steve Birkinshaw, as to the standard we should be aiming for. I do still practise.'

In 1987 Helene completed her first Bob Graham Round in 22-18. She had done a reasonable amount of preparation for the round. 'I hadn't been on all the tops but knew where the sections went. I probably couldn't have navigated my way round it all at the time even though I was safe and could have got off the hills, but I wouldn't have known the best lines. I basically got taken around.'

On that round she went up Broad Stand, using her experience as a climber. 'I think I stood on Martin Stone's shoulders and then hoiked him up,' she laughed. 'I think we left someone behind there. On each of my rounds I lost pacers.' The weather wasn't great, and photographs show them wearing thermals. Helene thinks people's attitude to using Broad Stand has changed, 'perhaps because it has got worse, much more slimy and very worn.'

Her supporters were people she knew mainly from climbing and who advised her not to set off with two or three other people. 'I believe that if there is more than one person setting off it can go wrong very quickly and I now say I am a particular person's pacer and make it quite clear.' Her view is that people can tend to go faster at the wrong time, for instance. She agreed with a comment that Billy Bland had made to me: that holding your own 'agenda' is really important.

Later that year she went with Alison Wright to Nepal to attempt to break the record for running from Everest Base Camp to Kathmandu. This is a 188-mile (303km) route which includes 42,000 feet (13,000m) of ascent. Both women completed the route in a record of 3 days and 10 hours. 'The Crane brothers had done the run from Kathmandu westwards to complete the Himalayan Chain. We noticed though that the Cranes had also done the Everest Base Camp run and beaten the previous record and thought that sounded interesting.'

She then talked about her ideas on going it alone on the Bob Graham Round in 1988. She recalls talking to Fred Rogerson. 'I was concerned about how to get a solo round validated.' Fred just laughed at her and asked, "Why would you cheat?". 'I explained I would leave cards at the road crossings so that if I didn't turn up someone would know which section I was lost on.' The only person who knew she was setting off was Andy Sheath, so that if she didn't ring at the end he could send out the rescue. It was planned and delivered as a solo/unsupported attempt. She had done a lot of practice navigation on her own, and was now confident. 'On the day really early on, I was climbing Skiddaw and took a bearing on a sheep in the dark,' she laughed. 'Fortunately, it didn't move before I got to it. That was a bit of a wake-up call.'

Helene's aim was to get round in under 24 hours, as no women had done that solo unsupported. Using the 1987 schedule she tried to see how much she could take off each section. However, Helene was really nervous setting off in the dark. 'I thought if I ran as fast as I could, I might be able to finish before it gets dark again and not have to navigate in the dark when I am tired. The worst patch was going up Red Pike; it is such a long pull. As I got to the top the Ennerdale race was going through, and it was a very hot day.' Here she had a conversation with one of the race marshals. 'He (and I don't know who it was to this day) spotted me, "are you doing what I think you are doing?", he asked. "You are nearly home". I felt fine running into the Moot Hall and I honestly felt better than I had on any of my other rounds. I had no idea what the ladies' time was', she claimed. She had set a new BGR women's record of 20-17.

'I still think that I enjoyed that solo round the most,' was her take on it. 'I could stop and eat when I wanted to, and where I wanted to. It wasn't at road crossing points, interestingly. It was usually where there were streams. I trotted through Dale Head and stopped at Hindscarth, as that was a better spot. The natural stopping points were when I was hungry, and I am sure that helped me have a fast round. I was eating when I wanted to and needed to, rather than when was convenient for a crew. I genuinely remember feeling OK and thinking this is rather nice.'

Looking back, would she choose to do anything differently with regard to that solo round? 'It is funny, because everything now is geared to times,' was her response. 'That wasn't my plan. I just wanted to get round the Bob Graham. I never set my sights to do a fast one, ever. I don't think you can set off to do a fast time like that – maybe some people can. I am sometimes not very confident, and my intention has always been to get round as comfortably as I can. I always feel that you are just a gnat's crotchet away from disaster, especially the further you go. The bigger, the longer, the harder it is, the closer you tread the line between having a good run and success, and a dire time and failing. You are only ever a twisted ankle, a blister, or a chafing away from failure.'

She didn't recall there being any point in the solo round when she thought she wouldn't succeed. 'It is incredibly easy to appear arrogant when you are young. I suppose it was because I honestly thought I could do it. It crossed my mind that I *might* not get round in 24 hours. I knew I could by then, so I just wanted to see if I could get round on my own. It wasn't for anyone else, or for a time, it was just for me. I think people make too much of these things sometimes.' She didn't worry about nutrition, just ate what was on the supermarket shelves. Nor did she worry about hydration, just drank water out of streams. There was obviously a need to navigate, as there was no GPS then.

Helene decided to carry a heavy cagoule, a bivvi bag, and a first aid kit. 'I thought if I do prang myself (there was no mobile phone then), I am going to be out at least twelve to fourteen hours before someone found me. I could stuff the bivvi bag with heather for insulation if I needed to, lying on the hillside with a broken leg.'

With her seeming desire to increase the level of challenge perhaps she had thought of doing a winter round? She had, and chuckled at the thought of it, as she told the story of that effort.

'I set off in January 2013 to do a solo/unsupported winter BGR. I had done all the legs in summer, and been round all the legs I was likely to have to do in darkness. Someone was going to check from a distance as I went through the road crossings for safety. I had a GPS for verification and also in case I got lost. I carried an ice axe, crampons, and kit weighing about 6kg. I set off up Skiddaw on a beautiful warm night. Because it was so warm the mist was thick and I kept wandering off the path (hidden under a deep layer of snow) going up Skiddaw, which wasn't a great start. I was well within the time at the top, but went slightly wrong coming off, and I remember thinking this is such a great night for a night run, but wouldn't it be better if I *wasn't* doing the BGR.'

'I carried on up Blencathra, and a shooting star went past which was glorious, and then I went back into the clag. All the time on that first leg I was well up on the schedule but kept dreading the next section along the Dodds, because of the dark and snow. I thought, 'The next section in the daylight will be icy but that is OK. Then it will be dark again and that will be grim.' I am thinking 'I am not looking forward to this'. All I can think about is how miserable the rest of this run is going to be. If I was only out for a little run I would be really enjoying myself. I had the revelation that I could go home – so I did. I had a really nice run out and bumped into someone else, who was also doing a solo BGR that night. He was making navigational errors too, so we caught up and ran off Blencathra together. So that was my attempt. It really is horrible out there in the dark for hours on your own. I had put a lot of effort into making sure my equipment was right, investing in decent head torches and spare batteries, and keeping them warm. I was ready to go, but it was just too miserable to continue.'

In 1988 Helene won both the women's events in the 31km Mount Cameroon race and the Mount Kinabalu race in Borneo; and she came third in the 100-mile (160km) Hoggar 'Super Marathon' in Algeria. 'There was never any question of a short course for the women at any of these events abroad,' Helene notes.

Then in 1989 Helene went really big, completing the Big 3 Rounds in one year. The first of her three was the Ramsay Round. She was then only the fourth person to successfully complete it and did so in a time of 20-24. One month later she ran the Paddy Buckley, which she completed in 20-08, beating the men's record (held by Adrian Belton) by two hours. Then finally the BGR was completed in 19-11, for a new women's record. Three rounds within a couple of months, an incredible achievement.

The following is from Helene's own account of her Bob Graham Round record, the last of the three:

> In the fell running tradition the decision to 'go for it' was made a mere 14 hours before the start. As gale force winds and showers were forecast it seemed ideal to make the attempt. Adrian Belton had decided that 18 days rest between records was excessive and he was also keen to complete his hat-trick. Hence a truce was drawn up and a mutual support party organised.
>
> Dawn broke descending to Threlkeld, where we had a wonderful breakfast of creamed rice and tea. We spent the Helvellyn section chasing Tim Maitland on his solo round, when I wasn't busy competing with him for the most pees per round.
>
> The cloud lifted, and with it our spirits. The work-to-schedule

> ruling by the pacers' union necessitated a mid-shift handover from Bowfell to Wasdale. I was bonking well up Red Pike, and Great Gable loomed out of the mist again, and again, as we had to double back to the summit to sort out a navigational error.
>
> At Honister a reception committee of 'I'd rather do the Buttermere' types waited like vultures at a painful death. Their encouragement propelled us up the final lumps and on to Robinson. The sun on the heather in Buttermere and the glowing evening light on the hills almost made it worthwhile.
>
> A quick change of shoes at the road, pick up more loo roll, and grit the teeth for the grind back to Keswick. The finale: dodging chip eating grockles, and ice cream wielding children, on the last 100m to the Moot Hall. A highly appropriate finishing tape of loo roll summed up my thoughts on the 3 completed Big Rounds.

Helene claims that doing the Big 3 Rounds in a year came about by accident. She wanted to have a go at the Charlie Ramsay Round:

> I didn't know Mark Rigby at the time, but Martin Stone said he was prepared to pace me on the understanding that if he could keep up he would continue to the finish. I said that was fine, and if necessary I would continue solo. We set off up Ben Nevis and along the ridges, and took turns to carry one rucksack between us. Rob Brown did the road support and met us for the tricky descent off the final summit. In the car going back we talked about the Welsh Round, and whilst it wasn't deliberately planned to be in the next month, I felt it would be good to use my current fitness. Once I had completed the Welsh Round I thought it really would be nice to finish it off with the third, so Adrian Belton and I teamed up for the BGR.

When asked about her training, she said 'what I did every weekend was to go for 12 hours plus Munro bagging running sessions. That was normal background for me, but when training for something specific I would do 4 days of that consecutively'.

'It was a really nice to finish all three rounds,' she says. 'I wasn't going for a time. I was on a high as everything was going well. We had a lot of friends out helping both Adrian and I do our three rounds that summer. It was like a party.'

Some people clearly wouldn't be able to do a decent fell race after a round, but Helene picked up after the first round and did two more right off. She claimed that she just didn't worry too much, just expecting everything to hurt. 'I think people analyse things too much these days, but this may push on performances', was how she looked at it. She has always put in the homework she feels is needed for an event. She worked on the basis that if she could get round the Charlie Ramsay Round she was probably fit enough for the others. Each one is progressively about an hour less than the last, according to perceived wisdom. 'The Charlie Ramsay is the hardest, by a long shot. Each hill is a good big hill. The technical difficulty both in navigation and terrain is significantly tougher. It is a hard round for pacers and runners alike. If you have a pacer who can support you on the Ramsay they can probably do it themselves. The Bob Graham isn't quite like that. You can pop up and do a couple of tops and pop home again and be done, none the worse for wear. The Welsh round is pretty rough. You find yourself dropping to a spot height which is defining the round and it is a bit frustrating.'

By 1990 Helene was playing with the big guns. When Hugh Symonds did his big run (the first continuous traverse of the 303 mountains of Britain and Ireland) she paced him on half a dozen of the Scottish Munros, along with Adrian Belton, Martin Stone, Mike Walford, Martin Moran, Mark Rigby and many others. 'We were all involved as the fell scene was quite small then, so all the fell runners knew what he was doing, and I think everyone helped out at some point. We all wanted to, it was such a remarkable thing to do.'

Apparently, people had often suggested Helene should do an extended round to take that record, but it didn't really fire her imagination. 'To do something like that you have *really* got to want to', was her view. She was also pretty clear on why many more do the BGR than the other rounds. 'Access is the biggie. It is easy to get people in and out, and is close to population centres. There is also the weather to consider as the further north you go the bigger the hills, the more iffy the weather and the smaller the window of opportunity.'

Helene was interested in running the Cuillin Ridge at one point, as no female attempts had been made. 'I thought of the Black and Red Cuillin as a round for a while. I went along the Cuillin Ridge with Rex Strickland and Adrian Belton and it took us fourteen hours to do just that. Hats off to anyone who can run it quickly.'

The next few years included some fell race records set by Helene. In 1990 she set a course record in the Wasdale Fell Race which stood until 1997 when it was beaten by Mari Todd. Helene equalled the Borrowdale record in 1991 and took the Lairig Ghru record. She also set a new record for the Langdale race in 1989, which was only beaten by Victoria Wilkinson in 2016. 'Langdale is raced in September and so was after the 3 Big Rounds. Every year I expected the record to go when there were good weather conditions. I am quite proud of that run as there had been a couple of championship races over the course in that time.'

Helene shared these memories of her record breaking Langdale run:

> I remember setting off on a misty day with wet rocks and thinking 'I shouldn't be up here with the fast men'. I was running with Scoffer I think and surprised myself by feeling OK. I decided to keep ticking over and see what happened. Going over Martcrag Moor it was really misty and I wasn't sure of the line as there was no trod then. I dropped back a little, but decided I'd better hang on to keep the line. Running towards Pike O'Blisco I kept thinking, 'I feel absolutely fine'. It was one of those days we all train for and hope is going to happen. One of those rare occasions where everything conspires to be absolutely right. I loved it. I had no idea what the record was.

Helene has had a brilliant set of results at the Borrowdale Fell Race, winning four times (in 1991, 1992, 1999 and again in 2006), with her 1999 time of 3-14-45 the second-fastest ever in the women's race, and within ten seconds of Menna Angharad's course record from 1997. Helene doesn't seem to get enough recognition for the fell running records she has set.

She tells an interesting story from 1999 when she set the Borrowdale record. 'I really badly gashed my foot coming off Scafell. I had cut through my shoe and into my arch on a pointed rock. I was coming along to the finish, hobbling along and Scoffer said, "come on Helene you can beat the record". I just tapped my watch and said, "No I've missed it". Scoffer turned round and said to Martin Stone, "I think Helene needs a new watch". I hadn't set off to go for the record but I wish I had known I was that close. I think sometimes if you set that sort of target for yourself and you don't achieve it you feel you had a bad run. I don't work well that way.'

In 1992, with Martin Stone, Helene entered the Dragon's Back race, a new 220-mile (350km) five-day race down the length of Wales. They had to navigate through foul weather and fought back to win after losing the lead on the final day, in 38 hours 38 minutes. The quickest female pairing were Sue Walsh and Wendy Dodds in 54 hours 6 minutes. The slowest finishers over the full course took over 68 hours and only sixteen of the thirty-two pairs who started made it to the finish. Helene and Martin had run together quite a lot and knew they ran well together:

> Martin was a last minute partner as my original partner fell through and I had asked Martin to be on standby, having reconnoitred the whole course. Everybody was racing flat out with different days suited to different people and pairings. Sometimes we may have pushed too hard and suffered, so others took advantage and then suffered too. It wasn't just us that were pushing. Mike Walford and Mike Cudahy were there, it was hard racing.

Remarkably, Helene Diamantides came back in 2012 to complete the Dragon's Back race when it was revised, finishing first lady in fourth place overall, twenty years after the first race. The Dragon's Back in 2012 was announced more than a year in advance. Helene asked her husband Jonathan what his thoughts were on her doing it. It would have been impossible without his support and her worry was the commitment required before the race, when the hard work, time and effort is put in. 'We then sat down and worked out how to get fit and planned the races up to it. I reconnoitred the mountain sections with the help of Cath Worth as I needed to fix the pattern of the event, and also buy a new set of maps as mine were twenty years out of date.'

In 2012, 'I was far more scared doing it as an individual, yet happier in that if it all went horribly wrong I would not be letting anyone else down. If I was injured, which there was a chance of, I'd rather drop out and know I could carry on running for another ten years than feel I had to keep going and get completely knackered for someone else's sake. Trying to tie in with someone else for training wasn't going to be easy either.' This time when she came to Crib Goch on the Dragon's Back she had the wobbles, saying she couldn't do it. 'I had previously done it in winter with my hands practically in my pockets. Fortunately, there was a lovely guy there who talked me through it. I was gripped having lost my head for heights since having a family, so any further ambitions won't involve rock climbing, that's for sure!'

When it came to training, Helene was mainly self-coached and, until she joined Ambleside AC at the end of the 1990s, it wasn't very structured. She just ran. She reckoned the folk at Ambleside were very good for her. 'They showed that you could have fun, train hard and get good results. I got back to track sessions in order to get faster on the fells as I realised I needed to do structured training. I also had a very memorable conversation with Anne Buckley in the early nineties over a pint after the Borrowdale race. She was saying essentially, that fell runners didn't know how to train, and until they did, she would always beat them on short races. I knew she was right.'

At the time Helene was trying to get into the teams to represent her country on the hills and finding she couldn't make it. She was even taken aside by someone who said, "You are more of a carthorse than a racehorse". 'I thought I will show you. People were representing my sport seeing it as an easy vest, track runners for instance who could run up a hill. I spent a lot of time training more seriously and represented Scotland for nearly ten years, mostly on the fells, but also at cross-country. I needed to make what I did count as I was always short of time. I had no time for junk mileage and I by then had found I could not train by doing the high mileages so popular back then.'

Jack Maitland was an early influence, after he showed Helene his diary in the 1980s. 'I remember being in the Sahara desert doing the 5-day Hoggar Super Marathon Stage race and he was writing something. He was keeping a training diary, with intensity, heart rate, how much sleep he was getting. I thought maybe I should be doing that. Better notes helped me understand what worked for me.' It was also due to watching Jack Maitland that made me think my style was OK. 'I saw him, all arms and legs hammering off Mount Cameroon at phenomenal speed, nobody told him to change.'

Then she met Martin Hyman, who she thinks was one of the most unorthodox people she has known. Instead of doing things by the book, he would question her on why she was doing what she did, recoveries for instance. 'He was a major force in changing what I did and how I did it. He would suggest HR monitor sessions I could do on my own. He was really understanding about me wanting to do things differently. I wanted to do the World (Mountain) Trophy and the World 100km Road Championships a week apart. That meant doing the selection for one, and doing a 35-mile road race two weeks before the World Trophy, which wouldn't be acceptable now. He thought it would work for me and it did, resulting in my best placing in the World Trophy with twentieth in both events. If I hadn't had Martin as a mentor, I wouldn't have achieved nearly as much.'

Later, when building up to the Dragon's Back in 2012 she

20 Angela Brand-Barker with the British Fell Championships Trophy, 1983.

21

21 Bridget Hogge at Moel Eilio, 1984.
22 Véronique Marot at the Sierre-Zinal race, 1984.
23 L–R: Eileen Jones (Burnip), Eileen Woodhead, Katy Thompson, Karin Goss (Taylor), Maureen Ashton. Front: Linda Bostock, at the Shepherd's Skyline race, 1988.

40
CA
1184
22

CLAYTON-LE-MOO
525
507
586
634
CLAYTON-LE-MOORS
509
587
23

24 Carol Haigh at the World Cup race, Keswick, 1986.
25 Helene Diamantides on the Everest base camp run, with Alison Wright, 1987.

25

26 Sue Parkin at Coniston, 1990.
27 Trish Calder at the Edale Skyline, 1990.

27

28

28 Ruth Pickvance at the Chew Valley Skyline, 1990.
29 Kirstin Bailey at the Sedbergh Gala race, 1987.

29

30 Anne Stentiford on her 24 hour Lake District Peaks Record round, with Colin Ardron, 1991.
31 Elaine Wright at the Sierre-Zinal open race, 1991.
32 Jackie Hargreaves, venue and date unknown.

31

32

33

33 Sarah Rowell at the Three Peaks, 1994/96.
34 Angela Mudge winning at Sierre-Zinal, 2001.

UBS
MIGROS
118
UBS
SKY RUNNER WORLD SERIES
SKY RUNNER WORLD SERIES
UBS MIGROS
UBS MIGROS

35 Nicola Davies at the Ingleborough (Inter-Counties) race, 2003.
36 Angela Brand-Barker handing the Olympic relay torch to Joss Naylor, 2012.

37 Christine Menhennet at the Ring of Steall race, 2016.
38 Wendy Dodds at the Three Peaks race, 2021.

worked with the late Pete Shields, a coach from Ilkley Harriers. She likes to know what is coming up and train properly. 'I did fourteen months of training with Pete's advice. I think it is invaluable having someone who can be objective telling you when something is not good and explaining why. I have had success and know what works for me, but you can't do what you have always done – your body changes and time constraints change. I think I got it about right in 2012.'

Helene reckons that her ability to run uphill and downhill has changed over time as well. She felt she was a downhill demon and used to love hammering down the hills, catching most people including the men. Later she counted on being able to climb past people. 'After you've broken a couple of bits, and your knees ache and your back jars, it is just uncomfortable.'

When Helene was funded as a Scottish athlete they repeated her lactate threshold testing and VO2 max a couple of times because they couldn't believe it was so low. She says she can't remember the numbers. 'It was part of the 100km enhancing performance programme. I had the lowest VO2 max on the 100km squad so they gave me threshold sessions but I couldn't do them. I was sick and jelly legged. However, it seems that I was unusual in my ability to sustain a level close to the threshold for very long periods of time. I was just efficient.'

She competed in a good few KIMMs, but it was not a main focus for the year. It was a challenge to see how well she could do, and she saw it as a good way of training. She ran with many different partners, which she felt was part of the fun. 'I think if you know the person you can anticipate whether it will work as a pairing or not. I really enjoyed running with Angela Mudge as we race well together, and whilst I am not as fast as her, we complement each other. The way I navigate is fairly coarse, but I may choose a better overall line. She is great at the fine navigation, finding a re-entrant for instance.'

Helene had some interesting thoughts on the early days, and being a female competitor. In an article in *The Fellrunner* in February 2004, entitled 'A Ladies Retrospective', she comments:

'As Muriel Gray facetiously pointed out in her book[20] – one needed facial hair to be accepted on the fells in the bad old days. I took to running with earrings, simply to avoid being mistaken for a "chap" – it didn't work, incidentally.'

As to inspirations, Helene cites Ros Coats for breaking down boundaries and her attitude to fells and running, and would have liked to meet her. She admires people like Angela Mudge and Wendy Dodds, who have won everything but still find huge enjoyment from the sport. 'People come and go, and race for different reasons. You see people who train inappropriately, and others that don't last. I don't mind being beaten; I'd rather be out there doing the thing I love than sitting in the house worrying about being beaten.'

Helene admits to being desperately competitive. 'I am glad I found a sport where that is OK in females, as I would have a go at anyone in front of me. Whilst I get the greatest pleasure racing on the fells, and if I can win, so much the better. That said, if I do my best that is even better than winning. One of my favourite races was when I came second to Jackie Lee at Wasdale when we were both faster than I had been sixteen years before. That was such a good run. I got so much out of it and worked so hard that I enjoyed being second and having a good go, even more so than some I had won.'

Asked about her own greatest achievements, she thought for a while before deciding it was different things for different reasons. 'The Dragon's Back certainly is what I am built for, physiologically as well as psychologically. The strategy required getting yourself from A to B in good nick day after day, that suits me, and I enjoy it as it doesn't really matter what other people do. I really enjoyed my solo unsupported Bob Graham Round. It was probably the best day out in the hills I ever had. I was running at my pace, I didn't feel pushed really, I could eat when I wanted to, not when the pacers wanted.'

Then interestingly: 'Getting a Scottish vest at cross-country

20. *The First Fifty: Munro-Bagging Without a Beard*, Mainstream Publishing, 1991.

was a real honour. I am old fashioned in that I put on a vest and I bury myself on the course. It is always such an honour to be selected. Even getting selected for Yorkshire at the age of forty-seven was a real thrill. It never wears off.'

Helene is still pretty fit, getting out running, biking, climbing, walking and swimming. 'I do enjoy racing still and like turning out when I can. It hurts more and I am less fit, so I do less racing but still get out on the hills as much as time allows. This is most weekends and if I have time midweek, I head to the local hills in the nearby dales.'

She took on a role working for the FRA juniors. 'I volunteered for the Junior Co-ordinator role for two years and am stepping down as planned. I really wanted to put something back into the sport, and as my girls were at every race, it seemed sensible to do something for the FRA youngsters. We are now growing out of the junior section and it's time to hand over to a fresh pair of hands.'

Helene Diamantides/Whitaker is a person who pushed herself very hard, and expected the same level of commitment from her pacers, whom she noted at one point were thinking of taking union action and 'running to rule' on one of her rounds. She pushed the boundaries, by constantly proving what women could achieve, in both races and endurance events.

CHAPTER 15

Going further

Even More Rounds: Joss Naylor Lakeland Challenge, Lake District 24 Hour Fell Record. Profile: Anne Stentiford

'Each contender has to be accompanied on every leg for safety reasons.'

A challenge with a difference was set up in 1990. The Joss Naylor Lakeland Challenge starts at Pooley Bridge and traverses thirty summits over a distance of 48 miles and climbs 17,000 feet. The inaugural run from Pooley Bridge to Wasdale was made by Joss Naylor, at the age of fifty-four, in very bad weather with heavy rain and strong winds. Joss completed the run to Greendale Bridge in 11 hours and 30 minutes. According to the website: 'The challenge is offered to fell runners over the age of fifty, male or female, to complete the run in set times according to their age group. The challenge is intended to be a "supported run" for individuals.'

In 1992 Monica Shone was the first lady, at the age of sixty-six, to do the Joss Naylor Challenge, and the second to repeat the Joss round, after Don Talbot had done so in 1991. The event report noted: 'Monica completed the run in 21 hours 47 minutes, well under the 24 hour allowance for her age group (over sixty-five). The weather was perfect for her attempt. With plenty of time in hand she opted for a swim in Lambfoot Dub on Great End. She was paced throughout by clubmate Wendy Dodds, with Linda Lord joining them from Sty Head. Monica is a lifelong athlete and outdoor enthusiast, having played ladies' cricket and lacrosse at national level, and instructed outdoor activities.' Monica Shone took over administration for the Joss Naylor Challenge in 1995, a position she held for several years. Sadly, Monica passed away in 2017.

The next runner to put their mark on the long distance scene was Anne Stentiford. She set a new fastest time for the Bob Graham Round in 1989, added a Paddy Buckley record in 1991, and then three years later extended the Lake District Peaks record.

In July 1994 Anne Stentiford added four peaks to Anne Marie Grindley's fifty-eight from 1979, as she set a new Lakeland 24 Hour Record. She came in in 23-17 having added Catstycam, Lingmell, Haycock and Grasmoor. To Anne Stentiford the extended round of sixty-two peaks was a natural next step. 'I knew Mark Hartell, who was in my club. He was very enthusiastic and keen to try and break the men's 24-hour record. He suggested I should have a go at the ladies' record.' Anne went on a lot of recces with him, and planned which peaks to add. She was working in the south as a computer programmer at the time and remembers spending time in the evenings poring over maps and pencilling in which peaks to add, and checking they were valid. Then she spent some time recceing those extra peaks to see how long they would take her. On the day itself she recalls, 'I had built in four extras, but I bottled out on doing Fleetwith Pike because I was feeling horrendous, with stomach problems. I thought if I did it, I might be outside 24 hours. Then I did start to recover and was going well again, so decided to pick up Grasmoor and knew that would take seventeen minutes and is a nice, grassy run out. I regretted at the end that I hadn't done Fleetwith Pike as I think I would have had time for it. I changed shoes at Newlands for the run in.' To get a feel for that achievement, this is a day out on the hill that is roughly equivalent to doing a Bob Graham Round in about 18 hours with an additional 5 hours run at the same pace. Anne became one of the few people to hold simultaneously the 24 hour Fell Record and the Bob Graham Round Record.

Anne Stentiford

I had spoken with Anne before in researching the sport but needed to expand on the events she was involved in that are pertinent to the theme of this book. A few email exchanges soon covered this, and a more fully rounded profile of her and her position in the sport emerged.

Anne Stentiford was born in 1965 in Hitchin, Hertfordshire, lived there till the age of ten and then moved to Congleton, Cheshire. She started running when she was about fourteen and joined Macclesfield Harriers. 'I did track running, high jump, cross-country and road running,' she said. 'I completed my first marathon at sixteen (in 3 hours 28 minutes), similar to Helene Diamantides.' At seventeen years old she was road running, but had met a few people who did the Karrimor International Mountain Marathons. 'They took me to a couple of local fell races, Shutlingsloe probably being my first.' Anne lived in London for a while, but, when she came back to Macclesfield, she got in with a group who were also doing long events. Her first husband, Geoff Pettengell, had completed the Bob Graham Round and said he thought she should have a go at it.

She was fairly new to fell running. 'In 1989, I met Mike Hartley and ran with him on his Pennine Way record run, from the White House near Littleborough to Edale, about forty miles. I was in awe of Mike and he inspired me to do the Bob Graham Round. I ran most of the sections with Geoff, and other club members.' Her first attempt on an actual round was a failure. 'I got as far as Wasdale,' she recalled. 'It had rained for about seventeen hours, absolutely torrential, so I had to call it a day.'

She went off then to the Pyrenees for three weeks, with Geoff Pettengell and John Amies, and ran/walked most of the High Level Route, which is a 500-mile high level traverse from the Atlantic coast to the Mediterranean coast. 'We all had the smallest of rucksacks with minimal kit: shorts and a T-shirt for running in, a Helly and a clean T-shirt for the evening, plus one pair of clean socks, lightweight waterproofs, light sleeping bag and a bivvi bag. Occasionally we would rinse our kit in a river, but even so we stunk to high heaven by the time we finished. We stayed in mountain huts when it fitted in, otherwise bivvied on the mountain. We lived on what we came to call 'chokies' (dry baguettes with a hunk of cheese or chorizo) and hut meals in the evening, if we were in a hut. Our days running/walking were approximately eight to twelve hours long. Sadly we didn't complete it as I got quite sick and on the insistence of a French lady who could see I was ill, we decided to call it a day.'

Anne got very fit doing that, as it was effective altitude training. 'A week after our trip, I thought I would have another go at the Bob Graham, with a very small group of pacers, about three or four. They worked harder than me, and I got round in 20 hours 35 minutes, as I recall.' This was later in 1989, at the age of twenty-four. She didn't do Broad Stand on that first round. 'No, on the very first one it was Lord's Rake. The pacers on that round didn't want to do Broad Stand.'

Anne says she didn't really have much idea of BGR times. 'I had started running on a twenty-four-hour schedule,' was her comment. 'Phil Cheek, who had done plenty of pacing for others, was getting excited as we were knocking off chunks of time. We were really flying, and he was thinking, "what is the record"? I was really pleased and was fine at the end.' She was well over an hour slower than Helene Diamantides' record.

Although quite young and green, she had done a fair amount of recceing. 'I went up to the Lakes when I could. Those I was running with often went up at weekends. There was always someone in the club wanting to run a section of the round.' The two Marks, McDermott and Hartell, were at Macclesfield, but were not a significant early influence. 'At that point I didn't know them,' Anne adds. 'The main influences at the start were John Amies, Phil Cheek (who was quite an inspiration), Colin Ardron and Geoff Pettengell.'

In 1991 Anne Stentiford went back to finish the High Level Route, spending another two weeks in the Pyrenees. Leaving there, she did the Swiss KIMM with Helene Diamantides. Anne was talking to Helene about possibly doing the Paddy Buckley Round, as she had recced a good amount of it already. 'She said, "you'll be fine, I'll pace you and you could have a go at the record" [*held by Helene at the time*]. I said, "don't be silly",' Anne recalls. A week or so afterwards she decided to have a go. She had recced all of the route in the summer and had a twenty-four-hour schedule. However, Martin Stone knew she was running well, and had secretly set a record schedule. 'So, we set off on the twenty-four-hour schedule, and two-thirds of the way along the first leg he said, "we're on record pace", so we switched to Martin's schedule. He kept his eye on both, but we stayed on record pace.' Martin Stone did leg one, but the problem was, they were so far ahead of the original schedule, the pacers weren't there. 'Martin ended up doing quite a lot with me, and then often people would end up doing a section later, all a bit chaotic,' she chuckled.

It seemed that Martin Stone was more confident than her in her ability. 'Yeah. I just didn't feel confident,' she agreed. 'I hadn't done huge amounts of ascents and massive mileage each week. I'd run both days at the weekend, which was often a day in the Lakes and then another long steady day, and maybe one or two runs in the week, but not the mileages others did. I never thought I could run quickly for a long time. I just ran how I felt.' On the Paddy Buckley she felt comfortable and enjoyed it. She had set a new record of 19-20. At the end of it, Martin Stone suggested she do the BGR, and even go for the record. 'That was a completely different kettle of fish. I set off a month later with the record in mind which made it much more stressful. The schedule was so much harder, starting off on record pace. I remember starting up Skiddaw and thinking this is hard, I can't possibly maintain this.'

Her start for the BGR was at 1.40am, banking on a quick round to make it in as little darkness as possible. The weather was awful and then got worse. It came in on leg two and deteriorated rapidly to torrential rain, hail and gale force wind. 'Later on, going up Kirk Fell we were crawling on all fours', Anne recalled. 'Fred Rogerson was waiting down in Honister; he said that in all his years on the fells, he had never been out in weather like that before. He was sitting in his car which was being rocked around by the wind and had assumed we had abandoned. He couldn't believe it when we came down and were ahead of schedule. As the weather got worse, I got stronger, physically and mentally. I was very together.' She claimed the weather doesn't bother her when she is doing something challenging, she just has to focus.

She says the pacers were all amazing. They kept her motivated while navigating in the horrendous weather. 'I knew them all well and they were a great team,' says Anne. 'Andy Thornton didn't know the route very well and had recently come back to England after living in New Zealand for five years. He was keen to get back on the hills and was a great motivator. There was a nominated navigator for each leg, including Martin Stone on legs 1 and 5. I had very little rest, maybe a couple of minutes at each section.' On the round she ate a lot of rice pudding and tinned fruit. 'I also seemed to eat a lot of satsumas for some reason. I managed to eat a lot early on, but from Wasdale, I couldn't get much down.'

Despite the deteriorating weather they didn't have any real navigation issues in the clag. 'No, I think it was spot on,' Anne remembered. 'We did Broad Stand with the aid of a rope set up by Stuart Gascoyne from Macclesfield Harriers. I hate exposed drops even though I'd done a lot of climbing, they mess with my head. It was fine as I kept focused. I wondered whether, if the weather had been better, I could have completed the round any quicker. It must have slowed us down significantly.' She had set a new record of 18-49, knocking twenty-two minutes off Diamantides' time. This was the eleventh fastest time anyone had done for the Bob Graham Round at the time. Anne never went back to try to run faster though.

Having said that, she is justly proud of her long-distance achievements. 'I think when I broke the ladies' BGR record it felt well-earned, as the weather was so awful,' she commented. 'My one regret was not being able to do the Ramsay Round. I was thinking of doing the Ramsay a month after but at the end of the BGR I could hardly walk. I had done something to my foot. I went to the hospital on the way home and they said it was an acute tendon injury. The doctor said it would have been better if I had broken my foot, and they put a pot [*a plaster cast*] on it for a month. So, that was the end of the idea of doing the Ramsay Round that year.'

A few years later, in 2009, Anne got very fit, maybe even fitter than when she did the BGR, and she had every intention of breaking the Ramsay record. 'It was an absolute disaster. We were driving at about 2am from a bunkhouse at Roy Bridge, for an early start from Glen Nevis Youth Hostel. Halfway there, we noticed loads of debris/greenery along the middle of the road. We stopped and got out to take a look. We spotted some car headlights in the ditch 100m away. We ran over and there was a car upturned in the ditch with a man trapped under the car, halfway out of the sunroof. He was still alive at that point. One of my support team was a doctor, but we could not save the man and he died less than a minute later. We rang the emergency services and all three came. We were there for several hours and interviewed to establish we weren't involved, and to all give statements. The Ramsay attempt was aborted as we were all in shock and had lost the will to start. I never did get the chance to have another attempt due to worsening knees.'

She did go to Nepal in 1997 though, to have a crack at the Everest Marathon. The start is at 17,000 feet, and they set off in a blizzard, with the first half of the route covered in snow and ice. It was the worst conditions the race had known. The second half eases as it runs downwards to Namche Bazar. Anne (running in Walshes) finished eighth, the highest position ever by a female at the time, and took 16-40 off the existing record with her 5-16-03 finishing time. 'The Everest marathon came after two months of travelling around Eastern Europe on my [second] husband Bill Johnson's Triumph Thunderbird motorbike, immediately followed by a month in India and two months in Nepal. We nearly didn't make it to Nepal as we went to Kashmir against government advice and were held captive on a houseboat on Lake Srinigar – but that is another story! We were backpacking on a shoestring budget and training in mountains wherever we went, in the Tatras mountains, or mountains in Poland, Croatia and Hungary for instance. Once in Nepal we trekked at a fast pace around the Annapurna circuit while carrying heavy rucksacks.'

'By the time we joined the trek to Everest base camp for the race, we were well acclimatised and fit for the marathon. We both found that trek quite limiting as the days were too short to allow everyone to acclimatise. We would get to the end of each day's trek before lunchtime – but there was great banter with trek leaders Andy Styan (the legendary fell runner) and Barry Johnson to make the trek entertaining. On the morning of the race it was minus 25° degrees with a strong blizzard blowing, deep snow on the ground and visibility almost zero. Everyone wanted to get going asap. The organisers said if we hadn't been at the start that day, we wouldn't have made it there due to the conditions. Although the race is overall downhill, you really notice the climbs due to the altitude – breathing suddenly becomes harder. By the time I finished, it was plus 25°, so a huge temperature range. I was eighth overall. Five of the runners ahead of me were Nepalese Sherpas or Gurkhas, including the winner Hari Roka. A fantastic event with fond memories.'

Anne didn't really think that these endurance efforts affected her other commitments. 'I wasn't into doing the champs races, although I have since,' she noted. 'I tended to run local races, coming fifth lady, or similar. I enjoyed races but didn't take them seriously. Usually preferring to spend weekends in the Lakes or Wales doing sections of the rounds. I wasn't a serious fell racer at the time.'

She offers three very different events as top memories. 'One of my favourite races is the Shuttlingsloe fell race, which I did most years from when I first started running at fourteen. Probably my all-time favourite race is Wasdale for its fantastic route and breathtaking scenery. The most memorable race was the 29km Guinness Mount Cameroon race in February 1992. I'd never been to a third world country before, so it was an eye opener. The intense heat and humidity, the smells, the poverty, and the smiling people. I loved it. I was in the company of Jack Maitland, who as a previous winner of the race was like a god to the locals. Wherever we went, a chant would start: "Jack, Jack, Jack". He was revered! A few days before the race I badly sprained my ankle while checking out the lower part of the route. It swelled up like a balloon and I was gutted. I decided to still do the race on a large dose of Ibuprofen. I wasn't travelling all the way to Cameroon not to run. The race starts at sea level and takes you through the tropical rainforest, then up to the top of Mount Cameroon, an active volcano. Steep uphill all the way, then a long descent back down to the start. I carried a litre of water and near the top, local competitors were trying to physically take it from me. I wasn't expecting to get into a fight! It was so hot at the top and despite sun cream, my arms were badly blistered with the heat. I made it back down to the finish, but probably set my ankle back a few weeks. A brilliant event.'

There were to be no more big rounds for her. 'My knees are bad', she said shortly after that. 'I don't think I am going to get back to the point where I can do long distances again. The consultant thinks they are pretty worn out. Grade four arthritis in parts, not much cartilage left. One is worse than the other.' Anne had a go at triathlon. Not being able to swim, that was her first target. She did move up to Olympic distance triathlons and duathlons and qualified for the GB age group team in both disciplines. 'I competed in the European Championships at duathlon in 2017, in Soria, and came second V50. Also in 2017, the European Champs triathlon in Kitzbuhel (finishing seventh V50) and the World Champs in Rotterdam (fourteenth V50).

My swimming was my big let-down as I'd only learned to swim when waiting to have arthroscopies on my knees. I was never going to be a Michael Phelps.'

She adds that in the last year she has stopped running/triathlons altogether as her knees are too painful. 'My latest achievements have been the Coniston end-to-end swim, 5.25 miles, in September 2020, and September 2021 the Marmotte Grandfondo Alpes sportive in the French Alpes. A fantastic event of 173km and 5,000 metres of ascent. Of just over 2,000 competitors, only eighty-nine were female. I was 3rd v50, 41st female and about 1,200th overall.'

Anne recalls that she had a strong emphasis on rounds and challenges and really does not, at the time or on reflection, think she was an innovator or pioneer. 'I don't think I'd describe myself as either of those things, but I'm always up for a challenge. I enjoy pushing my body out of its comfort zone and relying on mental strength.'

Anne had a very varied working life. 'My first job was as a forensic scientist, specialising in fire investigation, in London for the Met Police. That didn't fit in with fell running. I used to hitch every weekend up the M1 to go climbing or fell running with Clive Davies, a superb climber.' She is not working full-time now, though. 'Before children I was doing computer programming for ten years. I then retrained in reflexology and did that part-time. Now I help a friend out with dog walking – which fits in with my lifestyle.'

She hasn't worked, as such, for the last five years, apart from running their holiday let apartment in Grasmere. 'I spend the rest of my time out with our dogs, cycling, swimming and socialising with like-minded people. I love cooking and baking cakes which is a necessity for swimming outdoors all year. Last winter I carried on outdoor swimming with three friends as the water temperature plummeted to zero and we were breaking the ice to swim. The exhilaration and endorphin rush are a pretty good substitute for the runner's high.'

Anne Steniford/Johnson is another athlete whose feats may

not be well known. Her phenomenal endurance efforts stand as testament to her fitness and commitment to the sport.

In 2002, Wendy Dodds completed the first recorded women's '50 at 50' ('53 at 51', to be precise). She sprinted up to the Moot Hall in 22 hours and 38 minutes, nearly an hour faster than her original round of 42 peaks (on the Bob Graham Round), way back in 1979. This brought her great satisfaction: 'It really was much easier,' she claimed.

There are many other challenges, all of which can't be covered here. Some of those already mentioned have subsequently been bettered, as the bar inevitably has risen higher. The women mentioned in this chapter have very much set the standards for what is possible for female endurance athletes.

CHAPTER 16

To the millennium

The Late 1990s: More Stunning Records and Rise of the Veterans. Profiles: Nicola Davies, Menna Angharad, Angela Mudge

'Each year I was getting faster and breaking more course records.'

The 1994 season saw good women's fields in races and many more course records beaten. Among the record setters were Angela Brand-Barker, Ruth Pickvance, Andrea Priestley and Jacky Smith. The Fellandale club were having a fine year, winning both the women's British and English team championships, as well as the Hodgson Relay. Carol Greenwood was coming back from injury and was getting back to top form. On 31 December she won Auld Lang Syne, which was her fourth victory in five days. In the British Championships Angela Brand-Barker beat Andrea Priestley by a couple of points.

Nicola Davies was showing the way for women by winning races as a veteran, including that year's Borrowdale from Mari Todd. The women's course record spree continued in 1995, with some new faces joining in the fun. Sarah Rowell, Janet Kenyon, Nicola Davies, Menna Angharad, and Vanessa Peacock all set significant records in the year. Vanessa triumphed at the Grisedale Horseshoe race as a V40. At the end of the season the British Championship positions were: 1st Sarah Rowell 88 points, 2nd Angela Mudge 75, 3rd Nicola Davies 73.

Nicola Davies

Nicola's details came from another interviewee. When I spoke with her, she said, 'I don't really think I fit into the pioneer category. I think I was more the next wave.' A phone interview and an email follow-up gave a good insight into how things had changed by the mid-1980s onwards.

Nicola Davies didn't start fell racing until she was almost into the veteran category (i.e. then over thirty-five), but she had already done the Bob Graham Round in 1991. 'I did the BGR with my brothers and my caving friends. I came to it from hillwalking rather than fell running.' Nicola was born in London in 1958, and brought up in East Anglia and Scotland.

Nicola didn't come from a sporty background, but at university she joined the caving club (and still goes underground occasionally). The group would also go up hills in the Dales or across to the Lakes if it was too wet to go caving. 'Then we'd go to Scotland at Easter, or on caving trips to the Pyrenees, so I had plenty of hill and mountain experience before I came to fell racing. I moved to the Eden Valley in 1992, because I wanted to live near the Lakes, which I did when I was able to choose where I wanted to live. I started rock climbing which, as it turned out, combined well with fell racing when I was doing both quite a lot. If I did two races a week, my body was happy with climbing whilst my ankles recovered.'

She says ankles were always her weak point. On one visit to the orthotics expert, he suggested that 'when God gave out the running feet, you must have been at the back of the queue'.

With her late start she ended up racing a lot once she got into it, enjoying being in the low-key Borrowdale club. 'We never managed really to get enough for a proper women's team, but just really enjoyed the all-in-it-together camaraderie of fell running. I made some brilliant lifelong friends, and am still in Borrowdale, and still fell run, although I last raced the two short Patterdale races, in the year before Covid.'

She adds that the type of races she was best at were rough, with steep up and down. 'So, as little running as possible! I was equally good at both when I was at my fittest. As I have got older my ankles have failed me more, so now my downhill is pathetic.'

Nicola got a very good background in navigation experience from being a hillwalker. 'I was also a Lake District fell-top assessor for three winters in a row, up Helvellyn. I am happy on the hills, whatever the conditions really.'

She chuckles when she admits that she is not good at training, but really does like exercising outdoors. 'Racing was my training. I am still the same now. I am starting off my cyclo-cross season with no specific training. Once I have a few races under my belt I will get race fit. I have always kept a good level of base fitness just by doing stuff outdoors.'

Nicola has an amusing take on peaking. 'I probably never reached my peak because I started after it! People that start later can often carry on for longer than people who start earlier and trash their bodies.' She did have some peak performances. Nicola thinks the best race record she set was for the Scafell Pike. Her time of 1-03-24, which she set in 1999, has not been beaten at the time of writing.

She also reckons that she probably did some of her best performances in team situations, which was difficult with Borrowdale Fellrunners because they rarely had a full women's team. 'I love the Ian Hodgson because that is a team event. We had some really good mixed Borrowdale teams for that, and I am sure we won a couple of times. The Western Isles Challenge on the Outer Hebrides, I just loved that. It was for teams of four, with some really stiff runs, and hard navigation. You always try harder than you think possible for teams.'

Nicola speculated about the effect of the separate starts for men and women that used to happen in races. 'I think some women's records could have been better if the leading women had not been impeded at the start of races in the early days.' She reckons that her friend Menna Angharad was probably the best fell runner she knew, and that Janet Mclver was a great runner too.

Nowadays, Nicola Davies is really into racing, saying, 'I've done the Three Peaks Cyclo-cross race ten times or so, whereas I only fell raced it once. I've been successful in the Vet categories. I am now kind of pioneering the V60 category in the British Champs. I also got well into adventure racing. In fact, it took over from pure fell racing. I have always enjoyed lots of different outdoor sports and have never focused on any one thing. I've always done all right by being a fit diesel engine.'

She concludes that at her age (sixty-two at the time of the interview) she has lived all her life with gender inequality. 'It's part of our culture, and sport is just a small part of the bigger picture. However, the great thing about fell running is that it has always been, in my experience, a very inclusive sport. That has been the fun of it.' Nicola Davies was fairly late on the fell scene, but she confirms the life-giving camaraderie that exists in the sport.

The 1996 season saw Sarah Rowell win the British Championships again. After a great battle with Menna Angharad, Sarah won by just 2 points. Sarah set good records at the Three Peaks and at the Fairfield race early in the season. Angela Mudge was getting in on the act with a new best time at Ben Rinnes, whilst Menna Angharad was reaching peak form and duly replied with new records at the Coniston and Llanbedr to Blaenarvon races.

Menna Angharad

[I wasn't able to speak directly with Menna, but wanted to include her. I have summarised her career from published information.]

Menna Angharad was born in 1957 as Angharad Menna Cooper-Willis, but made the choice to use her first two names (in reverse order). Her profile in *The Fellrunner*, from 1997, notes that she only started fell running in her mid-thirties, seven years after the birth of her second daughter, having shown no interest in sport at school or university. Very much pursuing her own way through life she resisted attempts to persuade her to take part in mountain races once she had started jogging. In 1990 she reluctantly agreed to run the short Cnicht race. Ill-prepared, and wearing gym shoes, she dawdled to eat bilberries on the way down and came joint last, with no time recorded as the timekeepers had gone home.

Menna soon discovered she had talent for the sport. She claimed to never have been coached, never kept a training diary, never worked out in a gym, and knew nothing about the science of fitness. She first entered the record books with her win in the Peris Horseshoe race in 1995, finishing seventh overall, and beating a good Angela Carson record by twenty minutes. Moving on to the Borrowdale race later in 1995 she beat a long-standing course record with a time of 3-25-33, having never seen the course or ever run in the Lake District.

Then at the Peris Horseshoe race, in 1996, Menna ran head-to-head with Sarah Rowell. Menna finished fifteenth overall in a new record of 3-28-14, eight and a half minutes ahead of Sarah, who also ran really well that day, having led Menna for the first 6 miles.

Francis Uhlman suggested[21] that there were 'three outstanding women's records in major fell races in recent years. One is Sarah's at the Three Peaks, another Carol Greenwood's at Snowdon, and the third is Menna's at the Peris Horseshoe.' The percentage these three women's times were of the equivalent men's records (at the time) for those races was calculated by Graham Breeze (for an article in *The Fellrunner* in June 2006). Sarah's figure was 118 per cent, Carol's 116 per cent, and Menna's was 114

21. In a profile of Menna Angharad in the February 1997 edition of *The Fellrunner*.

per cent of the men's record. A cautionary note needs to be made. That is that the percentage figure does depend on the quality of the men's records, which Graham acknowledges. It does, though, back up the excellence of Menna's record at the Peris Horseshoe. I am sure an updated analysis would illustrate equally outstanding women's times and percentages.

In 1997 there was still talk at the FRA committee about separate starts for women at championship races. It was noted that it was agreed for 1998 for the British and English championship races. Selwyn Wright also reported from an ICMR meeting in the Czech Republic, which saw 'no progress with our desire to see ladies' courses the same as men's.'

Meanwhile, participation by women was healthy in many races. The Carnethy 5 that February had seventy-five women competing, out of a total of 400. Carol Greenwood, Menna Angharad and Mari Todd set a handful of new course records each that year. Mari's most significant was probably at Wasdale, where she 'won by over thirty-four minutes from a strong women's turnout in the hot, humid conditions, and placed a superb seventeenth overall from a quality men's field to hack over six minutes off Helene Diamantides' seven-year-old course record.'

Menna Angharad came back to Borrowdale and took on Sarah Rowell's record time from 1996. The report notes that 'just seven days after finishing third in the prestigious Nike International Snowdon Mountain Race, the forty-year-old pottery designer placed an astonishing sixteenth overall (from 256 starters) – despite going slightly astray coming off Dale Head.' She beat Rowell's time by almost a minute, recording 3-14-36.

At the end of the 1997 season the British Champion was Angela Mudge, beating Mari Todd by 9 points. Mudge went on to win the British Championship for the next three years, a remarkable run. The most consecutive wins by a male in the British Championships have been three, achieved by Kenny Stuart and Colin Donnelly, both in the 1980s, and by Rob Hope in the 2000s.

Angela Mudge

I made an approach to Angela out of the blue, via email, and fortunately she was happy to respond to my questions even though leading a very hectic life at the time. The respect with which she is regarded within the sport is not surprising when you consider her results and longevity.

Angela Mudge was born on 8 July 1970, in Plymouth. She didn't have a good start in life, as she was born with club feet, *congenital talipes equino varus*. In the 1970s parents were given two options; either an operation, or use plasters to gradually straighten the feet, which is much less aggressive, but takes much longer. 'My parents chose the latter option, and I had my feet in and out of plaster until I was two years old. My Dad would cut them off when they became too tight. Once I was walking, I regularly saw a podiatrist (until my early teens) who built corrective devices on the bottoms of my shoes. Orthotics weren't invented then! I still wear orthotics to correct my pronation.'

At secondary school Angela competed on the track at 1500m and 3000m, and at cross-country to county level. 'I competed at English schools on the track and over cross-country (eighteenth was my highest finish, in the Senior girls). Coming from Devon, I'd never heard of hill running as a sport. Tavistock AC was formed when I was in my Lower Sixth, prior to that one of the local dads, Pete Vale, took us (Janice, my twin, and his son) running at weekends. He wanted us to run as a team in his local half marathon, at Indian Queens – at fifteen!'

Angela had always swum, biked and hiked on Dartmoor. She completed the Ten Tors event several times at school. 'When I went to Leicester University I became disillusioned with the running scene – 2-mile relay races on the road or cross-country, so I joined the orienteering club. I was definitely an orienteer, running had become my second sport, until I was introduced to hill running.'

As a junior, and at university, Angela ran at county level. After she graduated, she never competed on the track again, having only raced to gain points for the club. 'I only ever enjoyed the first race of the season and then became bored with running laps. I've raced a handful of road races, only one marathon and one half-marathon as a senior, I ran Indian Queens at fifteen, sixteen and seventeen, plus a few 10km races. I still run cross-country, being a GB standard Senior.'

In 1991 Angela moved to Stirling to study for an MSc. Stirling University backs onto Dumyat in the Ochils. At lunchtime a gang of the university runners ran on the hill, so she joined them and found a discipline that she never knew existed. 'In 1992 we formed the Ochil Hill Runners, and the guys gave me lifts to races and training runs in the area. I was hooked and slowly ditched the orienteering for the hills.'

Angela explains that no one specifically had influenced her to try hill running, it was circumstances. 'If I wanted to train with a group, I joined them on the hill. I always loved rough and muddy cross-country, the tougher the course the happier I am, so it seemed a natural step. At Stirling I had no interest in joining the local athletics club and competing on the road and track. My plan was to avoid any club that would ask me to do a track race. I'd only ever lived in Devon, and Leicester for my undergraduate degree, so hadn't been exposed to the sport, or even heard of it. I enjoyed the lunchtime runs up Dumyat, so I just ran in more hills and travelled further north to explore Scotland's Munros. It was a natural progression given how much of my youth I spent on Dartmoor. My first hill run would have been Kit Hill in Cornwall when I was a teenager, but this was just considered the local 'hilly' run and definitely not an official hill race. I also ran Charnwood Hills at Leicester, but that was really a trail race.'

In Scotland, Angela's first race was the Carnethy 5, where she felt she was out of her depth. 'I'd only run in the Ochils, so didn't appreciate how steep and heathery hill races could be. I was a quick learner. Most of the running over the Winter was slow using head torches in the evenings, which back then didn't help much. So, over my first winter most of my training was just steady running. The club hadn't been formed at that stage so none of us were doing any quality.'

Angela claims never to have had a sporting hero, then relents and says 'Chris Hoy is the nearest you'd get from me. I can safely say I didn't look up to anyone in the sport of hill running, and didn't have a clue about the sport and who the pioneers/great athletes were. I just ran for enjoyment and spent my time studying for my Masters, which was pretty intense. I can remember watching the video of Hugh Symonds completing his Munro round at Adrian Davies' house with some of the Ochil runners and couldn't comprehend what he'd achieved, as my geography of Scotland was so poor. It made me realise that there was a lot more of Scotland to explore.'

After graduating from Stirling University, Angela spent eighteen months volunteering with Scottish Conservation Projects, and also ran – but it wasn't really training. 'I cycled 20 miles a day, was doing a physical job, so just ran up the Law several times a week, which made me good at steep climbs, but also very slow. Sadly, I didn't appreciate I had low iron levels during this period, I thought I was always tired because I was on my feet all day.'

Angela then moved to Edinburgh to work in a chemistry lab at Forth River Purification Board. She started training and racing with the Carnethy club. 'Training was an easy cycle to work, train at lunch and/or after work. It wasn't until I started a PhD in 1995 that things started to click into place. I had more time to train, found out I had had low iron levels for years and Martin

Hyman started advising me, so I added a lot more quality to my training instead of long and slow miles.'

Angela says she had no trouble fitting in. 'Both the Ochil and Carnethy clubs encouraged me early on. I was just one of the guys at training and completed the same sessions as them. I've never been in a club where females weren't encouraged and treated equally. I was on the committee for the Ochils purely because they needed a female on the committee – probably some ruling by Scottish Athletics. I was the only female in the Ochil club for some time.'

Angela says that in Scotland race organisers were encouraging, but that they frequently did not know the women's record, and doubts they knew the men's either. 'I never saw the sport as sexist. We raced the same distances as the men and competed against them. Women running shorter races was a thing of the past. The only race which treated women differently was the Braemar Gathering, where women were banned from racing. Helene [*Diamantides*] and I always talked of gatecrashing the race, but we never did.'

There was a strong feeling that in Europe females were definitely second-class citizens, echoed by Angela. This seemed especially so in Italy, where women had to race shorter distances than men and the prize money was much less. In races where 'travel expenses' were given women also received much less than the men. Angela adds that 'the pre- and post-race hype always surrounded the men not the women. Jonathan Wyatt was treated like a World Champion in 2001, whereas I was just another top female runner. I didn't mind as Jono was a world class athlete and won many global titles, whereas I was never going to dominate the sport.'

Like several others featured here, Angela says she never considered herself a pioneer. 'I started the sport in the nineties, and the generations before me were the pioneers. Women were already competing at a high level, we were racing the same distances as the men (domestically) and no one ever questioned your ability because you were a female. There were just a lot less females in the sport at the time – in all branches of athletics, not just the hills.'

She may not have felt that she was a pioneer, but Angela made her point about situations when she could. 'On the hills in the UK we were racing the same distances as the men, so I was happy. In cross-country the women raced shorter distances, so I ran the East District men's race after competing in the women's race and was prevented from crossing the finish line, but I had made the point. It took over twenty years for women to race the same distance as men in cross-country.'

On the world circuit Anne Buckley had tried to get the women to race over the same course as the men, as at the Worlds women raced a shorter distance. 'Anne lobbied the World Mountain Running Association. I supported her views, but wasn't active in lobbying. It fell on deaf ears for a very long time, and I expect the Italian officials were to blame.'

In the early days Angela's training wasn't very well organised. When she moved to Edinburgh it became more organised, including a weekly Tuesday and Thursday speed session and the traditional long run on a Sunday. 'In the mid-nineties I started training in some of Martin Hyman's sessions, and Martin took me aside and offered to help advise me with my training. He studied my training logs, ripped them to pieces and gave me some very good pointers to what I should be doing. As I improved and took on his advice, he left me to my own devices, knowing I'd learned how to organise my training and was putting in enough quality sessions to improve.'

Increasing her volume into her early thirties, Angela picked up a knee injury at thirty-four, and never did intense quality sessions on the flat again. 'My knee would react badly. It was an inflammatory response as soon as I looked at a track! So, I relied on more hill work and the bike for my fitness. Now in my fifties I do a lot less running training. I keep breaking down and find if I run hard then I end up injured. I have come round to just running hard enough to stay in one piece and am more than happy to go for a cycle or swim if I've got an injury.'

She says that she doesn't practise navigation as she's in the bigger hills most weekends and plays at orienteering, so gets plenty of navigation practice without trying.

Angela has never felt that she had to work on her climbing. As a child she lived on the top of a short steep hill, so all those years of walking home from school up must have had some training effect. 'I'm a climber, the steeper the better. I had to work on my speed and descending skills. Martin Hyman gave me one piece of advice years ago, which was there's no point working on your strengths, it is better to work on your weaknesses. I liked long and slow, so I had to work on short and fast to improve. In the mid-nineties, when I began to improve, I was religiously doing two or more speed sessions a week.'

Having great success in the late 1990s, Angela won the British Fell Championship four times in the years between 1997 and 2000, and considers 2000 perhaps her best year. 'In 2000 I won the British title, raced in the WMRA grand prix series, set course records, raced the Scottish Island Peaks race and won the World Trophy. I had a brilliant time in domestic races early in the season, competing in the races I loved and then went on to perform at the World level.'

Angela gives the background to winning that World Trophy. 'In 2000 I finished my PhD and decided to spend six weeks in the Alps, training at altitude prior to the Worlds. Previously I'd only spent short periods in the Alps. I moved around Switzerland, training or racing in a different valley each week. I had no idea where I was fitness-wise, as the majority of my training was done alone, and I had no set sessions to gauge my performance at altitude. I overcooked it early on in that period, but quickly learned you can't train harder at altitude without a lot of acclimatisation. The week before the Worlds I was camped in St Moritz. Richard Findlow was also there, and he gave me a lift to Bergen the day before the Worlds. So, I had no stress of travelling to the race, I just sat in his van and relaxed. Arriving the day before was a gamble as I had no idea if I'd race well or badly. I flew!'

Bergen is an uphill only race and Angela had raced it a few times before in the WMRA Grand Prix series. 'The race starts fast and I kept off the pace, joining the leading group a few kilometres into the event. Around the last third, where it gets steeper, I found myself in the lead. This was totally unexpected. I hoped to medal, but never dreamed of beating the home favourite, Brigit Sontag, who'd won everything that year. For the last few kilometres I was running scared, not wanting to be beaten when I'd led the Worlds. The race felt easy, a combination of a good performance and the altitude training having paid off. It took a long time for the surprise to sink in. I never fully appreciated it at the time, as overall Scotland had a really bad World Trophy team performance.'

Angela also has a slightly different approach to accommodation and travel for foreign events. 'In the 2000s I took my bike to the Alps and camped. My training was a combination of cycle touring, running and just big days walking in the hills after the morning training session. The first summer I took my jet packer, which was like a coffin and not the best option when it was pouring with rain for several days. The advantage of a bike and tent was you can turn up late and camp anywhere, then clear off early before anyone noticed you were camping illegally. It saved me a small fortune.'

The Grand Prix races would provide one or two nights of accommodation, which provided her a good opportunity to wash all her clothes in the sink and hang the tent out to dry. 'In 2006 I inherited two dogs, so long trips to the Alps involved taking the car and camping, so I could take the dogs with me. It proved a good way to get to know the locals, as everyone wanted to say 'hi' to the dogs. When racing the dogs would be tied up in random places and I just hoped they'd still be there when I finished. You knew the Swiss weren't going to steal them!'

Angela Mudge is the only UK athlete to win either of the Pikes Peak races, an event which has strong memories for her. 'I went to Boulder in 2003 for the summer to train for the Worlds in Alaska and wanted to race Pikes Peak whilst I was there. I had a great summer running the trails in and around Colorado and managed to bag several 14,000 foot peaks. But the actual racing scene was really disappointing. In the early 2000s there were very few mountain races in the States and only a handful of trail races. So, most of my races ended up being on the road!'

Angela recalls that it was difficult to get anywhere, with very little public transport and distances being a bit of a stretch on her bike. 'I hooked up with the trail runners in Boulder who took me to Manitou Springs, and I can remember being shocked that this classic race [*Pikes Peak*] was not the remote peak I'd imagined. The peak is just on the outside of Colorado Springs and not quite as I'd hoped. The race has history, so it's a big deal in America. I enjoyed the run up; it's not technical and is fast going in the middle section. I remembered reaching the turnaround point and falling over – there was very little air! Descending was like having an oxygen high, the further down the descent the easier it became as you could actually breathe. I was first woman and finished in the top ten, so was disappointed that the quality of the field didn't quite meet the hype surrounding the event. For my efforts I won a basket of foot care products, which was highly amusing given how famous the event is. Not surprising the top runners did not show when there was no cash up for grabs.'

That was not what Angela considered her finest achievement in the sport, though. That was breaking the record at Sierre-Zinal in 2001. 'I was the first woman to break 3 hours (2-56-41) and smashed Véronique Marot's long-standing record. That summer I camped on the course above Chandolin. I trained on the course, and on the day of the event I was flying, and it felt so easy. Coming down the finish straight, through the village of Zinal the atmosphere was electric. I was staying in Chandolin for the week of the event with a group of Carnethy runners, so it was great to have a good race and be able to celebrate with friends.'

That record at Sierre-Zinal, which is one of many she has set, is the one she considers the hardest and gives her most pleasure. 'I invested a lot of time and energy training on the course and lived that event for the six weeks prior to breaking the record. It's the only race where I camped out on the course and repeatedly ran sections of the course for a prolonged period. I normally prefer not to know a course too well, because if I'm having a bad day I know what's coming up! I dreamed of winning, but definitely didn't imagine breaking the record.'

Angela was injured in April 2004 when she felt her right knee go when descending on Arthur's Seat. 'In that August I had an operation for an oesteochrondral defect. I'd worn away a 1cm diameter of cartilage on my medial femur, so the bone was exposed. I had a micro fracture technique on the knee where they drill into the exposed bone and the bleeding forms a scab which acts as your cartilage. I was non-weight bearing for two months and didn't start running for four months. Rehab was really cautious due to the high rate of failure of the technique (my physio had worked with rugby players and had never had a successful outcome until mine). In 2005 I only ran a handful of up and down races to give my knee the best chance of success. I spent 2005 cross training, with many hours on the cross trainer and the bike as I was paranoid I'd never return to full fitness. I got really fit for climbing.' She came back from a holiday in the Alps shortly before the World Masters, in Keswick in 2005, and was fit from spending a few weeks at altitude, and managed to win her race.

Once when interviewed Angela said that she uses percentage time against race winners as a measure of her performance. 'I use a percentage time against the lead men, very often I'd win a race even when I ran (what I thought was) badly, so my position meant nothing in terms of performance. Using percentage time, I can gauge how well I'd performed rather than just taking the position. I rarely race with a stopwatch, but race by how I feel. This doesn't motivate me during the race, as I never check my time during the race, I only look once I've finished. I always ran as hard as I could or needed to on the day, depending on how important the event was.'

Angela calls Skyrunning just the sexy version of hill/fell running. 'Many of the races are on good trails with no exposed sections. The events have just become a brand, after some very good marketing. There are some amazing races, but it's far too commercialised for me. I had a great time racing them, but never liked the hype that surrounded the events. I prefer the low-key back-to-basics approach in hill running, where you pay a few quid for your entry then disappear off to the pub with your mates. In the Skyrunning Series the top athletes are 'presented' to the supporters on the start line, it's a very pressurised environment compared to the average fell race. I feel much more comfortable away from the public eye and just competing for the love of running rather than any kudos/financial gain that comes with Skyrunning. For me I would go back and race the Dolomites Skyrace again and again, a classic up and down race on a spectacular mountain.'

There were several female hill runners who were sponsored before Angela: including Helene Diamantides, and Sarah Rowell. 'Pete Bland Sports sponsored me in the nineties from my Championship performances and dropped me when foot and mouth appeared. I was very grateful for the support they gave me. Salomon sponsored me from the early 2000s. Tim Lloyd approached me and asked if I would join the Salomon team, as they were moving from adventure racing to mountain running, as Salomon had seen a gap in the market. It started off as a very low-key affair, some kit and the freedom to race where we wanted. As Salomon's market presence increased, we were expected to race more high-profile events and travel abroad, this led to me competing in the Skyrunning Series for three years and running in races like the Trans Alps and Trans Rockies. Some brilliant races.'

Angela Mudge had always wanted to race the Everest Marathon. She never considered going for the record, but ended up beating Anne Stentiford's record time. 'If I had been going for a good time I would have approached the whole event more professionally. Too many factors outside your control contribute to how you perform on the day. I didn't travel out early to fully acclimatise to the altitude, but flew out with the group and trekked in with the group. This gives you enough acclimatisation to finish the race but not enough to perform well. To really perform well you'd need at least several weeks at that altitude. The most important factor is getting to the start line well enough to race. Most of the competitors suffered from sickness and vomiting on the trek in, many picked up colds and others had altitude sickness. So, for many it was a case of just surviving the run rather than racing it.'

She says it's an amazing place, and that she just ran the race. 'I ran most of the course on my own and didn't set out to break the record. I set out to enjoy the scenery! I just went with what I was comfortable with. I didn't want to blow up and knew that was a huge risk if I went off too fast. I later lost my record to Anna Frost, but never considered our performances comparable as she went out six weeks beforehand, recced the course and stayed at high altitude, so her body was well acclimatised to the altitude.'

Angela won the British Fell Champs again in 2008, by which time there were just four championship races. 'I didn't race the British Championship for several years, because I couldn't finish the series as I was racing in the Alps during the Summer and would miss key races. I prefer the traditional six race format, you can use the series to your advantage. The four race format doesn't allow for injuries, if you miss the first race through injury you are out of the series. I've started the championships in the present four race format and failed at the first hurdle. In my last attempt I travelled to the Lakes (three of us crammed in the back with my dogs) only to get out of the car and find my back had gone into spasm and I couldn't move, all because I sat in the middle seat in a squashed position. I couldn't race as I could hardly move! Under the six race format you have a chance to play to your strengths and if you have a bad race you have a second shot at it. At the moment the British Champs isn't well supported, so I'm coming round to the idea of having a one-off Championship event. The race calendar is too congested, so perhaps all the top athletes would commit to a one-off event. At the moment, too few of the top runners commit to the British and the English Champs races often have better fields.'

Angela Mudge finished by noting whose records on the fells/mountains she was most impressed with. 'Finlay Wild, for winning the Ben Nevis race ten years on the trot, a local man winning this iconic Scottish race. Any record set by Hannah Horsburgh in 2021 (and hopefully longer!). Hannah is resetting the record book, her performances behind the lead men are phenomenal and she is achieving standards never seen in the hills before. It's exciting to see and hopefully she'll help raise the overall standard of the top females.' Angela Mudge came to the fore in the 1990s, and the range of events she has competed in, and her longevity, are reminders to women to keep on achieving.

The 1998 and 1999 seasons saw more course records being set by the likes of Carol Greenwood and Angela Mudge. Carol Greenwood had an interesting year in 1998, winning a fell race outright, and setting a record at Ingleborough that lasted till 2015 (when Hannah Horsburgh beat it), and also winning the Barnoldswick race for the third time, collecting her third bed from the sponsors, Silentnight. Runners highlighted earlier continued running well, defying the march of time. Several races were won by athletes in the V45 category, including Vanessa Peacock and Wendy Dodds.

Coming to the end of the millennium, women had plenty of race opportunities, welcoming clubs to belong to, British and National championships to enter, and endurance challenges to test themselves over. There were still issues though, of recognition, equality of prizes and sponsorship opportunities, and of appropriate media coverage, some of which sadly are still being fought for. Inappropriate representation of an athlete's image is something that many current female athletes see as a concern and there is an active move to eradicate it from media reporting.

On this latter point, when writing on women's sport,[22] Sue Anstiss noted that the Women's Sport Trust, in 2018, issued a statement saying that they believe 'women in the sporting environment should be judged by their sports appeal and not sex appeal. We've been working with Getty [Images] to establish visual standards for the depiction of sportswomen which focus less on what women look like and more on what they achieve.'

There was a setback for the sport of fell running at the turn of the millennium, when the foot and mouth outbreak of 2001 meant that all races were cancelled, and even access to the hills for training was restricted. The positive to take forward, as restrictions finally eased, was that the pioneers highlighted in this narrative had made it possible for females to do whatever took their fancy in the field of endurance and off-road running.

The profiles in the book illustrate some very extended running careers from these female athletes, who arguably have been under greater pressure than their male counterparts – particularly with regard to marriage, raising children and working choices – particularly in the earlier days.

Any sense of equality of opportunity (and reward) certainly took a long time to arrive in the sport of running, and to fell running in particular. We should remember those pioneers. I am sure that they have the respect (and thanks) of those that have followed. More recent barrier breakers, such as Nicky Spinks, Jasmin Paris, Beth Pascall and Sabrina Verjee, have been moving faster and faster over the same ground that those remarkable early female runners had trodden.

---

22. *Game On: The Unstoppable Rise of Women's sport*, Unbound, 2021.

CHAPTER 17

Relays

Mostly Relays: Pennine Way, Coast to Coast, Calderdale Way. The Hodgson and the FRA. Profiles: Linda Lord, Eileen Jones

'It inspired me to organise a women's team.'

As the club's women's sections increased their memberships, so they were able to consider putting teams together for the various relays that were being established in the 1980s. There are three types of relay that are relevant here: linear and looped courses that are run as inter-club races, and challenges, which are not usually races, such as the Pennine Way.

The Pennine Way was established in 1965, and a Clayton-le-Moors Harriers men's team established the first ever relay record on the Way in 1970. The 268-mile-long Pennine Way was probably the first of the challenges to be attempted as a relay by a women's team, by Clayton-le-Moors Harriers, who ran it in 1982. This became the women's record, which doesn't seem to have been beaten. There was heavy rain and high winds for the first half of the run. Seventeen women participated, although not all active racing members at the club, and a few joined solely for the relay, including Marjorie Talbot, who trained specifically for the event. The team was organised by Linda Lord and she also ran in the team, as she explains. 'The idea was sparked because earlier Clayton men had done the Pennine Way relay. We completed it in 44 hours 53 minutes. Although there has been lots of interest in individual attempts on the Pennine Way, there doesn't seem to have been any interest by clubs in staging a relay, so our record stands to this day.'

Linda Lord

Linda was very enthusiastic for the project when I contacted her and readily agreed to provide information on her involvement on the fells. She apologised, by saying 'I seem to have written a lot, but think I've answered the questions and hope they aren't too detailed.' They weren't, as she very much embodied the pioneer spirit I was looking for.

Linda Lord went on to have a long and varied career, concentrating mostly on longer races. She was born in Shipley, West Yorkshire, in February 1948. Her maiden name was McIntyre. At school she was mostly into gymnastics, dance and games, but did run and win the 440 yards at the school sports when she was fifteen. 'I only won because the favourite fell!', she says modestly now. The PE teacher suggested she should start athletics training, but she didn't get round to it. That was it for running, until Linda started fell running.

When she left school Linda Lord went to College in Ambleside to do her teacher training. 'I was there from 1968 to 1971. I taught in Blackburn primary schools and at a Children's centre from 1971 until just before my sixtieth birthday in 2008. It was whilst I was in Ambleside that I joined the college climbing club, started rock climbing, continued fell walking, got to know the Lake District mountains, and learned basic mountain navigation. My passion for the hills was sparked whilst at school when our geography teacher organised a walk up Ingleborough. I couldn't wait to go again, and explore the dales and moors which were a bus ride away from home. I continued with those sports after leaving college, getting married and coming to live in Lancashire.' Linda also eventually started cycling, mainly as an alternative discipline when injured through running, and that became another sport she found really enjoyable.

Mike Raine, a friend that Linda's husband Pete climbed with, had joined Clayton-le-Moors Harriers in the mid-seventies, and he suggested Linda enter the first women's Pendle Fell race when it was put on. Linda felt she was being coerced into entering the race but did some training on the route along with Mike's wife Susan. 'It was rare to see anyone out running or jogging, as the first London Marathon hadn't taken place, so there were very few road races, and anyway as a fell walker, fell running seemed the more natural discipline for me. By 1977 I'd done quite a lot of walking in the Dales, Lake District and Scotland. We don't have any children, so juggling childcare was never an issue', Linda adds.

That Pendle Fell race, in April 1977, was Linda Lord's first ever event, and she was very nervous at the start. She recalls now that she, 'wore a pair of totally unsuitable white leather trainers, and a full track suit. I remember feeling that it was really hard work, but once at the summit thought it would be a doddle to run downhill, but my legs had turned to jelly!' She immediately said, 'never again', at the finish. Once the pain and stiffness had worn off, something must have struck a chord, and made her think that she wouldn't mind doing another race. 'I do think the background of fell walking at least gave me some leg and cardio strength and fitness as much as the few training runs I had done in preparation for the race.'

Linda joined Clayton-le-Moors Harriers later in 1977, and there was only one other woman member, Anne-Marie Grindley, who had joined the year before. Anne-Marie took Linda under her wing and they trained together. Linda soon became involved in helping on the Clayton club's Bob Graham Round attempts, including Anne-Marie Grindley's record breaking one in 1979. Linda adds that, 'Anne-Marie was very much a person whom I admired and wished to emulate, as well as all the other Clayton stars at that time.'

Linda doesn't particularly feel that she was a pioneer, citing women like Brenda Robinson, Carol Walkington, Joan Glass, Anne Bland and others that had started a year or so before her as the true pioneers. 'Although running regularly by 1977, I didn't race much that year, concentrating more on walking, and did my first Karrimor International Mountain Marathon with my husband, Pete. There were so few fell races then, so I only ran the odd race and some cross-country. I didn't really get going with racing regularly until mid-1978.' She adds, tellingly, that she thinks, 'in addition to the above, the real pioneers were the women who ran unofficially in races before they were strictly allowed to do so, showing the powers that be that they were capable.'

That first Karrimor International Mountain Marathon Linda did with husband Pete was in the Howgills. 'We both had been doing running training as well as quite a bit of walking, so we were fairly fit, but Pete turned his ankle on the first day, and although we finished we were well down the field.' In 1978 Linda was competing in the Saunders Mountain Marathon wearing a pair of Walsh studs, which she says, 'were made from some new material and the soles partially separated from the uppers halfway through the first day, but somehow I managed to carry on.'

At the KIMM in the Howgills in 1988, with Eileen Irwin (wife of Pete Irwin), they were first in the Women's B Class; but at Threlkeld in 1989, with Eileen again, they retired on the first day when she developed a calf strain. 'I eventually decided that being out for a long day in the hills, possibly in bad weather as it could be for the Karrimor in October was a challenge enough in itself, without the rigours of an overnight camp using minimum lightweight gear, so I stopped doing mountain marathons by the early 1990s, preferring long races or LDWA events.'

Linda Lord had started fell running just as it was changing from the shorter courses, which were put on for women, to them running the same course in some races. Linda recalls that when they set off ten or fifteen minutes earlier than the men, so as to comply with AAA's rules that men and women should not compete in the same race, it was in a way advantageous to the women, as the faster men were continuously passing them, and tended to drag the women along (not literally).

Looking back on those early days, she finds it incredible that there were no rules stipulating the carrying of cagoules, or emergency kit. 'Coming from a fell walking background I tended to carry at least some gear with me, and it took the deaths of runners in several races over the years before we had the FRA mandatory kit rule.'[23]

Continuing her thoughts on the early days, Linda Lord adds that, 'there wasn't the sponsorship, hype and commercialism around races that there is now, except for the Three Peaks which was the 'blue riband' of races in the late seventies and eighties. I am glad I'm not starting out now, I somehow feel that the casual low-key feel around many races has gone. Having said that, fell runners on the whole still tend to be a friendly warm-hearted bunch.'

Gaining more confidence by doing recces, Linda entered her first long Lakes race at Langdale in 1978, and has vivid memories of it and doing it again the year after. 'I wasn't a confident or very experienced navigator and was apprehensive at the start (a fellow woman competitor asked me if the route was flagged!). Despite the bad conditions, mist and strong winds, I got round successfully, and Stan Bradshaw called me later that day to congratulate me on finishing – praise indeed! The following year, 1979, I was a bit blasé, and went off course, passed Esk Hause and got to Great End – the great Chris Brasher was following me because he "thought someone in a Clayton vest must know

---

23. There have been two notable deaths of female runners in fell races in the UK. Graham Breeze commented in *The Fellrunner*. 'First, there was the death of Carol Matthews in a Welsh Relay Race in April 1991. This prompted intense debate on safety in races – leading to the FRA safety rules in place today. The circumstances of Carol's death were slightly unusual. She was an inexperienced fell runner on a 6-mile solo leg of a new relay run in poor weather who went off route. The tragedy prompted the FRA to buy radios for use by Race Organisers and to sanction runners who broke its safety rules. Unfortunately, 3 years later the experienced and well-equipped Judith Taylor died during a well-established fell race – the Kentmere Horseshoe – prompting further changes to make the sport safer.' There had been deaths of male runners earlier – including at the Three Peaks (1978) and Ennerdale (1981), which also caused reviews of safety.

where they're going"!' She adds that she wasn't the only Clayton Harrier who was followed by Chris Brasher, 'in a conversation with Anne-Marie Grindley a few days ago, she said that he had once tagged on to her in the Kentmere race. I don't think she got him lost though!'

Linda Lord ran the first Haworth Hobble (30 miles) in March 1980, partnered by a new Clayton member, Maureen Barlow, whose longest run until then had been nine miles. 'It was a beautiful early spring day but with three inches of snow on the ground it was hard going. We finished in just under nine hours (having briefly stopped for a half of shandy each in the pub at Heptonstall).'

In 1980 there were very few fell races in the winter. Along with many other fell runners with nothing much else to train for, Linda ran the Barnsley Marathon (her first marathon). Notable names in that race were: Jeff Norman (winner in 2-22-31), Billy Bland (15th in 2-32-21), Hugh Symonds (19th in 2-33-02) and several other fell runners from that decade. Amongst the women finishers were: 1st Véronique Marot 2-55-38, 2nd Anne Bland, 4th Pauline Haworth, 6th Miriam Rosen. Linda Lord was 8th in 3-30-04.

Later in 1980 Linda competed in the 19-mile Moffat Chase on a cool, October day, with low cloud, wind and rain. It was a small field of ninety starters, including eight women. 'I was out on my own for much of the time, but my navigational skills got me round OK, although I was passed a couple of times by club mate Tony Peacock and several others who had gone off route.'

Linda reckons she didn't ever encounter any problems at all with race organisers. In fact, most were encouraging and welcoming, but she recalls that prizes could be a bit pointedly sexist. 'I remember winning a flower arrangement in one race, as did other women prize winners, when the men got a bottle of beer or wine! We weren't given a choice between the two, but neither were the men.'

Linda says she doesn't particularly think of any of her results as being an 'achievement', but that she enjoyed the longer challenges in the early days, including the following two:

> Her first Three Peaks Race was in 1980, which she completed in 4 hours 13 minutes. It was only the second year women were allowed to enter, and it felt like it was a real achievement, as she had previously walked the route and watched the race several times.
>
> The Lakes 4 x 3,000's, also in 1980, run totally in walking boots, including down Borrowdale on the road. At that time the event was organised by the Ramblers Association, usually around the longest day in June, setting off from Keswick Rugby Club. As it was a walkers' event, open to all including runners, women competitors weren't unusual, although very much a minority.

Clayton-le-Moors was one of the first clubs whose women's team took on relays. An all-women Clayton team did the Derwent Watershed in March 1981, and completed it in the worst ever conditions. Forty-four teams started, and only thirteen finished, with their team ninth. Linda was never enamoured of the route, and never did it again. It is perhaps better known as the High Peak Marathon, and is a 40-mile race round the Derbyshire Moors, for teams of four, setting off from Edale at three minute intervals. 'It starts at 11pm – just to make it hard!' chuckles Linda. 'That year we were definitely the only women's team entered – I'm not sure if we were the first ever. There could have been women in other teams in 1981, but the results don't indicate women competitors. The event has now been cancelled altogether because of access difficulties. One comment by the organiser on the result sheet for that year states, "The all-ladies' Clayton team finished in a good time and looking better than the men in all respects." I don't think there was any problem about having an all-women team in the event when we entered – it was accepted unequivocally.'

Linda's club was not that much different from other clubs

regarding women members in the early days. 'Anne-Marie Grindley was the first to join, and I do recall her telling me that there was some questioning by certain committee members about having females in the club when her name came up for membership in 1976. So, she was certainly a pioneer in our club as well as generally on the fell scene. By 1981 we had about ten women members who were running regularly, although not necessarily fell racing, and that number included some exclusively road or cross-country runners.'

The Calderdale Way relay was first held in 1984. As Clayton women's team captain at the time Linda Lord organised a team, but there were no other all-women teams entered, although Bingley had a mixed team. 'It seems unbelievable now, but only twenty-two teams entered – and we finished eighteenth. Even Clayton men hadn't entered a team. I have the results sheet, and Peter White, the then organiser, put a note on the reverse saying he would probably set the limit of thirty teams in 1985. How things change! There was no questioning of us entering an all-women's team – it wasn't a case of being invited, I simply entered us and assumed it wouldn't be a problem, and it wasn't. Other relays I've been involved in are the Bob Graham Round relay, and the Coast-to-Coast relay (with Clayton teams).' Clayton had an all-women's team in the first Ian Hodgson relay in 1986 and have done so ever since, and the FRA relays every year.

The Fellsman Hike became Linda's favourite. She completed it five or six times, and won the women's event in 1985, jointly with Vanessa Brindle (Peacock). 'I had already done the Fellsman a couple of times, when Vanessa, who had become a good friend, and I agreed to do it together in 1985. She was just starting out on her fell running career; she wasn't a confident navigator, and was still unsure of her capabilities. I like it because it traverses some of the countryside I love and am very passionate about, having spent my early fell walking days there. The event has always been very well organised by the Scouts, with good refreshments at the checkpoints. In the early days the kit check was very strict – Alan Heaton once told me they held his cagoule under a tap to make sure it was waterproof! Boots were also mandatory at one time, but that was before I did it. The event used to start at midday so it was more or less guaranteed that competitors would have a night section to make navigation even more tricky. I have good memories of doing recces with Anne-Marie Grindley and her husband. I also ran with Vanessa in the first Old County Tops 1988 – we won the ladies' category, by default, as we were the only ladies' team entered.'

Linda only raced abroad once, at the Gold Rush Ultra Half-Marathon in 1989 in the foothills of the Rockies, California, which was 15 miles long. 'We would call it a trail race now, quite a bit of climbing, but all on marked tracks and trails. I was first lady V40, and third woman overall. I had always intended entering the Sierre-Zinal race, in Switzerland, which many Clayton members were doing, but regret never getting round to it.'

She is not someone you might think of as a record beaker, but Linda Lord had her moments. The Lyke Wake Walk is a long distance trail over the North York Moors, with an annual race along it every July. Linda ran it four times, in 1980, 1981, 1982 and lastly in 1985, and she lowered the record each time, which she says she looks on as one of her greatest achievements. Then she mentions that, 'the record has since been broken', before adding, 'one other record I held for around twenty years, (along with partner Judy Makinson) was for leg 5 of the Calderdale Relay, which we set in 1997.'

Like many people from the era, Linda Lord thinks Joss Naylor is one of the most impressive fell runners ever, as even at his now advanced age he is still out there enjoying the fells, having set numerous long-distance records. She adds, 'I was also full of admiration for Jean Dawes, the first successful woman BGR contender, and I have a great respect for my (former) club mate Wendy Dodds. Her love and dedication to the sport – not only for fell running, but orienteering and other mountain activities – is unbounded. She is the most motivated and driven runner I have ever met. She is still a prolific racer, and like me has managed to continue running even into her seventies.'

Linda Lord puts her longevity in the sport down to a couple of things. One is motivation and a deep desire, if not a need, still to run and race. 'An addiction, or a way of life more than a hobby', is how she puts it. 'I only have to look at a few pages of the latest *The Fellrunner*, and I'm looking at which race to do next. Having said that, I do far less than I used to, age has taken its toll, and I tend to do races which would take me no longer than a couple of hours at the most.' Over the last ten years she averaged around fourteen or fifteen races a year, with perhaps a LDWA event thrown in where time taken isn't a constraint. 'I go out for long days on the fells at my own speed, and am hoping to do the George Fisher's 30 mile Tea Round sometime.' The Tea Round is a challenge event in the style of the BGR or Joss Naylor Challenge (JNC). For the past few years Linda has been doing long distance training with a couple of her friends from Bury. 'Sheila McNulty and I had a go at the JNC at age seventy-plus in 2018, but after a long spell of dry warm weather, we were unlucky enough to choose the first wet, very windy and cold weekend for weeks, and had to retire.' They decided rather than make another attempt, they would try the less arduous Tea Round, which has no time constraints, 'so we may do it together, depending on how the training (or lack of it) has gone.'

The other factor for her longevity is pure luck, she says. 'I haven't over the years (fingers crossed) had any injuries that haven't been resolvable. So many club mates have had to stop running – largely because of knee/back or other long-standing problems. I struggled with Achilles problems on and off for years and spent many hours on the couch at Denise Park's clinic having treatment. It would frustratingly sideline me for weeks at a time and I found that cycling was a good way to keep fitness levels up, as it didn't aggravate the injury at all. I tried custom made orthotics, but they don't fit well into fell shoes, when your footfall changes continually. Eventually Denise Park and Wendy Dodds pointed me in the direction of eccentric calf stretches which genuinely work, and I've had only a little recurrence in the past ten or fifteen years. I take glucosamine/chondroitin for joint protection, and have done so for twenty years – my doctor reckons it's debateable whether it's effective or not – it could be the placebo effect, but I'll carry on taking it anyway. It seems to have worked well for my friend's ageing dog! Cycling is now part of my exercise regime, and I enjoy it as a sport in itself, and have done quite a bit of touring – I even tried time trialling in the past, but decided it wasn't for me.'

Linda had in fact done the JNC in 2008, as a V60, as she now explains. 'I was worried that I hadn't done enough long-distance running for a decade or so, and was dubious that I had it in my legs. Wendy Dodds and Monica Shone kept egging me on to have a go, so the pressure was on. Even so, I decided to wait until reaching sixty when I had eighteen hours' time allowance. We had reasonable weather mostly, but from Dunmail there was heavy rain and mist for about two hours, and we lost about twenty minutes trying to locate High Raise. Then my intended route down the gully off Great End had to be abandoned, as my pacer wasn't confident about it (we had to change pacers at the last minute) and going the longer way past Sprinkling Tarn added time, but luckily the weather improved from Sty Head to the finish. I was pleased to be well inside the allotted time. Joss wasn't there to meet me. Unfortunately, he was on holiday.'

Linda Lord seems to have been strangely ambivalent about her performances in the British Championships at the time. 'When I look back at 1982 at coming second in the British Fell champs, and the accolade that it is now, I remember how unimportant it seemed to be then. The champs weren't being contested by any of the real women stars, and I had plenty of points to win, if only I had turned up for one of the races later in the year – I don't recall which one – I would have beaten Sue Parkin on points, although she was a faster runner than me. Instead, we went to Pete and Sarah Haines' wedding, but I didn't even consider missing that to do that all-important (as it seems now) race. I feel pleased that I can still compete at seventy-plus, and even if I missed out on winning the British Champs in 1982, I've made up for it to a large extent by winning the V60s and V65s in more recent years.'

Linda also reflected on the early days and on who moved the sport on for women. 'I think the comments by others about the early fell championships being "all a bit of fun at first" about sums it up. I certainly never envisaged it would become the accolade that it is now. It is difficult to say who came along to make it more competitive – simply more women coming onto the scene definitely upped the standard. Women like Jean Lochhead, Pauline Haworth and Ros Coats were already at the top of the sport in the early eighties.'

In the early 1980s, most of the Clayton fell runners were very active distance racers and many were attempting the Bob Graham Round. By then Linda Lord had already done lots of distance challenges and a lot of the long Lakes 'A' races. Again, it was someone persuading her (Anne-Marie Grindley this time) that she could do this that made her think perhaps she could. 'Clayton's well-oiled and disciplined BGR machine provided the ideal support for any member having a go. I did the Clayton traditional anticlockwise route, and had near perfect conditions, except for thick mist on the Helvellyn range in the night, and losing about ten minutes finding Raise. At a particularly low point, my pacer, Don Barton, was talking to me about the then current Test match. I wasn't interested in cricket at all then, but am an avid fan now! Seeing Fred Rogerson and Stan Bradshaw waiting at the Moot Hall was a wonderful bonus. I finished in 22 hours 35 minutes and was the seventh woman to complete it.'

Linda comments on how things have changed since her round in 1983. 'The BGR is still a big physical challenge, but now made easier in many ways by the use of GPS, dedicated maps, the plethora of nutrition advice available, and much improved gear. A couple of years ago on a training run round the Blencathra/ Skiddaw leg I noticed well-worn easy-to-follow trods on much of the route.'

She concludes by saying how lucky she is to live where she does. 'I live close by Pendle, in Sabden, a village in between

Clitheroe and Burnley. I can easily access Pendle which borders my back garden without having to cross a road, and we are twenty minutes' drive from the Bowland Fells, and thirty to forty minutes' drive from the Yorkshire Dales, including places like Ribblesdale and Wharfedale.'

Linda Lord is one of the very few runners who can say that they ran in the first 'official' women's fell race, at Pendle in 1977, and is still competing now, an amazing achievement.

After their success on the Pennine Way, the linear Coast to Coast route was the next that Clayton women ran as a relay, in 1987. The women's section showed their strength in depth when they took the route on as a relay on 20 and 21 June that year. From St Bees Head to Robin Hood's Bay, it is a distance of approximately one hundred and ninety miles, which they divided into fourteen sections, varying from 5.75 to 19 miles. Each leg was taken by an individual runner (who sometimes had company), who followed Wainwright's route from his guidebook. *The Fellrunner* report noted that they 'decided to pass on a small, rounded pebble, picked up from the beach at St Bees, from runner to runner'.

The first of the looped routes to be organised in relay race format was the Calderdale Way. Peter White and David Cleminson recced the route and ran it together in October 1978. In 1980 White suggested to fell runners at Halifax Harriers that the route could be broken down into sections with one or two runners on each leg. In December 1981 ten club members completed the relay. In 1984 it was opened out to other clubs to compete and the first race took place. Clayton were the only women's team in that first race, finishing 18th out of the 22 teams. In 1985 Bingley women beat Clayton's women, in 30th and 32nd places respectively. These two clubs dominated the women's results for the next few years, with Bingley repeating their win the next year over Clayton, but with those positions reversed for the next five years.

Reviewing the history of the Calderdale Way Relay, Peter White says that the event has now turned into the largest relay of its kind in the country, attracting over 1,200 runners from a hundred clubs throughout the UK. He explains why he thinks these events are so successful: 'The main ones being the spirit, camaraderie and effort required not individually, but collectively from the whole team and club.' The entry is capped at a hundred teams now.

The Rossendale Way was first opened in 1982, and Rossendale Harriers and Athletic Club first ran a relay race round the 45-mile route in 1987. Horwich won the women's event in 7-15-15. It wasn't held in 1988 and 1989, but was revived in 1990, over six legs instead of the original four. For the women, Clayton beat Rossendale, and same result was recorded in 1991. The first Pennine Bridleway Relay (over 47 miles, with five legs, ten runners), was held in 2004, replacing the Rossendale Way Relay, although this event is no longer held either.

In 1986 a relay race was inaugurated that has become one of THE races for top clubs to target, such is its prestige. The race was first run as the Ian Hodgson Relay. Ian and his partner, Jem Wilson, won the Score Class of the Karrimor International Mountain Marathon in 1985, but Ian was tragically killed in a cycling accident the day after the event. Delays in circulating the result in those pre-electronic times meant Ian never knew that he had won. The Hodgson family decided to organise an event in his memory and because he was always keen on team sport chose to make it a Relay event. The chosen race venue was Sykeside campsite, Brotherswater, and the course was planned in the fells surrounding Patterdale. The route is 24.5 miles and includes High Street and Fairfield, some of the same ground as that KIMM had been on, and is for teams of eight who run four legs in pairs for safety reasons.

Despite doubts about whether the event would be successful, as the FRA had just turned down a proposal for a Relay Championship, it attracted an entry of thirty-six clubs. The Spring 1987 issue of *The Fellrunner* doesn't mention any women's teams for that year, but Linda Lord says she ran in a Clayton team that year. At the event in 1987 and 1988 Clayton women won both times. For 1989 the Hodgson Relay incorporated an FRA Relay, with Clayton beating Rossendale. In 1990 Clayton won in a new women's record, with their 'B' team coming second. For 1991 other clubs began to show their women's strength, with Livingstone setting a new record, winning from Keswick. The Hodgson relay has more recently moved to Patterdale Playing Field, and is now known as the Hodgson Brothers Mountain Relay.

Looking back, Clayton runner Eileen Jones feels the 1980s were an exciting period for women, especially with their participation in the various relay events. 'I was women's fell captain at Clayton for a few years, including when we did (and won) the first ever Hodgson relay, and the first Calderdale Way relay, in 1984,' she explains.

Eileen Jones

Eileen and I were discussing photos in one of my other book projects[24] *one day and she asked me what my next project was. Telling her of this manuscript which I had just started resulted in her admitting to have run the fells and having a few stories to relay. One Zoom call later and I had a long transcribing job to pull together her material.*

Eileen Jones ran as Eileen Burnip when she joined Clayton-le-Moors, but went back to her maiden name after she separated from husband Steve Burnip. She was born in Fairfield Hospital in Bury in April 1952, and now lives with Fairfield (the mountain)

24. *Fell and Mountain Running: Through the Eye of a Lens*, self-published, 2020.

at the end of her street. Eileen showed no particular talent for sport at school, or inclination towards it. 'Absolutely not', she laughs. 'I hated sports, was frightened of the ball in netball and rounders, couldn't run for a bus without getting a stitch.'

She did love walking though, and went to the Lakes for the first time at the age of sixteen and got hooked. 'For many years I walked the fells, and wanted to do something a bit more challenging when my mum and dad started walking and doing everything I did! I tried rock climbing for a very short time, but it was not for me.' Much later on she got to know some women in Hebden Bridge whose partners were runners, and they got a group together to run on Saturday mornings. 'We didn't want to be grass widows. Hardly any of them lasted, but I loved it. I was thirty-one and I'd never run a step in my life before. The running group was the extra thing that I was looking for.'

Kay Pierce, who was an established runner, came along and joined the group later. She and her husband Bernard (a very good marathon runner in his day) took Eileen under their wing. 'Along with another local guy, Lawrence Sullivan, they persuaded me to join Clayton-le-Moors. Back then the only local running clubs were in Halifax (mostly road) and Todmorden (very few women); with the Calder Valley club not being formed till 1986. Clayton already had a number of women runners, and it was suggested that I'd get a chance to run in relays if I joined them. My first race was at Otley Chevin, Boxing Day 1983. I was never very good, just enthusiastic!'

Eileen ran Pendle and a few local races in 1984, and then did the Fairfield Horseshoe in 1985, her first Lakes fell race. 'I got round in 2-07, and was not last. A year later I did it in 1-52, and in 1988 was eighth woman in 1-46, probably my best ever performance. I found the results recently and was astonished to see who was behind me, including blokes from my club [*Clayton*] I hadn't beaten before!'

In March 1986 she had entered and won the Haworth Hobble, as she explains. 'It was a very special day. I'd watched Kay [*Pierce*] and Lawrence [*Sullivan*] doing the Hobble the year before, and never dreamed I could do that distance. In the summer I was race-watching at Wasdale with Judy Sharples [*then Makinson*], and she asked if I fancied doing the Hobble with her. It was just a pairs event then. She'd done it before, I think with Susan Raine. I was both flattered and awe-struck. I'd done a couple of road marathons – Windermere 1984, in 3-59, and Manchester 1985, in 3-38 – and knew I wanted to concentrate on the fells, so I started training with a Clayton group every weekend. Judy and I had a wonderful run in the Haworth Hobble, and didn't realise we were first women until well over half way when a supporter pointed out that the two "ladies" ahead of us were actually Sylvia Watson, and Geoff Webster, who had longish hair. We won in a very slow time of 6-14. A year later, after training harder, we knocked half an hour off that but only came fourth, as some proper runners turned up, including Véronique Marot and Angie Pain, who set a new women's record.'

Later in 1986 Eileen ran the Borrowdale race, in atrocious conditions, with rain and strong winds, proper Lakes weather for August. 'I ran part of it with a guy called Mike Farnworth, who would yell at me to drop to the ground when he knew a gust of wind was coming. Vanessa Brindle had a male escort on either side of her, I gather. The same year I also did Ben Nevis, in a respectable time of 2-14. Karin Goss [*Taylor*] took NINE minutes out of me on the descent; we were neck and neck at the top. She was an amazing descender, and she's still competing.'

Eileen trained specifically for the fells in her local area. Living in Hebden Bridge she had Stoodley Pike as an obvious training run target. 'I ran mostly on the fells, in the area around Hardcastle Crags, and on the Widdop moorland. I was working for the Yorkshire Post in Leeds and would also do lunchtime runs on the road. I'm not built for running. I have very short legs, and hopeless feet, and I had to train so much harder than others to achieve what I did. I got very competitive. It was the whole scene, being my social life at the time.'

There were no problems, and no special treatment, from race organisers for women at this time, according to Eileen. 'I just felt like "one of the lads", though weirdly we were vets at thirty-five years old, and the women's prize lists were poor. Very few women were running on the fells, relatively. A male friend at Clayton once tried to flatter me by saying I was certainly in the top twenty of English women fell runners, till I pointed out there were probably only twenty-one of us! I once came second at the Gunson Knott race behind (a long way behind) Winkie O'Neill and won a box of bath cubes.'

On the day of the Coast to Coast Relay, in 1987, Eileen hadn't run for three weeks because of injury. 'I thought I have got to do this because I am team captain. I ended up running 19 miles. I can't remember what the injury was now. I have got flat feet and my toes turn the wrong way. I was always having injuries. The amazing Monica Shone, who must have been over sixty then, ran two sections that day.'

Interestingly, Eileen feels that she didn't see any barriers at the time. 'I'm lucky that all my life – professionally, too – I've either not encountered barriers, or simply ignored them. It was good to see more and more women coming into the sport, people like Clare Crofts and Jacky Smith. I witnessed the amazing development of Carol Haigh/Greenwood, and was a good friend of Yvonne MacGregor who stormed onto the fell scene for a year or so, won everything in sight, and then went back to cycling, where she won Commonwealth gold and Olympic bronze.'

Eileen says that when she joined Clayton-le-Moors and met Wendy Dodds, Linda Lord and Vanessa Brindle, they became her heroes. 'Kay Pierce was my guiding light. Then Ruth Pickvance, when she joined Clayton, and we've stayed good friends (though we lost one another for a very long time somewhere!) They were real runners in my eyes. Above all, Monica Shone. We met when she beat me at Pendle. She was fifty-seven then, and had only just started running. She was persuaded by Linda Lord to join Clayton and she became one of my most reliable relay team members. I recall doing a Calderdale recce with her, and she admonished me: "Use it or lose it, Eileen!" She was doing the World Masters Championships in Keswick at the age of seventy-nine and very cross because she had to fit in with the "over sixty" category.'

Eileen thinks she joined Clayton in 1984. 'I have a plaque for being the third member of the Clayton women's team in the Manchester marathon in 1985, behind Vanessa and Kay. I've had a few life-changing experiences in my time, and joining Clayton was one of them. I made some wonderful friends and was part of a tradition that included Stan Bradshaw, Alan Heaton, George Brass. In my first cross-country race, Stan shouted "well done Clayton" as I ran past on the first lap. Then he must have asked who I was, because on the second lap he shouted "Well done, Eileen". I nearly burst with pride.'

Clayton was a strong and very big club, with members across a wide area. 'We had terrific teams in relays, and wonderful camping weekends for races like the Borrowdale and Wasdale. In the winter, when we couldn't run off road in midweek, I'd leave work in Leeds and drive all the way to Clayton (and then later, home to Hebden) just to run six miles round the streets of Accrington. It was my entire social life.'

Eileen raced maybe every other weekend, usually Saturdays, so she would do a long run on a Sunday, 20 miles or more depending on what was coming up. 'I also tried to get to the Lakes as often as possible. My navigation was OK. I did once follow a group of men in the direction of Red Pike in the Wasdale race in the mist, and eventually had enough confidence to announce, "this is wrong". I turned back, and one of them came with me. The others all got timed out.'

Eileen started a family late. 'I no longer wanted to train or run at the same level, because I wanted to spend every moment I could with them. Of course, I dragged them to fell races almost as soon as they could walk.'

Eileen says she never wanted to do the Bob Graham Round. She explains her involvement in the Clayton Rounds. 'I'd rather be giving help than accepting it. Clayton had a BGR machine that would get people round: navigators on each section, bag carriers, jokers, jelly-baby feeders, but I didn't want to be the focus of attention like that. I was a great crew member, road support, doing sections in training and on the day. Always anticlockwise, in the Clayton tradition. I still can't understand why anyone would CHOOSE to run the last six miles on the road, doing it clockwise. I've helped again in recent years, and absolutely love being part of it.'

She also adds that she was backroom manager for Paul Tierney's 2019 Wainwrights record. Her front room was mission HQ. Eileen explained her role and how it came about. 'Just about everyone in my street runs for Ambleside AC. I had offered to help in the week, not on the hill but as a basecamp. All the requests from the hill came to me, a need for plasters or paracetamol, or that Paul wants fish and chips, and I would make calls out to the people that were driving around supporting him. I had a spreadsheet of all the supporters, and I had to let them know whether they were needed ahead or behind schedule. I also did the laundry.' At one point she had a whole washing line of men's underpants – Paul was sponsored by a noted underpants supplier.

Eileen only raced seriously on the fells for a few years in the 1980s. 'I've done fell races since the family came along, but I simply didn't have the time any more to train at the level I needed to really enjoy it, because I'm not a natural. I did another Hobble, very slowly, and I've done races on Pendle, and Stoodley Pike, and I did enjoy the Lakeland Trails events, especially Keswick with its fantastic descents. Since moving to Ambleside, I've done the Loughrigg race a few times but usually finish last. After a while, it's no fun being so far off the back of the pack, and I feel guilty that the marshals are up there shivering, waiting for me. That's why parkrun became my salvation, but that's another story.' For that story, see her book on the subject.[25]

Eileen is now involved on the committee for the Ambleside Sports. She says she still had to prove herself when she offered to join the, mainly male, committee. 'I proved myself to the

25. *How parkrun changed our lives*, Gritstone Publishing, 2021.

committee by going out with the hound trailers with the smelly rag to set the course. You can't use the paths as shoes move the scent on. It meant doing much of the Fairfield Horseshoe below the skyline which was really hard going. I am accepted now.'

She responded with two very different answers when asked what she felt was her finest race or achievement in sport/life. 'Completing the Bens of Jura, and not being last! It was in 1988 and I spent a week on the island, scaring myself silly training over bits of the route. It paid off. I found my way round, and was joined by a much faster Clayton runner, Len Farnsworth, who stuck with me because I knew the way. I'd always been fond of Jura whisky, that's why I always wanted to do the race. The other thing I'm proud of is the relay I organised in 2021 (in lockdown) to launch my parkrun book.'

As far as other runners on the fells are concerned, she is most impressed with Billy Bland's Bob Graham Round record which stood for so long. 'I thought he was an amazing runner. Also Kenny Stuart's Ben Nevis record. Will that ever go?'

Eileen has led a filled and fulfilled life, with plenty more to come. The mileage is less than it used to be, and her focus is now mostly on parkrun. At the end of 2021 she even persuaded Joss Naylor to have a go at his local one.

In the early 1980s the FRA had been pressed to agree to a British Fell Relay Championship, with Dave Hall taking a lead in the representation to the FRA committee. They finally agreed in 1988, and the first one was held within the Hodgson Relay in 1989. The FRA then decided to offer the organisation of the event to FRA affiliated clubs, both to spread the workload and the geographical location. Pennine Fellrunners organised the second championship and based it at Edale (Dark Peak women winning from Macclesfield), with Bingley Harriers holding the 1991 event around Kettlewell, with one runner per leg (Pudsey and Bramley women winning from Clayton). Later, in the 1990s, it was changed to be a short solo leg, followed by a longer pairs leg, a longer pairs 'navigation' leg, followed by a final short solo leg.

CHAPTER 18

Professional versus amateur

Encounters with the Professional Scene.
A Barrier Breaker.
Profile: Kirstin Bailey

'I showed that females could run in this prestigious event.'

For around one hundred years there was an uneasy parallel world of professional fell races and the amateur versions. The professional events tended to be shorter races, up-and-down one hill, attached to the local country show, and offered prize money. The amateur races were normally longer, sometimes included multiple summits, and often required navigation skills, and followed the 'amateur code'. The first professional race is reckoned to be the Guides Race, held at Grasmere (in the Lakes) in 1868, while the oldest amateur race is considered to be the Hallam Chase, held on the outskirts of Sheffield in 1863. The full story of the professional-amateur divide is told in the author's book *It's a Hill, Get Over It.*[26]

Having the two codes in place produced some ridiculous situations, which even affected young athletes coming into the sport. There are stories of some of those youngsters being noted as 'professionals', and subsequently being disallowed from competing in their own school athletics teams. Roger Ingham was very involved in organising country show races, such as Kilnsey, and coaching young athletes from his area. He recalls taking some of them to a schools' race, where it got completely out of hand.

26. *It's a Hill, Get Over It: Fell Running's History and Characters*, Sandstone Press, 2013.

'In 1978 some of these youngsters were going to the English School cross-country finals. Some had only run in the Kendal Winter League, just the odd race. Somebody had filtered the names through to bigwigs at the English Schools (authority). It was at Lincoln that year with eight in each county team. They were going into the starting pens. There were 300 on the starting line and they are saying they are professionals (but they had never run for a penny in their life) and they are not allowed to run.'

From the early days the professional side of the sport was closed to female runners. Changes did begin to happen, though, with junior events being added for young athletes at the country shows. Two of the biggest and most prestigious of these were the Grasmere Sports and the Ambleside Sports. At Ambleside there had been Junior Guides races (for boys) – for the under 14 age group (from 1955); under 12 (1959); and under 17 (1962). Equivalent girls' category races were added – for under 12 and under 14 in 1986, and under 17 in 1991. The winners of all these races are listed in Marjorie Blackburn's booklet[27] '*Our Traditional Lakeland Sports: Ambleside and its Sports*'.

Roy Lomas' excellent history of the Grasmere Sports[28] tells this story well. Privilege, and charity, prompted a significant event that was noted in Lomas' report on the 1984 Guides Race. 'Ladies featured in most events for the first time this year. Lord Lonsdale's daughter, Caroline Lowther had trained for the Cumbrian marathon earlier in the year, in order to raise money for a Carlisle hospital. She did it [*the Guides Race*] "for my fitness and the hell of a cheer I got when I came back in".' Separate under 14 and under 12 categories, for boys, were also introduced for the Guides race that year.

Girls began entering the youngsters age groups from then on, and the next female to compete in the Senior Guides was K. Bailey, in 1988. That was Kirstin Bailey, who had caused

27. *Our Traditional Lakeland Sports*, Ambleside Sports Association, 2000.
28. *The Grasmere Sports: The First 150 Years*, MTP Publications, 2002.

quite a stir by wanting to compete at the Braemar Highland Games in 1986. These are the highland games that the royal family often attends, and the organisers did not allow females to run. It is quite a story. They met their match in Kirstin Bailey though. At the time she was just fourteen years old and had a short haircut, so she decided to pass herself off as a boy. She takes up the tale.

'All the other competitors were in on it and aimed to shield me from the organisers. However, some of the officials got suspicious and started asking questions. They even threatened me by saying they would manhandle me into a tent to check my gender. At this I became quite frightened, but at the same time determined to make a point. So, I joined in the race as the runners left the arena. I ran the whole course running on adrenaline and maintained a high position. On the way back through the crowds towards the arena I made sure I was tucked in behind another runner. At this the officials saw me and tried to grab my arm, they even had a crook and tried to get me with it, but I slipped past them into the arena. Even now I remember the feeling it gave me and the deafening sound of 20,000 people clapping and cheering, all the spectators got off their seats and gave me a standing ovation as I raced a man round, leading up to the line the man gave way. It was a truly memorable moment for everyone who was there. The officials took no further action.'

Kirstin says she was going to the Braemar Games at such a young age because it was one of the races that BOFRA promoted. Traditional historical fell running. She just enjoyed being part of it and had great family support. She says that: 'my goals and dreams have not changed. If you asked me as a kid what I wanted to be when I grow up, I would answer "Happy", that's what mum supported me in. She supported me in my education, my mental health, my physical fitness and associated goals, to enjoy life, to not give up. It is what mums do, I suppose.'

Kirstin Bailey

Kirstin's contact details were given to me by Roger Ingham, who used to take her to races when she was a young athlete. Her perspective on how young athletes were disadvantaged, given in two long emails, was an excellent addition to the narrative.

Kirstin Bailey went on to have a successful running career. She was born on 29 September 1971, in Blackburn. She was a county standard athlete at school, and Bradford school 1500m champion. As a child, and adult, she was very sporty. At various times participating in trampolining and gymnastics, swimming, track running, netball, hockey, tennis, cross-country, and then fell running.

She explains what led her to running on the fells. 'I love the countryside and farming, so loved the country shows, where they had the short fell races. I enjoyed exerting myself up and down the hills.'

The first event she ran was the egg and spoon race at primary school, where she won a Mars bar. Her first proper race was a cross-country, at Barton on Humber as an under 11. She ended up in a sprint finish where the girl next to her stopped and started crying, so she stopped too and put her arms around her to see if she was OK. She recalls, 'mum was proud of that, but I had to learn the art of competitive sport. One of my most memorable early fell races was when I ran the Rombalds Moor Fell race (organised by Skipton AC) as an under 11 and beat all the boys. The gold medal was awarded to the first boy who came in behind me in second place overall! Everybody was so upset about this as I had won the race. Carol Haigh (now Greenwood) was at the event, and she made a complaint to the officials.' Kirstin has strong memories of the day, adding, 'at the same event I actually locked the car keys in the car, and it was blowing a gale and we had to run through deep mud!'

These were all official races, sanctioned by the AAA, as they were cross-country events. Moving to the fells, the first fell race she won a trophy at was under 11 Eldwick Gala fell race (organised by Bingley Harriers). She still has the trophy – it was two glasses, a sherry and a wine glass with a pheasant on them. A strange choice for that age group.

At this time, she was very young and didn't train at all. In fact, she says, 'I have not ever done a vast amount of training, as I was always investing my time in lots of other areas of life as well. I would walk round Harden Moor as a child.'

Soon Kirstin was joining her local athletic club. At first, she was in Keighley AC, then Bingley Harriers. In 1986 her mother (Ellen Bailey) and Paul Buckley formed Keighley Hill Runners (which merged with Keighley Road Runners – and now is known as Keighley and Craven AC). 'So, I joined that for a while before re-joining Bingley. Since having the kids, I have run for Mercia and now Staffs Moorlands.'

Although she was not running till the 1980s, Kirstin feels she was something of a pioneer. 'Absolutely. At the start females where not recognised in the sport, there were no prizes, so you had to get in the top three overall and even then, officials would not award the prize to you because you were a girl. I stuck at it and eventually girls became recognised and got the prizes they deserved.'

She has been running since the age of eight and competed on the fells from the age of nine or ten and still does some of the BOFRA races. In 2019 she won the BOFRA V45 category.

Looking back, she reflected that her finest race was the Kilnsey Crag Race. 'I think I have won this event at least six times over the years and still hold the record, of 9-58.' This time doesn't tally with that quoted for a different runner on the FRA website, so what is the explanation? Kirstin reckons, 'records were not kept very well back then, the time of 9-58 is the time I recorded on my stopwatch on the day and subsequently wrote in my diary, that's why I know I still hold the record. It's never bothered me much what other people think or believe, it's only important to me that I know.' Unfortunately, neither the

BOFRA website, nor the Kilnsey Show one, list all the results from this period.

Kirstin was engaged to John Taylor, who sadly died of cardiomyopathy in 2002, and she was instrumental in setting up The John Taylor Foundation, whose aims were to: give financial assistance to young amateur athletes in the United Kingdom to allow them to pursue opportunities in amateur athletics; and the promotion and preservation of good health by raising public awareness of the condition of cardiomyopathy in athletics.

She has been married to fell runner Simon Bailey since August 2006, and they now run a sheep farm and a sportswear and lifestyle brand called 'gr8ful'. She notes a weird quirk, in that: 'I already had the same surname as my husband, but we are not blood related.'

We finished our discussion by Kirstin being asked to give a list of those that had the most impact on the sport in the 1970s and 1980s (male or female). She came back with, 'Kenny Stuart, Bill Teasdale, John Bulman, Stan Edmondson, Joss Naylor (he offered me a pair of boots once) and Roger Ingham. To name but a few.' And whose record on the fells is she most impressed with, looking back? 'Simon Bailey, eight times English Fell Running Champion, an absolute legend', came straight back.

Kirstin Bailey gives an insight into the issues faced by female young athletes in those early days, and shows how being someone who challenged the status quo could change the situation.

From 1995 anyone could legally compete in races like the Grasmere Guides, Ambleside Sports and Kilnsey Crag races – which they had been doing recently anyway, but 'unofficially'.

That year, at Grasmere, Jonny Bland won the Senior Guides race from Gary Devine, whilst Victoria Wilkinson won the women's category there. In effect the sport was fully open from then onwards, and women could test themselves in whatever events they wanted to.

CHAPTER 19

Women coming first

Wonderful Winning Women – Outright:
Sarah Rowell, Helene Diamantides, Carol Haigh

'I knew women were capable of winning outright,' claimed Helene Diamantides.

Throughout history women have been treated as the weaker sex. This is indeed true if you just consider muscle power. The fastest women tend to be 10 to 15 per cent slower than the leading men over the distances that fell races are typically run over, but that difference can often be a little less over the longer distances. In pure endurance events though the physiological differences between the sexes can be quite insignificant. There is also evidence that women's mental approach when the going gets really tough can also help them close that gap. In the period that this book covers there have been several instances of these circumstances coming together to result in an outstanding women's performance on the day. They CAN beat all the men when this happens.

A performance in 1926 anticipates this, admittedly in endurance swimming rather than running. Gertrude Ederle had recently won a gold medal, and two bronzes, in the pool at the Olympics in Paris when she took on the challenge of swimming the English Channel. She became only the sixth person to complete the 21-mile swim but was two hours faster than the fastest of the five men that had achieved the feat before her. Her women's record stood until 1950.

The first outright victory by a woman in an off-road endurance running event was Sarah Rowell's win at the Beachy Head Marathon in 1986. Known as the Seven Sisters Marathon at the time, she won this tough event in 2 hours 49 minutes, a time that was only beaten at that event by two men in the next twenty years.

Gareth Webb's profile of Sarah Rowell (in *The Fellrunner* in June 1996) gives the background. 'Injury, brought on by running on the roads, was soon to force Sarah to have a career re-think and in 1986, after consulting with her coach Cliff Temple, she came to the conclusion that either she succumbed to the succession of troublesome back injuries or moved off the roads. She didn't need much convincing. "Cliff and I talked about it and said wouldn't it be fun if I won [*the Seven Sisters Marathon*] because no female had ever won it." I remember running the race off a 100-mile training week and it was just one of those things really. I was running so well at the time and was on such a high for several weeks after. It was a great feeling.' She chose to take to the fells with serious intentions shortly after this. But there was another hitch. She had also been troubled by post-viral fatigue syndrome, which kept her out of the sport for over a year and held back her training once she started training again. As we have seen though she made a lasting impression in her fell and mountain running career from 1989 onwards.

As a multi-day event, the first Dragon's Back race, in 1992, was a real test of endurance, fitness, and mental strength (together with good recovery). It traversed the highest mountains of Wales, over five long days. There was a field of around a hundred, of which three were women. The mixed pair of Helene Diamantides and Martin Stone, after taking and losing the lead over the five days, then came through to win. In an interview Helene said she didn't necessarily think it was anything to be surprised about. She said: 'I was aware that Sarah Rowell had won The Seven Sisters Marathon outright. I'd run a few of the big rounds in the fastest overall times. I knew I could do well.' When it was next held, twenty years on in 2012, the event had 232 starters, of whom thirty-one were women.

The only known outright win by a women in a standard FRA fell race was the Erringden Moor fell race (in Calderdale), on April 18 1998. In June 1998 *The Fellrunner* had a short report on Carol Haigh/Greenwood's fantastic achievement. 'Carol Haigh managed the unthinkable. She won outright over a demanding 9-mile course with almost 2,000 feet of climb. Carol had held onto second place until the second major climb, at around halfway, from Withens Clough reservoir to the Pennine Way, near Stoodley Pike, when the leading man missed some flags and ran around two miles off course. Carol met the hapless would-be winner going the wrong way down a bridleway after she had completed a large loop of moorland, and began to apply the pressure on the final climb from London Road to Stoodley Pike and over Erringden Moor to the Mytholmroyd finish, where she set the inaugural record time of 1 hour and 12 minutes.' Despite the unfortunate mistake by the lead male, it should be noted that Carol beat ALL the men in that race. She also had top six finishes in other races when she was at her best.

The situation is perhaps best summed up by a further quote from the Helen Diamantides interview about the Dragon's Back win. 'I guess it was outsiders looking in that took most interest in the gender thing. I think if you're good enough to be there, it doesn't matter whether you are in your sixties or female. The good thing about fell running is that everyone stands on the start line and does the same thing in the same conditions on that day.'

Following on from that last thought, I feel that the message of the book is the value of getting out in the hills for both its physical and mental benefits. Women have fought hard for the right to run freely, and particularly to compete in the sport of fell and mountain running. I hope this book does justice to their struggle for recognition, using their voices from the hills. Attend a club training session, a fell race or a challenge round these days and you will see huge numbers of women involved, supporting and challenging each other and their male friends and rivals. The true spirit of fell running is on show and out there for all to see, and be part of.

Some of the biggest stars in the sport, with the highest profiles, are now women. That this is possible is a direct result of the actions over the last fifty years of pioneering women runners, many of whom are highlighted within this book.

Acknowledgements

I would like to acknowledge the many people that have helped me, in their different ways, to bring this manuscript together. As an author it sometimes feels like you are working in a vacuum but compiling the acknowledgements makes one realise that is in fact very much not the case. Having said that, I have felt very remote sometimes, particularly when lockdown restrictions were in place during the Covid pandemic. It meant that face-to-face interviews were out of the question, which I find the most fascinating, and enjoyable, aspect of researching a book such as this.

In the early days I was unsure whether I should pursue the idea that I had for the book. The first person I talked to about it in depth was Rebecca Robinson, when I shared the synopsis with her back in the autumn of 2020. Her encouraging response clinched it for me. Massive thanks for your positivity. Rebecca also helped immensely by suggesting a list of people I must speak to, which I duly used as a starting point. Showing great encouragement early on was Hugh Symonds, who also had some good suggestions for contacts to pursue.

One of the early leads enabled me to contact Duncan Macpherson. As the son of Kathleen Connochie, he was able to shed some interesting light on his mother running the Ben Nevis race in 1955, which is a pivotal point in the story of women on the hills and mountains. In a similar way, fellow author Victoria Benn introduced me to her father, Roger Ingham, who had some fascinating memories of early days at the county show races. He has so many stories he should write a book of his life in sport.

The extensive network that I have established when writing my previous books proved really useful for reaching out to women responsible for breaking down barriers. Nick Barrable, Eileen Jones and Malcolm Patterson all provided useful contacts, and in Malcolm's case some cracking tales, as per usual. Anthony Kay, Dave Hall and Joe Ritson all came in with some background stories, not all of which made the cut. Norma Hughes was very helpful in explaining her husband Danny's crucial role in organising races, via the Cumberland Fell Runners Association, and in a wider sense in the sport, both in the UK and internationally. Norma also loaned me several copies of the CFRA booklets from the early days. Rob Grillo was very helpful in suggesting books I might usefully read in the early research phase. Thanks to Rob I have now read more running club histories than is healthy for anyone.

Huge thanks go out to the following for help with finding photos, and allowing their use in the book: Dave Woodhead, David Hughes, Pete Todhunter and Tommy Orr; and to the athletes who are profiled, for going back through their own photo collections and providing some great illustrative material. Moira Chilton applied her consummate artistic skills to provide the chapter sub-division artwork, which are of (in my view) the most recognisable skylines in England, Scotland and Wales respectively. These are respectively the Langdale Pikes (Eng), the Cuillin Ridge (Sco), and the Snowdon Horseshoe (Wal).

A big thank you goes to Katie Holmes for checking the early sections of the manuscript, and for some very helpful feedback. It was good to reach out to another solo researcher and share some information both ways where we have common ground. I owe a massive debt to Graham Breeze, who took on the task of being my critical friend. Graham knows his fell running, and it was pleasing to find that he was fascinated by the detail of lives he thought he knew, and that in a couple of cases where he really knew someone well that he could 'hear' them talking when he read their profiles. His observations and suggestions on reading the manuscript in full were detailed and on point. Acting on them I am sure has made for a better book, whilst any errors that remain are solely my responsibility.

At Sandstone Press I have again been brilliantly served by my editor, Robert Davidson, and the rest of the Sandstone Team, particularly A. Smith (indexing) and Dave Middlemas for his diligent proof-reading.

This book would amount to nothing without the insights gleaned from interviews with the many athletes who were active from the 1970s onwards. Necessarily, Zoom or email often had to be the medium used, due to Covid not allowing 'normal' interactions. A massive thanks are due to all of the following, who took the time to talk to me, and then answer what may have appeared naïve or irrelevant follow-up questions: Carol McNeill, Joan Glass, Carol Walkington/Campbell, Bridget Hogge, Anne-Marie Grindley, Pauline Haworth/Stuart, Joan Lancaster, Ros Coats/Evans, Jean Lochhead, Sue Parkin, Véronique Marot, Jean Dawes, Wendy Dodds, Fiona Wild, Brenda Robinson, Vanessa Brindle/Peacock, Christine Menhennet, Carol Haigh/Greenwood, Sarah Rowell, Angela Carson/Brand-Barker, Ruth Pickvance, Tricia Calder, Jackie Hargreaves, Alison Wright, Elaine Wright, Helene Diamantides/Whitaker, Anne Stentiford/Johnstone, Nicola Davies, Angela Mudge, Linda Lord, Eileen Jones and Kirstin Bailey. I hope I have used their 'voices from the hills' wisely. They have all added something different, and personal, to the story.

Many publications have provided source material, or been used to corroborate information provided by contacts, whilst in the research phase. Several magazines and papers proved particularly useful in this aspect, including: *The Fellrunner, Compass Sport, Up and Down*, and the *Press and Journal*. Many books were dipped into, in particular: *Stud Marks on the Summits* by Bill Smith, *The Ben Race* by Hugh Dan MacLennan, *First Ladies of Running* by Amby Burfoot, *Grasmere Sports: the first 150 years* by Roy Lomas, *Game On: the Unstoppable Rise of*

Women's Sport by Sue Anstiss, *Staying the Distance* by Rob Grillo, *Pedestrianism* by Matthew Algeo, and *Our Traditional Lakeland Sports* by Marjorie Blackburn. Finally, the following booklets all proved the value of recording events in detail: *Ten years of Dark Peak Fell Runners (1976–1986)* – part of the DPFR club history, *History and Records of Notable Fell Walks, 1864–1972, Within the Lake District* by Fred Rogerson, *50 years of the Welsh 1000m Peaks Race* by the Gorphwysfa Club, *42 Peaks* by Peter McDonald, and *Fifty Years Running* by the Lake District Mountain Trial Association.

Index

Note: Page numbers followed by "*n*" refer to notes